The spread of economic ideas

The spread of economic ideas

Edited by

DAVID C. COLANDER and A. W. COATS

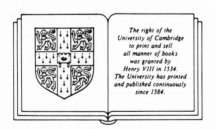

CAMBRIDGE UNIVERSITY PRESS

Cambridge

New York   Port Chester   Melbourne   Sydney

Published by the Press Syndicate of the University of Cambridge
The Pitt Building, Trumpington Street, Cambridge CB2 1RP
32 East 57th Street, New York, NY 10022, USA
10 Stamford Road, Oakleigh, Melbourne 3166, Australia

First published 1989

Printed in Canada

Library of Congress Cataloging-in-Publication Data
The spread of economic ideas.
1. Economics – History. I. Colander, David C.
II. Coats, A. W. (Alfred William), 1924–
HB75.S686 1989   330′.09   88–35363

British Library Cataloguing in Publication Data
The spread of economic ideas
1. Economics. Theories
I. Colander, David C.   II. Coats, A. W.
(Alfred William), *1924–*
330.1

ISBN 0-521-36233-4 hard covers

This book is dedicated to
ROBERT JONES,
a good friend of Middlebury College

Contents

Tables

Figures

Preface

The papers in this volume were originally presented at the Annual Middlebury College Conference on Economic Issues, which was funded by the Institute of Economic and Monetary Affairs. The institute has made it possible for Middlebury College to play a larger role in the economics profession than most other undergraduate schools. In doing so, it has exposed our students to a larger sense of economics than would otherwise be possible. We at Middlebury are extremely thankful to the institute for making that possible.

Running a conference is no easy task. Without the support of many individuals it would be an impossible undertaking. Two people stand out: Sheila Cassin, the Economics Department Secretary, and Helen Reiff, who acted as conference coordinator and saw that all went smoothly. They did the work and I took the credit: a simple arrangement, the inequities of which I am quite aware. Here, in the preface, which few read, I acknowledge my debt to them.

As you read the volume you will quickly see that this isn't a mere reprinting of conference papers. It's a book that fits together like a puzzle. The puzzle took a while to solve and had me piecing parts together – adding something here, subtracting something there – taking bits and pieces of the conference transcripts and getting the authors to turn them into full-blown papers. Doing so takes diplomacy (of which I have little), effort (of which I have lots), and a background spanning all of philosophy and the humanities. (My co-editor Bob Coats is strong where I am weak and I sincerely appreciate his efforts in helping me make the pieces of the puzzle fit together, even as he traveled the globe.) We, with help from a reviewer, my Middlebury College Senior Seminar on the Spread of Economic Ideas, and Helen Reiff, managed to "sort of" fit the pieces together. I thank them heartily.

Once the pieces "sort of" fit, the finishing crew came in. At Cambridge, that included our editor, Ina Isobe, whose diplomacy and

charm rivals my co-editor's, and our production editor, Louise Cala-
bro Gruendel, whom I thank profusely for a superb job of editing and
for keeping the book on schedule. Together with my personal editor,
Helen Reiff, who smoothed my rough edges and provided me with
general insights and specifics as well as an index, they made this into
a polished manuscript. The end result is a neat fit. I thank them all.

Middlebury College   David C. Colander
Middlebury, Vermont

Contributors

WILLIAM J. BARBER teaches at Wesleyan University, where his fields of specialization are the history of economic thought, the economics of energy, international economics, economic development, and "economists as policy advisors." After graduating magna cum laude from Harvard he went on to Oxford University, where he obtained his Ph.D. He is the president of the History of Economics Society and is on the editorial boards of *World Development* and *History of Political Economy*. He has held many fellowships and other teaching posts. He is the author or coauthor of six books, some of which have had several printings in as many as six languages and/or have run to three volumes. He is the author of numerous articles, monographs, book reviews, and other contributions. Currently he is working on studies in American economic thought and policy in the years between World War I and World War II and studies of American economic thought in the 19th century.

ROBERT W. CLOWER is the Hugh C. Lane Distinguished Professor of Economic Theory at the University of South Carolina. Previously he taught at Northwestern and U.C.L.A. He is one of the few economists in the United States who says what he thinks. Moreover, he does it eloquently. He is an original thinker and has published several works in both micro and macro theory, most of which he now disowns. He has served time as editor of *Economic Inquiry* and the *American Economic Review,* but is now free on bail. He has recently published an intermediate microeconomic text and a collection of his articles entitled *Money and Markets* (edited by Donald Walker). He maintains a strong interest in the history of economic thought.

A. W. "BOB" COATS has been research professor of economics at Duke University since 1984, and is also emeritus professor of economic and social history at the University of Nottingham, where he was head of the department in that subject from 1964 until his early retirement in December 1982. He has held visiting appointments at fourteen different universities in the United States, Australia, Canada, and Israel. He obtained his B.Sc. and M.Sc. in economics from the University of London, and his Ph.D. from The Johns Hopkins University in 1953. Professor Coats has written extensively on various aspects of the history of economic thought and policy with special reference to the economics profession, the role of economists in government, and the methodology and sociology of economics. He has edited or coedited a dozen books, and has contributed many journal articles and reviews. In 1985–6 he was president of the History of Economics Society, and has been a fellow at the Netherlands Institute for Advanced Studies (1972–3) and the National Humanities Center, NC (1983–4).

DAVID C. COLANDER is the Christian A. Johnson Distinguished Professor of Economics at Middlebury College and the organizer of the conference from which these chapters derive. He is the author and editor of numerous articles and of ten books, including *MAP: A Market Anti-Inflation Plan* (with Abba Lerner) and *History of Economic Thought* (with Harry Landreth). He serves on the executive board of the Eastern Economics Association and on the board of advisors for the *Journal of Economic Perspectives.*

COLIN DAY is the director of the University of Michigan Press. After several years as lecturer in economics at Stirling University in Scotland, he joined Cambridge University Press as economics editor. While working for Cambridge in New York, he mastered the art of playing both sides of the street: both contributing to this volume and considering it for publication.

JAMES K. GALBRAITH received his Ph.D. in economics at Yale in 1981. He is currently associate professor at the Lyndon B. Johnson School of Public Affairs at the University of Texas at Austin. He was executive director of the Joint Economic Committee of the Congress of the United States in the early 1980s. He has also taught at the University of Maryland. He has written articles on all aspects of political economy and is the joint author of *The Economic Problem* with Robert Heilbroner. His most recent book is *Balancing Acts: Technology, Finance and the American Future,* 1989.

CRAUFURD D. GOODWIN is the James B. Duke Professor of Economics at Duke University, where he has also served as vice-provost and dean of the graduate school. He is the editor of *History of Political*

Economy and has published widely on economic policy, including books on inflation and energy policy. He is editor of the Cambridge University Press Series *Historical Perspectives on Modern Economics* and is coauthor with Michael Nacht of *Abroad and Beyond* (Cambridge University Press, 1988).

CHARLES P. KINDLEBERGER, Ford International Professor of Economics, Emeritus, Massachusetts Institute of Technology, retired in 1981. He was Christian A. Johnson Visiting Professor of Economics at Middlebury College in 1981–2. He is the author of a number of books including *Economic Response* (1978), *Manias, Panics and Crashes* (1978), *International Money* (1981), *Financial History of Western Europe* (1984), and *Keynesianism vs. Monetarism* (1985).

DONALD S. LAMM graduated from Yale in 1953. After serving in the Counterintelligence Corps of the U.S. Army, he did graduate work at Oxford University. Since 1956 he has been with W. W. Norton & Company, after becoming president of the publishing house in 1976 and chairman in 1984. He has twice been a guest fellow at Yale University, giving a course on book publishing, and was the 1987–8 Ida H. Beam Distinguished Visiting Professor at the University of Iowa. He is chairman of the board of governors of Yale University Press and a trustee of the Roper Center.

JOSEPH J. MINARIK is a senior research associate at the Urban Institute, specializing in taxation and income distribution issues. He was a research associate at the Brookings Institution from 1974 through 1981, and served as deputy assistant director in the tax analysis division of the Congressional Budget Office until he joined the Urban Institute in 1984. He is the author of *Making Tax Choices* (1985), and was named to "150 Who Make a Difference" in the nation's capital by the magazine *National Journal.* In 1989 he became executive director of the Congressional Budget Office.

DANIEL H. NEWLON is director of the National Science Foundation's Economics Program, where he has developed innovative ways of making grants in order to cushion the impact of federal budget cuts on the economics research community. Prior to joining NSF in 1974, he taught economics at the State University of New York at Binghamton. In addition to getting his Ph.D. from the University of Virginia, he has studied at the London School of Economics and Political Science, the University of Koln, and the University of Mexico. He has published a book and articles on energy policy and on the volunteer army. His current research interests include science policy and public finance in developing countries.

JAMES A. SMITH is a historian teaching in the Graduate School of Management and Urban Professions at the New School for Social Research. He has taught at Brown, Smith, and the University of Nebraska, and served on the staff of the Twentieth Century Fund, a New York policy research foundation. During 1988–9 he was resident scholar at the Rockefeller Archive Center. He is the author of a book on think tanks.

ROBERT M. SOLOW is institute professor in the department of economics at MIT, where he has taught since 1949. He was on the staff of the Council of Economic Advisers in 1961–2, Eastman Professor at Oxford in 1968–9, and overseas fellow of Churchill College, Cambridge, in 1984. He is one of the authors, with Robert Dorfman and Paul Samuelson, of *Linear Programming and Economic Analysis* (1958) and of *Growth Theory: An Exposition* (1970; 2nd ed., 1988). He is currently working with Frank Hahn on a book on macroeconomic theory. He won the Nobel Memorial Prize in Economics in 1987.

GORDON TULLOCK was born in Rockford, Illinois. He is a graduate of the University of Chicago and the holder of Doctor of Jurisprudence honorary degree from the Chicago Law School. He has also studied Chinese and related topics at Yale and Cornell. He was a member of the American Foreign Service from 1949 to 1958, specializing in China and the Far East. He is past president of the Southern Economic Association and the Public Choice Society, and is on the board of the American Political Science Association. He is the editor of *Public Choice* and coauthor, with James Buchanan, of *The Calculus of Consent*.

DAVID WARSH is an economic columnist who keeps close tabs on new developments in the field. He writes for the *Boston Globe* and is the author of *The Idea of Economic Complexity* (1984).

CHAPTER 1

An introduction to the spread of economic ideas

A. W. COATS and DAVID C. COLANDER

Given the importance of ideas it is strange that the process, and institutions, through which economic ideas are transferred from individual
brains into the general inventory of ideas and eventually into policy
has not been considered seriously. Upon reflection the reasons become
clear. The concepts are vague, the institutions hazy, and the process
messy. Studying the spread of ideas is like studying subatomic particles
with half-lives of nanoseconds.

About the only way that we will be able to say anything meaningful
is by limiting our focus, and the papers in this volume concentrate on
the recent spread of ideas in the United States, within the profession
and from the profession to the common reader. The popularization of
economic ideas, as such, is not considered because it is too large and
amorphous a subject. The volume is divided into four sections: Part 1
considers the nature of the economics profession, whether it has any
ideas to spread, and how ideas spread within it; Part 2 considers the
spread of ideas from economists to the lay public; Part 3 considers the
spread of ideas from economists to politicians; and Part 4 considers
how the funding of economic ideas influences their diffusion.

The difficulty of the subject is not the only reason for its previous
neglect. According to standard scientific methodologies – positivism,
falsificationism, and modernism – it is a nonsubject. These standard
methodologies implicitly assume that the "best" ideas necessarily win
out.[1] If this is the case, why study the process? The relevant issue is
not how do ideas spread, but rather how to disseminate "sound" ideas.

---

[1] Joseph A. Schumpeter held that controversy between schools of thought is a waste of
energy, for "There is no use fighting something which life will sooner or later eliminate
anyway.... All we can say is that if in science something wins through it will have
proved its right to exist, and if the thing is not worth anything, it will surely wither."
From his farewell speech at Bonn, June 20, 1932, "The Whence and Whither of our
Science," cited in Erich Schneider, *Joseph Schumpeter: Life and Work of a Great Social
Scientist,* trans. W. E. Kuhn (Lincoln, NE: Bureau of Business Research, 1975), p. 40.

Over much of the past century we see economists taking an active role in propagating "sound" economic ideas through such organizations as the Political Economy Club of London, the Anti-Corn Law League, and the Shalckenbach Foundation (devoted to Henry George's doctrines). Although there remain a number of influential and well-endowed foundations devoted to the promotion of free enterprise and libertarian ideals and policies, recent developments in methodology have removed this sense of mission from many economists. Most modern economists are not preachers. They would rather see themselves and be seen as scientists, more interested in knowledge for its own sake than for its potential policy implications.[2]

With the emergence of rhetorical and sociological approaches to methodology the process by which ideas spread becomes an important subject. These alternative antipositivist methodologies allow for a potential difference between the "best" ideas and those that "win out," and as soon as one accepts this distinction the dissemination process becomes an integral part of the discipline's subject matter and attaches to its history. Whether "truth" is attainable, or whether unambiguous criteria of "best" ideas can be established, are matters that can, for present purposes at least, be left to the epistemologists and philosophers. The current view among students of economics is profoundly skeptical, for they are acutely aware of the persistence of popular fallacies.

As noted at the outset, the concept of economic ideas is elusive and it is advisable to begin with a definition. Unfortunately the dictionary versions cover a wide spectrum extending from carefully formulated and fully specified theories, doctrines, or intellectual systems through a miscellaneous variety of assumptions, postulates, statements, propositions, claims, and predictions to the most casual types of assertions, hunches, and speculative guesses. Concentration on strictly professional economic ideas narrows the range somewhat, but it raises problems of scope when the spread of ideas is under consideration. In order to avoid overintellectualization we consider that the processes of persuasion, simplification, translation, redescription, and distortion that are directly or indirectly alluded to in this volume are most fruitfully considered by reference to concrete examples. We therefore propose to define an economic idea narrowly as "a conception or notion of something to be done or carried out; a plan of action." Examples include

---

[2]For perceptive and amusing comments on this topic, see the title essay and "Do Economists Matter?" in George J. Stigler, *The Economist as Preacher and Other Essays* (Chicago: University of Chicago Press, 1982), pp. 3–13 and 57–67.

proposals for an industrial policy or tax-based incomes policies and deregulation. Advocacy of such proposals is obviously not confined to professionals; their proponents include many who do not fully grasp either the underlying logic or the practical political and social implications. Some of the economists' intellectual systems, such as Keynesianism, monetarism, or supply-side economics, have widespread currency among members of the public who lack the requisite professional knowledge and technical capacity to comprehend them. The permeability of the division between professional and amateur economics is one of the crucial problems economists encounter when they seek to influence public opinion or government action.

As Richard Whitley has noted:

for the many intellectual fields whose vocabulary and concepts are quite close to ordinary language and whose results are of clear public interest, such as most of the social sciences and the humanities in many historical periods ... lay standards and terms are involved in intellectual debates and controversies so that what counts as knowledge is often affected by successful mobilization of lay elites and/or diffusion of doctrines to a wide audience.[3]

The point can be amplified as follows:

[T]he topics which economics purports to deal with are important everyday issues and the terminology of economic analysis is close to ordinary language even if technical definitions of these terms are quite distinct. Profit, for example, has a technical meaning in microeconomics which is not the same as usages in conventional accountancy – which themselves vary. In their internal discussions and rankings of intellectual significance of contributions economists use their technical concepts and their own standards of evaluation, yet they also make policy pronouncements and seek to intervene in everyday debates and discussions where terms are not technically defined and they do not control usages. Indeed, it seems unlikely that economics would receive so much financial support if it was not thought that its subjects and problems were strongly connected with everyday phenomena. Thus, within the professional fraternity, performance and significance standards, and technical terminology, are fairly strongly controlled by the reputational elite but there is also considerable overlap with commonsense terms and concerns which legitimates public support and sometimes affects standards. As with the problem of demonstrating effective control over phenomena, this difficulty is resolved to some extent in economics by separating analytical economics from fields of application and insulating it from external influences to a very high degree.

---

[3]Richard Whitley, "Knowledge Producers and Knowledge Acquirers: Popularization as a Relation between Scientific Fields and Their Publics," in Terry Shinn and Richard Whitley, eds. *Expository Science: Forms and Functions of Popularization,* vol. IX of *Sociology of the Sciences* (Dordrecht, Holland; Boston and Hingham, MA: Reidel, 1985), p. 8.

Thus economics is a hybrid science in which divergent features are combined so that the core exhibits different characteristics to the peripheral subfields.[4]

In the spreading of ideas language is crucial, and debates within the economics profession, as among the laity, can easily degenerate into misunderstandings and disagreements about the meaning of terms. Among professional economists the protracted controversy over the terms "savings" and "investment" provoked by Keynes's *General Theory,* and the more recent confusion over the various meanings of Keynesianism and monetarism, are classic examples. Disputes of this kind, at times resembling medieval theological disputations, undeniably diminish the economists' collective intellectual authority; but they may be unavoidable, and they have significant implications. The "politics of meaning" is a subject of growing interest to social scientists.[5]

An unusual, perhaps unique, example in economics was Alfred Marshall's ability to shape the accepted terminology in use in neoclassical economics around the turn of the century. It was of direct importance in creating and strengthening the influence of the Cambridge school which dominated British academic economics from the 1890s to the 1930s, and it also had important implications for the reputation of British economists in the wider community, both at home and abroad.[6] Terminological agreement or disagreement is an important determinant of the degree of consensus among professional economists, a matter of some discussion in recent years. Samuel Brittan's stimulating book, *Is There an Economic Consensus?,* reveals a substantial measure of agreement among economists on a range of politically charged and controversial topics, such as the pricing of public transport, air purification (antismog) policy, the provision of subsidized housing for low-income groups, and the relationships between private and public interests. He found that the disagreements among the economists were less than those between the economists and the "politicians," and not because the questions posed were either esoteric or technical. Moreover, with respect to such objectives as employ-

[4]Richard Whitley, *Intellectual and Social Organization of the Sciences* (London: Oxford University Press, 1984), pp. 255–6.

[5]Peter Sederberg, *The Politics of Meaning: Power and Explanation in the Construction of Social Reality* (Tucson, AZ: University of Arizona Press, 1984).

[6]For discussion of this matter see A. W. Coats, "Sociological Aspects of British Economic Thought, Ca. 1889–1930," *Journal of Political Economy,* 75 (Oct. 1967), especially pp. 710–11; also John Maloney, *Marshall, Orthodoxy, and the Professionalization of British Economics* (Cambridge: Cambridge University Press, 1985).

ment, growth, the containment of inflation, and international monetary stability, on which there was apparently a strong political consensus, there was "a readiness to follow professional opinion if only it would point the way."[7] However, according to F. A. von Hayek, as cited approvingly by Brittan,

> those who gain the public ear consist of two elements: the communicators, who are expert at putting other people's ideas or information across, but are amateurs in the substance; and professional people theorizing outside their own field, doctors reforming the political system, engineers putting the economy to rights, and so on. . . .
>
> Unfortunately [Brittan continues], partly as a result of growing specialization and technicality within the subject, there has been, as Stigler has pointed out, a retrogression in the ability of economists to communicate with other intellectuals. The difficulty is not just that economists are bad popularisers or that their message is unwelcome. It goes much deeper. The real trouble is that economists are no longer sure what it is that they wish to communicate to a wider public. Individual economists feel passionately on particular subjects in opposition to other economists. But they are far less sure of what it is that they can put forward which would both reflect a professional consensus and also convey a relatively simple message to the educated laymen.[8]

Brittan's views are debatable, but they are worth quoting, however impressionistic, for he is probably the most distinguished and influential contemporary British economic journalist. There have also been two other more-or-less systematic efforts to gauge the degree of professional consensus among economists, one a multinational study of agreement, disagreement, and uncertainty on a range of specific propositions, the other a study of views on free trade among economists in a single large economics department, at Michigan State University.[9] The latter study illustrates both the need to ascertain the reasons why economists hold the views they profess, as well as the actual views held.

---

[7]Samuel Brittan, *Is There an Economic Consensus? An Attitude Survey* (London: Macmillan, 1973), p. 74.

[8]Samuel Brittan, *Capitalism and the Permissive Society* (London: Macmillan, 1973), pp. 11–13. Supply-side economics is cited as an example of economists' uncertainty about what they wish to communicate in Philip Mirowski, "What's Wrong with the Laffer Curve?" *Journal of Economic Issues*, 16 (Sept. 1982), p. 823.

[9]They are, respectively, Bruno S. Frey, Werner W. Pommerehne, Friedrich Schneider, and Guy Gilbert, "Consensus and Dissensus among Economists: An Empirical Inquiry," *American Economic Review*, 74 (Dec. 1984), pp. 986–94, and Warren J. Samuels, "Economics as a Science and Its Relation to Policy: The Example of Free Trade," *Journal of Economic Issues*, 14 (March 1980), pp. 163–85.

Previous work on the spread of ideas

The nature of ideas

The "plan of action" definition of an idea adopted above is associated with the American pragmatists, Peirce, James, and Dewey, who avoided Hume's skepticism by abandoning the "image" theory of thinking. However, pragmatism has been a minority view in the history of philosophy, and although it is currently enjoying a vigorous revival, especially in the United States, it should not be allowed to obscure the duality involved in the term "idea," which covers both the representative percept (the mental image) and the object of conceptual thought. In the current philosophical climate there is a strong tendency to blur the distinction between ideas as such and the properties of things in the physical world.

It is usually risky to assert that a given idea is generally held, for there are differences within the economics profession and among members of the general public, and between these two categories. Thus it is obviously sensible in principle to differentiate the various forms or stages of an idea and follow it through from one group to another. However, this is more easily said than done. Tracing the history of ideas is an intellectual activity usually associated with the work of A. O. Lovejoy and his followers, who focused on "clusters" of "unit ideas" such as "nature," "reason," "romanticism," and "being," a type of study that has been described as the "cartography of ideas." This approach produces "thread" accounts of what Schumpeter termed the "filiation of ideas." The intellectual history approach to ideas is, by contrast, a much broader, less well-defined field of research. It can be a form of retrospective sociology of knowledge, dealing with either or both the history of the intellectual classes and the spread of ideas among ordinary as well as educated people. It includes studies of the relationship among ideas, drives, and interests, that is, intellectual and nonintellectual factors in individual and social psychology, and while encompassing such vague notions as "the spirit of the age" or the "climate of opinion," it also considers the role of ideas as the driving forces in history, an issue that links history with the social sciences.

Most pertinent to this volume is the new light intellectual historians are shedding on the transmission of ideas through various media and to differing audiences. Generalized expressions of concern or dissatisfaction with economists' relations with the public, including the business community and government, are abundant, especially in the institutionalist and left-wing literature.[10]

*Previous work on the spread of economic ideas: some
examples*

Our introductory observation that the spread of ideas in economics has not been seriously considered was an overstatement since some interesting exploratory work has been undertaken. For example, some twenty years ago a group of scholars examined the transmission of economic ideas among cultures,[11] and more recently there have been similar studies and investigations of the variety of roles economists play in particular societies.[12] Fritz Machlup's monumental project on the production and distribution of knowledge is also highly suggestive.[13] A preliminary effort to provide an analysis of the spread of economic ideas was made by Craufurd Goodwin who distinguished twelve possible unidirectional linkages. The most important of these were between economic theory and professional views on economic policy; economic theory and nonprofessional opinion; and among public opinion, events, and professional economists' interests and activities.[14]

---

[10]Underlying the discussion of these issues is the sensitive issue of the relationship between professional or scientific economics and ideology. An unusually well-argued example of the critiques of economics is Edward S. Herman, "The Institutionalization of Bias in Economics," *Media, Culture and Society,* 4 (July 1982), pp. 175–91. He "suggests the possibility that the entire drift of the science . . . may be decisively shaped by market forces" (p. 285; also see pp. 288–9). For more general treatments see Warren Samuels, "Ideology in Economics," in Sidney Weintraub, ed., *Modern Economic Thought* (Philadelphia: University of Pennsylvania Press, 1979), pp. 467–85; and Benjamin Ward, *The Ideal Worlds of Economics: Liberal, Radical and Conservative World Views* (New York: Basic, 1979).

[11]J. J. Spengler, "Notes on the International Transmission of Economic Ideas," *History of Political Economy,* 2 (Spring 1970), pp. 133–51, and references cited therein; and Craufurd D. W. Goodwin and I. B. Holley, Jr., eds., *The Transfer of Ideas: Historical Essays* (Durham, NC: Duke University Press, 1968).

[12]For example, A. W. Coats, ed., *Economists in Government: An International Comparative Study* (Durham, NC: Duke University Press, 1981); George Rosen, *Western Economists and Eastern Societies: Agents of Change in South Asia, 1950–1970* (Baltimore: Johns Hopkins University Press, 1985).

[13]Fritz Machlup, *The Production and Distribution of Knowledge* (Princeton: Princeton University Press, 1962); and his incomplete series of studies, *Knowledge, Its Creation, Distribution, and Economic Significance,* 3 vols. (Princeton: Princeton University Press, 1980–4).

[14]Craufurd D. W. Goodwin, "Economic Theory and Society: A Plea for Process Analysis," *American Economic Review,* 62 (May 1972), pp. 409–15.

8   A. W. Coats and David C. Colander

Unfortunately, this model has been largely ignored by historians of economic thought.

In a recent collection of essays on the popularization of scientific ideas there are two essays on economics, one by Max Goldstrom, dealing with the popularization of classical economics in school textbooks, based on an earlier book-length study, and one by Gregory Claeys, on the concepts of productive and unproductive labor, both of which reveal the complexity of the multilevel processes involved.[15] There is also a scattering of relevant articles and books and a wealth of occasional and anecdotal material relating to professional conduct and ethics, but no systematic effort has been made to collect and analyze this material. The possibilities for revealing research on the dissemination of economic ideas to the wider community are considerable, as revealed by T. W. Hutchison's studies of British economists' public pronouncements (often pontifications) on major policy issues.[16] Using a wide range of contemporary newspapers and magazines, sources unduly neglected by most historians of economics, and comparing economists' statements before and after the events, he produced an account highly embarrassing to many of the authors cited. "The publishing outrage of the year!" one victim expostulated. But the serious side of the exercise was its implications for the profession's reputation and for the question of professional responsibility. Somewhat similar issues arise in discussions of the roles of professional economists and economic journalists.[17]

An adequate understanding of the spread and influence of scientific or professional ideas is directly dependent on knowledge of the structure and functioning of the discipline in question, matters on which sociologists of science have made significant advances in the two decades since the publication of T. S. Kuhn's masterly *Structure of Scientific Revolutions.* As Richard Whitley has observed, until recently the views of the dissemination of scientific knowledge have rested on an inadequate and ahistorical conception of the sciences that exaggerates both their unity and their privileged status. In reality,

scientific fields vary considerably in their degree of internal cohesion, of intellectual pluralism, of standardisation [*sic*] of research procedures, of control

[15]Shinn and Whitley, *op. cit.*
[16]See his *Economics and Economic Policy in Britain. Some Aspects of Their Interrelations* (London: Allen and Unwin, 1968), and *Knowledge and Ignorance in Economics* (Oxford: Blackwell, 1977), Chapter 5.
[17]Leonard Silk, Bernard D. Nossiter, Henry C. Wallich, Richard F. Janssen, and John Schnittker, "Economists Consider Economic Reporters and Vice Versa," *American Economic Review,* 62 (May 1972), pp. 373–90.

over performance and significance standards and of formalization of symbols.[18]

Consequently, it is no surprise that while some parts of economics are of greater interest and are readily communicated to a lay audience, others are more esoteric and protected from public scrutiny.

There are numerous methods by which ideas can spread – mental telepathy, dreams, communication, printed words, conversations, reported conversations, and so forth. Tracing and evaluating the spread of ideas requires an understanding of these lines of communication and the institutions which control them. Though there are many means of communication, the most important institutions are colleges and universities, publishing houses, the press, research institutes, foundations, political parties, and lobbying organizations.

Individuals in these institutions have a variety of agendas. For example, academic economists need to publish articles to enhance their status within the scientific reputational system and they tend to choose media and forms of presentation that achieve that end. Journalists need stories which fit into their space constraints and they are obliged to adopt a style designed to capture and hold their readers' attention. Politicians need new ideas to get themselves elected. Research institutes need to be financed and unless they have an adequate permanent endowment they will tend to choose research agendas which achieve that end, or go out of business. All these spheres interact, for there are overlapping media and styles of presentation. The study of the spread of ideas is the study of this complex interdependent network of communications.

As ideas move from the originator toward acceptance in theory or in policy, there is a constant interchange among individuals at these various institutions. For example, universities train legislative assistants, reporters, editors, columnists, and foundation staffs. Once these students graduate into the real world their decisions determine what articles will be written, what ideas will get funding, and what ideas will eventually become enshrined in laws. Thus, over time and indirectly, the teachers of ideas, not all of whom are in academic institutions, influence the choice of policy. But the flow also goes the other way. What the press reports influences what economists study, often with a substantial time lag. When a former student, now a legislative assistant, calls and suggests that some idea is interesting to her boss, the professor may redirect his or her research interests. Foundations influ-

---

[18]Whitley, in Shinn and Whitley, *op. cit.*, p. 11.

ence ideas even more directly. By channeling money to certain scholars they can influence which ideas are spread.[19]

When we consider this complicated set of interdependencies, a central question is whether the agendas of these institutions interact in such a way that the outcome is, if not the ideal, at least an acceptable method of spreading ideas. Answering that ill-specified question is not easy. Often, contradictory ideas exist simultaneously. For example, graduate schools have long since stopped teaching ideas such as the balanced budget multiplier or the consumption function, but these Keynesian ideas still figure prominently in introductory teaching. Similarly, textbooks used in high schools focus on institutional economics whereas in college neoclassical economic ideas predominate with little or no discussion of institutional influences and conditions.

A final general comment is that ideas evolve: at one point in time a set of ideas might be considered outlandish but subsequently become accepted as orthodoxy, or part of the conventional wisdom. For example, in the 1930s and 1940s, "liberal" interventionist economic and social ideas were in vogue; in the 1980s conservative economic ideas moved from kooky to respectable. However, rather than an evolutionary process, this may simply reflect changes in fashion.

The foregoing general reflections raise a variety of other questions: Is there a competition of ideas? Do the "best" ideas win out? Is there a natural process through which all ideas proceed? Is there a cycle of ideas so that the same ideas reappear in different form every so often? Generally speaking, intellectual historians shy away from these comprehensive issues, and we will do likewise.

Three models of the spread of ideas

Apart from bibliometrics, most studies of the spread of ideas have followed a humanistic approach, arguing that the more precise the elements compared and measured, the more potentially relevant infor-

[19]Serious research on the role of foundations in economics is now, at last, under way. See, especially, Earlene Craver, "Patronage and Directions of Research in Economics: The Rockefeller Foundation in Europe; 1924–1938," *Minerva*, 25 (Summer–Autumn 1986), pp. 205–22; and David M. Grossman, "American Foundations and the Support of Economic Research," *Minerva*, 20 (Spring–Summer 1982), pp. 59–82. For earlier, more impressionistic, observations from two Nobel prize winners, see George J. Stigler, "The Foundations and Economics," in Warren Weaver, ed., *U.S. Philanthropic Foundations: Their History, Structure, Management, and Record* (New York: Harper & Row, 1967), and Theodore W. Schultz, "Distortions of Economic Research," in William H. Kruskal, ed., *The Social Sciences, Their Nature and Uses* (Chicago: University of Chicago Press, 1982), pp. 122–33.

mation is eliminated.[20] Economists, however, have a proclivity for models and modeling and it therefore seems appropriate to outline some possible models of the spread of ideas. The three models we consider are the following:

1. the infectious disease model;
2. the marketplace for ideas;
3. the information theory model.

The infectious disease model

The spread of an idea can be likened to the spread of a disease. Epidemiologists model the spread of disease by dividing the population into subgroups: for example, in the easiest case, the sick and the healthy. They then attempt to measure the number of contacts among individuals of both types and to predict the rate at which an epidemic will spread. As applied to our topic, the economic ideas would be analogous to the disease, while contacts between individuals and groups constitute the spread points. Thus, we might expect an idea to gather momentum, spread rapidly, and eventually decline as a larger and larger proportion of the susceptible population is contacted. Elements such as novelty and the length of the audience's attention span are obviously relevant. But it would perhaps be overambitious to suggest that attempts might be made to apply the mathematics of dissipative structures to this subject matter.[21]

It may, however, be useful to distinguish between the population's receptiveness to an idea and that idea's actual spread. The emergence and spread of AIDS, for example, provides an awesome contemporary parallel, for as the course of that scourge has shown, it may first be necessary to break down barriers before an idea can spread. This is the essence of the propagandist's and the popularizer's function.

---

[20]In commenting on his attitude survey, Brittan said, "I shudder to think, however, what this enquiry would have yielded if it had been undertaken by the fashionable computerised methods, in which only rigidly specified alternatives would have been digested by a literal-minded magnetic tape incapable of reading marginal comments, or accompanying letters of widely varying style, form and length." *Is There an Economic Consensus?, op. cit.,* p. 25.

[21]The potentialities of this approach should not, however, be dismissed entirely. See, for example, Milan Zeleny's general study, *Autopoesis: The Theory of Living Organisations* (Oxford: Oxford University Press, 1981) and *Autopoesis, Dissipative Structures, and Spontaneous Social Orders,* which Zeleny edited for the AAAS Selected Symposium 55 (Boulder, CO: Westview Press, 1980). Also see Ilya Prigogine and Isabelle Stengers, *Order out of Chaos: Man's New Dialogue with Nature* (Toronto: Bantam, 1984).

The marketplace for ideas

The market model directs attention to the supply and demand for ideas and the competition among them. The supply of economic ideas comes mainly, though by no means exclusively, from economists, while the final demand for ideas comes from policymakers who need the ideas as inputs into policy proposals; from businesspeople, whose interests are mainly in the application of economic ideas, whether in forecasting, in reducing costs, or in setting prices; and from individuals, such as students and laymen, who are trying to understand the economy (or simply trying to get a degree which certifies that they understand the economy).

Economic theory tells us that if we want to understand which ideas spread and why, we must look at the incentives influencing the disseminating or receiving institutions and their clients, including the lay public. There are various audiences for scientific/professional ideas; for example,

1. the scientific community: science is a reputational system in which the scientist's status, autonomy, and access to funding and research resources will depend largely on his success in persuading his peers of the importance of his work to his fellow specialists and to specialists in related fields (i.e., intrascientific communication);
2. the lay public; and, in between,
3. more specialized groups, such as, in the economist's case: congressional committees, government departments, individuals or groups of businesspeople and bankers, research foundations (which initiate and/or support research), international economic agencies, etc. In some instances there are substantial feedback effects that directly influence the content, scale, and distribution of knowledge production.[22]

The diffusion process is inevitably selective, highlighting certain ideas or aspects of a system while obscuring or fragmenting others. Which ideas work their way through the system and how the ideas are changed as they proceed depends on the incentives of individuals in the particular institutions and on how those incentives and institutions interact. These interactions emphasize certain aspects of ideas while fragmenting others. The Keynesian revolution in economics provides

[22]Adapted from Whitley, in Shinn and Whitley, *op. cit.*, p. 4, ff., where this issue is discussed at length.

a striking illustration. In Keynes's *General Theory,* there is little or no reference to monetary or fiscal policy, but in what became known as Keynesian economics, monetary and fiscal policy were virtually the only Keynesian policies considered. This explains why it is cutomary nowadays to distinguish between Keynesian economics and the economics of Keynes.

And as if the aforementioned interactions were insufficiently complex, the incentives vary over time. Thus in considering why a particular idea caught on, it is not a trivial statement to say that the idea was at the right place at the right time. The conjuncture of content and context is crucial; but chance also plays a part. If Arthur Laffer hadn't had a convenient cocktail napkin, supply-side economics might never have emerged – or at least it might have developed in a different form and manner. Only by understanding the creation and diffusion process can we even hope to determine whether the spread of ideas is effective or can be made more so.

The market metaphor implies competition in ideas, and mainstream economists – insofar as they consider the matter at all – tend to assume that the spread of ideas works rather well, according to an invisible hand species of argument. So long as there is perfect or effective competition, all will be well: true or sound ideas will tend to prevail over ignorance, error, and vested interest. Would that this were so! But unfortunately, in the market for ideas perfect competition is no more likely than elsewhere.[23] The prevailing situation may perhaps best be described in terms of dynamic competition, with an uneven distribution of power among disseminating and receiving individuals and institutions. With respect to individuals, reputation and position are crucial: the cost of effective dissemination falls sharply the more widely the individual economist is known and respected. Here decreasing marginal costs obtain, and the same applies to institutions.

There are, of course, exceptions. Reporters look for controversy, stirring it up deliberately if necessary, and thus a critic of the received professional wisdom may be able to get a hearing more easily than can a minor mainstream economist. Because many reporters have few reliable criteria by which to assess the quality of professional economic ideas – though they often demonstrate a healthy skepticism of the more novel or esoteric offerings – the determinants of access to the media are likely to be such factors as personality (is the economist

---

[23] *Cf.* Schumpeter's view cited *supra,* footnote 1. Also see the interesting discussion, "Economics of Scientific Publications," in Joseph Agassi, *Science and Society: Studies in the Sociology of Science* (Dordrecht, Holland; Boston and Hingham, MA: Reidel, 1981), Chapters 12 and 13.

good for an arresting quotation?), availability (does he or she live in the area?), and luck (did they meet at a recent cocktail party, press gathering, or conference?) rather than the quality of the ideas.

So, although there is real competition in the spread of economic ideas, it is messy; no single simple model will suffice. With respect to dynamic competition the issue is whether it is workable. Does the propagation process serve informational or monopolistic purposes? Are there significant unfair practices, and, if so, what are they? Do particular groups or organizations exercise control over freedom of expression, whether within or outside the economics profession, and, if so, by what means and with what effects? How can presenting and participation be fostered?

Obviously there are many issues here that deserve careful study. Since our purpose in this volume is to raise issues, not to restrict discussion, it is appropriate to suggest that the spread of economic ideas, in the United States at least, seems to be becoming more, rather than less, complex, despite the speed of modern media communication. Thus, in the case of the Washington "economics industry," to cite Herbert Stein's expressive term, we find that both the number and the variety of professional and quasi-professional inputs into economic policy discussion have increased rapidly of late, and with bewildering effects – a view shared by Alice Rivlin, another eminent contemporary observer.[24] A significant new ingredient in the mixture is the emergence of a new type of activist foundation dedicated – unlike earlier foundations, which were ostensibly designed to promote unbiased research – to the propagation of certain ideas and the combatting of others. In so doing they are, of course, changing the nature of the competition of ideas.

The information theory model

Our earlier definition of an idea as a plan of action leads directly to another way of viewing the spread of ideas – in terms of information theory. The basic concepts here are the source and the receiver of information linked by transmission channels. Information dispatched from the source is encoded, in the transmission process it becomes interspersed with noise, and it is eventually decoded by the receiver.

The structure can be useful for organizing our thinking. Information corresponds to ideas, with the economists as sending agents, policy-

[24]Herbert Stein, "The Washington Economics Industry," *American Economic Review* Papers and Proceedings, 76 (May 1986), pp. 1–9; Alice Rivlin, "Economics and the Policy Process," *American Economic Review,* 77 (March 1987), pp. 1–10.

makers and members of the lay public as receivers, and the various individuals, groups, and institutions as the transmission channels.

The economist's job is to think up ideas that may be useful to society and encode them so that they can be efficiently transmitted through the institutions. The job of the transmission institutions is to send out the ideas with an optimal amount of noise and to decode them so that the policymaker can use them to improve society.

Structuring the inquiry in this manner leads to questions similar to those discussed earlier. For example:

1. Are the transmission institutions the most appropriate?
2. Is the code used in the transmission process the most appropriate?
3. Is the decoding process correctly carried out, so that it is the most efficient process and it receives ideas that reflect those being sent out?
4. Is the feedback process through which economists are trained to send out ideas the most efficient?

Although these questions are similar to those to which the economic model directed us, the framework of analysis and the issues information theory directs us to consider are different.

The general feeling at the conference at which the papers in this volume were presented was that although these three models were suggestive, the processes through which ideas spread were too numerous and diverse to model formally at this time. Thus, in this volume there is no general theory, or even specific theory, about how ideas spread. Nonetheless, we believe the papers in this volume add insight and understanding to the process.

Organization of the volume

The volume is divided into four parts. Part I discusses the spread of ideas within the profession. The first three papers in it consider the state of the profession. The papers by Robert Clower and David Colander argue that the ideas with which much of the profession is concerned are no longer relevant to the functioning of the economy or to policy. Most of what economists do, including most of their formal modeling, is not even pertinent to the realm of pure ideas; it is primarily a means toward self-promotion and fame within the profession. Clower put this view neatly when he asked, "How many footnotes do we need?" Robert Solow provides the reasonable mainstream response to Clower and Colander, arguing that they are too cynical.[25] Most economists are doing Kuhnian-type normal research: some is good, some bad, but the median is near O.K. He argues that the formalism that Colander attacks is an essential means to clarity, and that clarity is the goal economists should shoot for.

The next paper, by Charles Kindleberger, offers one economist's view of how ideas spread and considers some examples from international trade. He discusses how he processes the flow of information and then takes up five categories of ideas. He points out that supposedly "new ideas" are often simply old ideas held by younger economists who are not familiar with the history of the discipline.

Colin Day's paper views university presses as communicators of economic ideas from highbrow to middlebrow readers, a function complementing the work of professional economic journals. In writing specialist articles economists need not adjust to the audience, which is usually well-defined, and they can adopt a well-recognized standard style. Books, however, are different, and he considers the various types – such as the research monograph, the integrative volume, the "original" contribution, and the "synthesis for the middlebrow." He also draws attention to gaps in the supply.

Part II treats the spread of ideas from economists to the public, starting with Solow's complaint that in the process economists' ideas turn to mush. The reasons for this are complicated, but he is especially concerned with economists' methods of handling empirical data. If economists were to use simpler, more robust models, and were more judicious in using evidence, their effectiveness might increase markedly. Lacking this, he favors a little more silence.

David Warsh's paper is a case study written from an economic journalist's perspective. He shows how the idea of strategic trade policy spread and undermined many of the arguments for free trade.[26] He argues that the idea followed two parallel tracks, one through the popular press and one through academia, and argues that the role for an economic journalist is to mediate between the two.

In the final paper in this section, Donald Lamm, a publisher, offers a series of trenchant observations on economist authors' predominant style and subject matter, and their tendency to leave the big issues to

[25]Initially we wrote "mainstream response," but after Solow pointed out to us that the "real mainstream" response would be much more "scientistic," we added the adjective "reasonable."
[26]Strategic trade policy is closely related to the question of increasing returns in international economics, which Kindleberger argues is not so new after all. Charles Kindleberger, "How Ideas Spread among Economists: Examples from International Economics." Chapter 5, this volume.

nonacademic writers. Publishers must also share the blame, but "as long as economists insist on placing the highest value on exchanges with other economists, the common reader will remain an outsider, convinced that in contemporary economics the situation is hopeless, but not serious." He provides a vivid illustration of the manner in which specific institutional characteristics can determine which ideas are accepted and which are neglected.[27]

Part III deals with the flow of ideas between economists and policymakers. The first paper, by A. W. Coats, reviews the professional economists' collective experience of employment by governments and international agencies since World War II, mainly with reference to the United States and Britain. He is concerned both with the economist's role as adviser to policymakers and with the value and limitations of economic knowledge and techniques within bureaucratic structures.

Next, William Barber maintains that, in general, "arguments derived from political opportunism will win out," a disquieting conclusion from the economists' standpoint. He notes the large and expanding role that economists are playing in government and shows that although there are a number of established pipelines through which economic ideas flow into government, these pipelines provide "no assurance that new economic ideas will be effectively spread."

In "The Exchange of Favors in the Market for Commitments" James Galbraith looks at the issue from a slightly different perspective. He argues that the exchange metaphor best fits the way economic ideas are treated in the political sphere, and explains how specific institutional characteristics determine which ideas are accepted and which are dropped. The final paper in this section demonstrates that the flow of economic ideas into the policy process does not always run smoothly. Examining the course of events leading up to the tax reform legislation of 1986, Joseph Minarik shows how, in this instance, the conventional wisdom was overturned and some of the leading legislative actors reversed themselves, even in defiance of the law of political gravity.

Part IV considers the funding and the spread of ideas. Craufurd Goodwin considers the recent history of the funding of ideas, looking specifically at the Ford Foundation's changing role in spreading economic ideas. In a fascinating and illuminating article he recounts how a marriage seemingly made in heaven has ended in a trial separation largely because the economists' professorial beliefs and expectations,

---

[27]I think I learned more from this paper than from any other – except my own, in which I learned once again how little I know (A. W. Coats).

on such matters as philanthropy and human welfare, were incompatible with the Foundation's aims and expectations. From both parties' standpoint it was a sadly missed opportunity.

Next, James Smith considers the role of "think tanks" in spreading economic ideas, pointing out that these private bodies were instrumental in creating in-government think tanks such as the OMB, GAO, and CBO, and that these have reduced the direct impact of private think tanks. He also points out that research studies have only a limited influence on legislators who have little or no time to read them. Instead, the most effective channels are indirect. He says that because early practitioners set the fact-based, objective mold in their pragmatic approach to ideas, thus leading to a narrower and narrower emphasis, some modern-day denizens of conservative think tanks have been able to challenge pragmatism and gain a comparatively wide audience by delivering ideas instead of "mindless accretions of facts." They follow Richard Weaver's maxim: ideas have consequences. Economic ideas are digested into Op-Ed pieces and magazine articles where they may be read by legislators or their assistants. The new conservative think tanks have used this knowledge and tailored their output to exert maximum effect, and their strategy creates considerable difficulties for the older think tanks.

Daniel Newlon's paper examines the funding of ideas within the profession, looking specifically at NSF's contribution. He provides a wealth of statistical material documenting who and what NSF has funded, and ends with a vigorous defense of the NSF's role in the funding of ideas.

In his concluding summary of the conference proceedings, David Colander points out that much economics research is funded indirectly, because many academic economists have quantities of "free" time after fulfilling their teaching commitments. Whether this free time is used efficiently, however, is another matter. It seems likely that the additional funding supplied by NSF and private foundations has, however, a much larger impact in directing research than does the indirect academic provision since NSF's and the private foundations' comes with strings attached. Colander challenges Newlon's assertion that the NSF has been successful, suggesting that there is a degree of faddishness in its funding and a replication of mainstream ideas. However, there are numerous other private funding agencies, such as the Sloan Foundation, so that while the funding system for ideas is not perfect, it may not require a radical reformation.

The final paper in this section, by Gordon Tullock, is a look at the funding of ideas from another angle. He sees the problem of funding ideas as being the nonexistence of intellectual property rights. Funding economic ideas should be done with the idea of mimicking the nonexisting market. Turning his attention to some moderate proposals for reform, he questions the value of the current peer review process and proposes the awarding of prizes for work that has already been done. These, he argues, would help reduce the current strong pressures for faddishness in research.

Conclusion

As will be obvious to the reader, these papers do not provide the final word on the spread of economic ideas. They do, however, provide an insightful look at the process and will, we hope, stimulate further research on the subject.

PART I

From economist to economist

CHAPTER 2

The state of economics: hopeless but not serious?

ROBERT W. CLOWER

In thinking about the spread of economic ideas, we must first consider the state of economics and what ideas economics has to convey. While I was mulling over these issues, I was reminded of the characterization of the political situation in one of the Balkan countries as "serious but not hopeless." In economics, the situation is perhaps the opposite: hopeless but not serious. Much of economics is so far removed from anything that remotely resembles the real world that it's often difficult for economists to take their own subject seriously. Publishers have sometimes asked why we economists don't write as if we were intellectually engaged; why don't we produce books about the marvels of our science? The answer is simple. Economics doesn't have much to marvel at. Once you've got beyond some elementary arguments, it's as though most of economics dealt with footnotes to material that has already been spelled out a hundred years ago.

How many grand ideas are there in economics that are worth talking about? How much of economics is just dressing up common sense in difficult language? How many footnotes do we need? Adam Smith's contribution to economics is important not in terms of technical detail but because he indicated the solution to a paradox: How can an economy where people are turned loose on one another – an economy which is driven by competition and greed – yield any kind of order if no one directs it? Adam Smith's great accomplishment is to have provided a Newtonian picture of the economic system. At least as a long-run proposition, Adam Smith shows that there will be an orderly disposition of resources, an allocation of goods to those who most desire them, an allocation of activities in efficient directions, and so forth. In that system, no one intends the orderly result, but somehow individuals are led to cooperate in spite of their pursuit of self-interest. That's a grand idea, but it isn't something we need to talk about all that much these days.

Unlike many other professions, economics combines a vast array of different kinds of talents. Those who call themselves economists are not all academics, or even specialists in economics. And most academic economists pride themselves on being sufficiently versatile to handle theory, applications, politics, sociology, and almost anything else. They need not and don't stick to specialized work. If you think about a field like physics, there's an elite group of people whom *no one* knows about except those in the physics profession, and this bunch of people deals with the grand ideas of physics. (People learned about Einstein because he was a Nobel laureate, but he didn't get his laureate for relativity theory; he got it for a heuristic analysis of the photoelectric effect.)

In economics, what is that elite group? It includes the more erudite of the mathematical economists. When, for example, one of them some years ago was nominated for the J. B. Clark medal, his name was not familiar to half or more of the members of the AEA executive committee. There are a few people of this sort in economics, people who are not well-known, who deal with the highest reaches of economic theory, and who are still busying themselves improving on Adam Smith's vision. I don't think they have anything to communicate to the general public because Adam Smith already said about all that is worth saying, and he said it in an intelligible way.

Another group in the economics profession, probably the majority, fancy that they are engineers, social planners. They read theory; they understand the basic ideas. Some of them are extremely adept at working out problems. They don't pretend to develop grand ideas – they don't see any to be developed. They're just elaborating models. I think there's a good market for this, but it's not the sort of thing that yields many books.

And then the economics profession has a big group of people who are much like high school or junior college teachers of physics. Because of the paucity of grand ideas in economics, these people believe that they already know all that's worth knowing. It would be nice if we could communicate with them, but you can't expect to deal with them on anything but a pedestrian level.

All things considered, the profession has few people who are capable of writing for the general public in an exciting way. So if Donald Lamm is looking for interesting books that W. W. Norton, Inc., can publish, he's going to find them as scarce as good books on physics or chemistry or molecular biology. There are few great scholars who can do this kind of thing. Einstein could write on relativity. How many other examples are there? Perhaps Max Planck ... but he got out of economics because he found it too messy. "Difficult" was the word he used, I think, but "messy" is surely what he meant.

Our problem these days is that we feel economics is a mess but the situation is perhaps not that serious. The reason it's a mess is that since the Keynesian revolution we've had to deal with the short run. In that area we're all in a state of confusion and muddle. It isn't that we don't have a fairly clear conception of the long-run forces of self-interest and competition and how ultimately they will work out to some kind of coherent disposition of resources. We've got the long run adequately analyzed. The trouble is that we live in the short run, and nowadays we're working with issues that don't bear any relationship, typically, to the kinds of issues that were dealt with – and dealt with successfully – by the nineteenth-century economists. We're dealing with Keynesian problems of short-run adjustment. We think we're going to be forecasters and engineers and we think we have the necessary tools at our command. The tools look scientific – as precise, often, as the tools of physics. This is the kind of *hubris* that the classical economists would have eschewed. Most of them did not try to work with short run adjustment processes and short-run consequences of particular government actions because they knew they didn't have the tools to do it.

Since the 1930s, economists have developed the attitude that we're not really academics, we're not really intellectually involved, but instead somehow or other we've got to get involved in the political and social melee, and we have something useful to say there. I think most of us who have tried to say something useful have discovered that what we have to say is very often wrong, misguided, or impractical. That's because we don't, in fact, have an understanding of how the economy actually works, or if we do have such an understanding it doesn't fit into any model of how the economy will respond in the short run to shocks. Three months, six months, a year ahead – we cannot forecast worth a damn except by extrapolation.

These are very complicated problems. Are our existing paradigms, the kind of thing that comes out of Smith or Walras or Marshall, suitable for handling them?

You might get a clue from Marshall himself. You won't get a precise model in Marshall because he did not believe that you could go from the long run to the short run to the market period using the same kinds of basic constructs. He's just fuzzy the whole way, because he does not believe it's meaningful to talk about a thing like "the short-run supply curve," much less short-run demand. He didn't develop much of a theory of oligopoly because he could see that once you started talking about the tactics of business firms in the short run, you deal with how prices are actually set, and how markets actually operate. In these matters, there isn't much to say at a general level that would fit into a decent textbook.

Most economists today are still looking for some kind of grand scheme to handle these short-run processes, and I don't think it's there. You certainly won't find it in Keynes's *General Theory*. I was fascinated recently by Frederick Lavington's book on the trade cycle, a short little book. It repays reading now. It was published in the early 1920s. It's a far more intelligible account of the general theory than *The General Theory* is. It covers much of the same ground as *The General Theory* and covers it with a focus that is dead right, expressed in a way that the most casual businessperson or common reader could instantly grasp. The language is straightforward, the background is there, the theory that is needed to understand what he's doing is set forth. He doesn't go far, but he has some notions that are very nice.

Wicksell in one of his early works said it should not be the main business of economists simply "to make common sense difficult"; but economists seem to have concentrated on doing just that, elaborating the obvious in ever more complicated ways. We've produced a collection of theoretical constructs that give us satisfaction for teaching, and we can terrorize our students with them, but they don't help us much in arriving at an intellectual understanding of the world in which we live. Bob Solow is clear, and he's right, that you can tell from a theoretical model what a person is saying. But an equally important question is: What is the person talking about? We're forced to interpret for ourselves most theoretical models because there isn't sufficient background provided to indicate what they refer to – and as often as not they have no empirically sensible interpretation.

Most economics classes nowadays are made up of large numbers of students, and it would be nice if we could expect them to read something. After all, if the student is confused by the textbook, he's likely to turn to the teacher – who will confuse him even more. To deal with that confusion, the student should read two or three principles books and then go back and read one of the treatises on which they are based. He should read Marshall, for instance. He should read Adam Smith – a little bit. He should read Robert Heilbroner's *Worldly Philosophers*, and he'll find a lot of things are sorted out that are never sorted out by talking to any professor. But the idea of students actually being required to read and the idea of professors actually being able to check up on them have gone by the board as class sizes have expanded from 20 to 30 to 240.

The intermediate economics classes at places like UCLA run anywhere from 150 to 200 students. These are advanced undergraduate courses in monetary theory and intermediate micro. What can you do in that kind of a situation? Students don't read unless they get intellectually and emotionally engaged. It's a real trick to pull 200 students into that. I don't think we can do it by directing their attention to all these policy issues. Big issues aren't why students are in college. Students are in college to have their intellects provoked – and very often they just don't get that from economics.

I've had a long stint as a journal editor, and that's an interesting experience if you want to know the connection between the spread of economic ideas and publishing. I used to think that I was responsible for attracting good papers and getting their messages into print. In retrospect, I realize that what I was getting was just what the profession was producing. The editor doesn't have much impact. An editor can filter out certain kinds of things – but not much, certainly not in a journal such as *Economic Inquiry.* When I moved on to *The American Economic Review,* I felt that there, at least, I would be seeing a more representative collection of papers come across the desk. Maybe I did. It's hard to tell whether a collection is representative. But the experience turned out to be shattering. What was remarkable was the absolute dullness, the lack of any kind of new idea, that predominated in the selection of papers I got. Close to a thousand manuscripts a year – and I swear that the profession would be better off if most of them hadn't been written, and certainly if most of them hadn't been published. Most of the published papers could have been left in discussion paper form, with a great benefit to everyone and a great saving of resources.

If, as some people have suggested, textbooks are a major outlet for thoughtful ideas, God help us. The typical principles book is pretty obviously a commercial proposition. You try something out and if the balloon doesn't fly, you take it out. The neoclassical synthesis entered textbooks in the 1950s largely because books that packaged "radical" Keynesian ideas in "conservative" neoclassical wrappings had better commercial prospects during the McCarthy era. I think the strategy was successful – or maybe it was just that McCarthy died. Then we got doses of Marxian economics. The reason Marx is leaving textbooks now is that it no longer sells.

If you look at textbooks generally, it's amazing how the standard course these days is patterned after the original Samuelson; we haven't had any fundamental changes. Take macroeconomics. What do these texts do? They set forth a simple view of how macroeconomic equilibrium is achieved and then put us through eight, ten, maybe fifteen chapters of drill on meaningless and mindless multiplier exercises. One of the first things the text teaches us is that there is no reliable relationship in the short run between consumption and income, but then the relationship is used in multiplier exercises in the rest of the chapters. How can that be? How could one write a textbook that said as little as what's said? How would you teach a course on the subject? We do it – but a lot of it is just mindless activity.

The economics profession is in rather a sad state at the present time. I don't know whether it's because of our detachment from the humanities or our detachment from the history of economic thought. I try to persuade myself that what's being talked about now is important, but the truth is that in contemporary monetary theory I'd be happier using an 1802 book by Thornton than any other text. I don't see anything better than that around, anything more intelligent or more comprehensive in its coverage. I'd supplement, of course, with a couple of essays by Hume. That would be about the end of the course – and there would be no lack of interesting and relevant things to talk about.

What about price theory? Well, I guess you would have to introduce your students to something modern there. Even so, I sometimes think that we could use Edgeworth's *Mathematical Psychicks,* introduce the students to an Edgeworth Box, and have done with general equilibrium and welfare economics – because a lot of the rest is simply footnoting.

It isn't that I don't think there are unsolved problems. On the contrary, I do think so. But the real difficulty in economics is that there are empirical problems to which we do not have adequate solutions at the present time. There's a lot of interesting and important work going on in specialized fields that deal with this. A book such as Arthur Okun's *Prices and Quantities* is just full of interesting unresolved problems that need to be worked on. It's in this kind of area that one sees interesting papers. If you want to know where the real action is, look at conferences like this one. Every conference volume – not the journals – will have one or two papers where you'll find out *why* a man was thinking in a certain way. Maybe it will come out some time – but up to now none of this stuff is percolating into textbooks. The core of economic theory that we are teaching is not being affected – and that's a pity.

Keynes once said, "If some day we could manage to get ourselves thought of as humble, competent people, on a level with dentists, that would be splendid." I think that if we could ever convince ourselves that we were competent, we'd have no reason to be humble. And there would be no dearth of good books – even decent textbooks. There would be shorter courses, but with more meat in them. But the way things are going, in many cases, we persuade ourselves that the world out there, even in the short run, looks like our model of a purely competitive economy. That is the world many economists, even if they know it isn't there, think it convenient to work with. As long as we're not willing to deal with the real messiness of our subject, we're going to be in a "crisis" – not just in macro but also in micro. Economists are trying to say too much about things where they haven't the knowledge to improve on refined common sense. That's why our situation is serious. If we can't somehow do a better job of fitting our grasp to our reach, our situation may also be hopeless.

CHAPTER 3

The invisible hand of truth

DAVID C. COLANDER

In his biting critique of the economics profession Robert Clower suggests that much of the profession is irrelevant, more concerned with techniques and game-playing than with ideas. Because it is irrelevant, many economists do not take their own subject seriously. He asks, "How many footnotes do we need?" In my view, Clower's critique of the profession is correct; the spread of economic ideas is seriously undermined by the educational institutions that have developed in the United States.

Arguing that much of what economists do is irrelevant goes against what is currently in vogue in the philosophy of science; most scientists seem implicitly to believe that there exists an invisible hand which guides science to the truth. In this normal science view, scientists search after understanding by dividing up a set of questions, and trying to answer one small subset of those questions. Their answer to the question: "Does this lead to Truth?" is, "Yes, each researcher is looking at only a small part of the puzzle, but, combined, economists' research is the best way of approaching truth." Solow argues below that this normal science view is the generally held view of what economists do within the profession. Yes, he agrees, there are some minor problems; some researchers are doing irrelevant work, but these are problems of any scientific profession; in total, economics is not that bad and no worse than any other field.

The view that Clower, I, and many other critics of the profession hold is that in economics normal science has run amok. The invisible hand of truth has lost its guiding influence. Clearly, some normal science, and some advancement in understanding, takes place, but that advancement is the exception, not the rule, and may not even be large enough to replace what is forgotten. The reason why economics has run amok is to be found in the sociological approach to economics which focuses on the internal dynamics of the profession: who is allowed to become a member, who gets promoted, who gets paid what, who gets the laurels, as opposed to the external dynamics which considers how truth-seeking individuals can best find truth. Philosophers of science have given short shrift to the internal dynamics (which they see as external to science); they assume that researchers have a desire to find the truth and do their best to answer questions that will advance science. They believe that if they can specify a scientific method which will most likely lead to discovering the truth, then researchers will follow that scientific method. But that is simply an assumption. They do not logically show why people want to discover the truth.

The sociological approach to methodology which I follow is more agnostic; it allows that people may have an inherent desire to discover the truth, but they may not, either because they aren't interested or because the internal dynamics in the profession directs self-interest toward other ends. There is a connection between self-interest and discovering the truth – the individual who advances knowledge advances in the profession – but it is a loose and often tenuous connection, and frequently the two diverge. The reasons they diverge are numerous: the requirements for advancing understanding change quickly while the institutions within which that search for knowledge takes place change only slowly. Deriving the financial support for research requires different skills than does actually doing research, and there is a difficulty of deciding what advancement is.

Combined, these leave most academic disciplines in a quandary. Some, like English literary criticism, make no pretense of advancement. They simply try to maintain a steady state of knowledge. Others, such as sociology or political science or anthropology, become fragmented, and each group does its own thing, with little agreement about what is advancement. Economics is amazingly coherent compared to the other social sciences. It has a "grand theory" accepted by a large majority of the profession, and an accepted methodology. However, that coherence does not come from a well-defined set of questions which researchers are trying to answer; rather, it comes from a core of knowledge that almost all economists believe should be mastered by an economist. That core knowledge is embodied in the core curriculum of graduate school economics programs and consists of a set of techniques and problem-solving algorithms. Economics is tied together not by a common set of questions, but by a common set of techniques.

The lack of a well-defined set of questions which, if answered, everyone agrees would advance understanding, is in part explained by the difficulty in empirical testing. Other formerly considered hard sciences – for example, modern physics – are becoming more conjectural as the costs of empirically testing various theories become more forbidding.

Such a state of affairs is most conducive to internal rather than external dynamics guiding the profession. In the absence of an agreed-upon specific set of questions researchers are attempting to answer, most research is done and most papers are written to establish positions for internal reasons. Economics research has become more a move in a game of chess than a search for understanding reality. An example is the recent spread of rational expectations in macroeconomics.

Rational expectations is a neat idea and makes the analysis of expectations an integral part of economic analysis. Early on, it was apparent to many, if not most, economic researchers that there were limitations on rational expectations as applied to macroeconomics. These included multiple equilibria making the delineation of a unique rational expectation impossible; informational problems; and game-theoretic problems. These difficulties, which most economists now agree make the rational expectations hypothesis untestable, did not stop economists from developing large numbers of rational expectations macro models which differed from one another by an assumption here or there. The result was the New Classical Revolution. Younger Keynesians quickly got in on the game; finance-constrained rational expectations models soon appeared which provided a theoretical justification for Keynesian policies even assuming rational expectations. By developing these models, graduate students and professors demonstrated that they could jump through hoops; the more hoops they could jump through the higher their income, chances for promotion, and standing in the profession. For many economists economic research has become the art of devising clever models and in doing so demonstrating one's technical virtuosity.

Rational expectations is only one example. There are many others. Econometric work often is done to demonstrate mastery of new techniques, rather than to answer questions. General equilibrium models with an infinite number of traders, optional taxation models, screening models – all fit the same mold. Empirically they are difficult, if not impossible, to test. Impossibility of empirical testing does not, and should not, stop economists from writing about a subject. But it does change the optimal form which the writing should take. If an idea can't be tested, it should be conveyed in as understandable a way as possible because ultimately others will judge it by the commonsense test. Does it make intuitive sense? Is it reasonable? The formal models that fill the economics journals are difficult to judge by the commonsense test, or can't be judged by that test at all. But nonetheless they are conceived and published. The reason is simple. The incentives in the economics profession are for articles, not ideas.

To remain an academic economist one must get tenure. Getting tenure means getting published. Economists who follow the academic route must publish their ideas in the form of articles, preferably in the best journals. Books, for some reason, count for little in the academic economics profession; books that are readable by the lay public count for less than nothing and can be the cause of an otherwise qualified person not getting tenure. John Kenneth Galbraith, who stopped writing for the profession and began writing directly to the public relatively early in his career, has stated that if he were advising a young economist today, he would advise that economist to write highly mathematical articles and not follow the route he himself took.

To say that the incentives within the system are for articles, not ideas, is not to say that the profession does not value ideas. If most economists were asked, they would respond that it is good ideas and insights, not articles, that should get a person tenure. However, because ideas cannot be quantitatively measured and articles can, generally schools rely on articles as a proxy for good ideas. And when one is up for tenure, any article that can get published is a good idea.

If there were a relatively close correlation between ideas and articles, this proxy would be acceptable, but there is not. Generally, the easiest impressive-looking articles to write do not involve exploring new ideas or ideas useful in policy; they involve using a new technique, or formalizing a simple idea that is well-known. Thus, that type of article predominates. Differentiating nonformal articles that say something from those that do not is exceptionally difficult. Thus, to write a good nonformalist article that will be perceived as being good is risky, if not downright crazy, especially when the individuals deciding what is good take a formalist approach.

The incentive system is readily ferreted out by economists. In a study Arjo Klamer and I did of graduate economics education, we asked students what would put them on the fast track. Approximately ninety percent said that knowledge of mathematics and knowledge of modeling were important; only about three percent said that these were unimportant. Only ten percent said that knowledge of economic literature was very important and only three percent said that knowledge of the economy was very important. Sixty-eight percent said knowledge of the economy was unimportant (Colander and Klamer, 1987). In my view, these answers suggest that something is terribly wrong in the economics profession and in the incentives that economists perceive.

No one is saying that, where possible, a formal model is not preferred to an informal model. But when mindsets become so fixated on formal models that individuals cannot deal with ideas outside of these models, then it is not surprising that many believe that economics has lost its bearings.

An example of the problem is the way in which economists deal with institutions. Put simply, in many of their models they assume them away, not because they believe institutions are unimportant, but because institutions cannot be neatly modeled. The needs of formalist expression overwhelm the needs of common sense, and clarity of the models gets in the way of clarity of meaning.

At dinner one night I described a proposal that I had written to an economist – a graduate of a top graduate program. After listening to my account of the proposal, he asked if I had a formal model for it. When I said no, he said that he didn't believe, and could not even think about, a proposal that wasn't formally modeled. Now, I am not saying that the idea was good or bad; what I am saying is that informally expressed ideas should be able to get a hearing within the economics profession. Generally, they cannot.

If the experience described above were unique, it could be dismissed. But it is the rule, not the exception. The majority of young economists today either will not, or can not, deal with ideas not presented in formal models. In their pursuit of logical rigorous models, they have lost their common sense.

Creating the current economics mindset does not come easy, and the molding of students starts early. Most undergraduate economics courses are courses in models and modeling. Much of the institutional richness which characterizes applied economics is removed from the analysis. Anyone who cannot accept modeling for the sake of modeling drops out. The few nonconformists who somehow nonetheless continue their study of economics into graduate school are usually weeded out in the first year.

In a perverse sort of way, the focus on modeling for the sake of modeling nicely serves the interest of the profession. Strong incentives toward modeling exist in both the suppliers and demanders of economic ideas conveyed in textbooks. Consider, first, the students' incentives. Students' immediate interest is to get good grades, or at least to pass. If they learn, too, that's nice, but for most students, their immediate concern is grades. In many ways, they prefer neat models because such models offer a closer correlation between study and grades than do less formal methods of conveying information. When one learns models, if one studies, one can assure oneself of an A. Studying ideas is necessarily vague and will likely lead to a wider variation in grades. Then, as modeling gets built into the courses, students who don't like modeling don't stay in economics. Faculty also have an incentive toward modeling: Teaching models is much easier than teaching ideas. It takes less time to prepare and less thought. Thus, models meet both students' and faculties' needs.

For both of these reasons, ideas that work their way into textbooks are often skewed to what is teachable and graphical, rather than to what makes the most sense in some larger context. I would go even further and suggest that unless an idea can be reduced to a simple graph, it has almost no chance of entering the core of what is taught in economics at the undergraduate level.

It is not simply the incentives within the economic profession but it is also the incentives within the entire academic community. For example, almost all ideas have political and social, as well as economic, components, but the fragmentation of social science disciplines, like restrictive work practices, limits how those ideas can be passed on.

The above arguments have been suggestive, rather than conclusive. They have, I hope, been sufficiently suggestive to provide a prima facie case that internal incentives within the profession should make one question whether the invisible hand guiding economics toward the truth is not, instead, an invisible foot stomping on anyone with the audacity to scream that the emperor has no clothes.

An addendum

The above discussion has been critical of the economics profession, and I want to end on a more positive note, so that I will not be misinterpreted. All real-world systems involve perverse incentives. The perverse incentives in any real-world system must be judged in relation to the incentives in other real-world systems, not those in ideal systems. I am not making the argument that economics is uniquely perverse. Much in the world is perverse. Thus, when considering alternative institutions, it is important not to condemn a system automatically because it exhibits perverse incentives. My argument is simply that the system deserves to be considered more carefully than it has been. How should we change economic institutions is a complex question of comparative institutional analysis. It is, however, a question that should be addressed.

CHAPTER 4

Faith, hope, and clarity

ROBERT M. SOLOW

In the papers by Clower and Colander, which capture the mood of many of the critics of mainstream economics, there is a sense that our profession is marked by utter confusion and loss of confidence and bearings. I do not share that feeling, not at all, nor do most of the functioning economists I hang out with. There are obviously lots of important things I don't know and know I (we) don't know. I think that's inevitable, because I think economic truth is history-bound. There are very few permanent economic truths. So the questions keep changing and the answers to even old questions keep changing as society evolves. That doesn't mean that we don't know quite a bit that is useful, at any given moment. At any time there are bound to be some economists who think it's all a mess. Skeptic though I am, I find the hand-wringing and concern expressed in these papers grossly overdone. Most of the professional economists in the United States are out there doing normal science. They are about as happy in their work as any analogous group. Their research ranges from very bad to excellent, with a median somewhere near O.K. If Clower thinks that economists do not have much to say about the world, he should listen to what other people say. For example, I would argue that anyone who understands the contents of a standard macro text and has a grasp of the main economic magnitudes and the reliable econometric parameters knows vastly more than anyone who doesn't. I might roughly estimate what he/she knows as a sixth of what one would like to know and maybe two-thirds of what is knowable at this moment.

Colander and many critics would have us go back to earlier days when philosophy and the other social sciences were intertwined. He even argues that we should go back to the vague generalizations of Adam Smith. I yield to a dozen people or so in my admiration for Adam Smith, which is not unbounded. I do not regard *The Wealth of Nations* as a theory; I do not regard it as anything with policy implications. There isn't anybody in the whole economics profession who doesn't quote and claim to be a descendant of Adam Smith, capable of intuiting the most variegated implications from his book. (It has taken two centuries to understand when The Invisible Hand works and when it doesn't. Smith didn't know.) I need something more precise – something less amorphous, less vague, less Rorschach-ink-blot-like. I don't need something, necessarily, like the DRI model with one thousand incomprehensible equations. Somewhere in between I find my optimum. If asked where, I'd say that the optimum is something between three and seven equations.

A second complaint of the critics is that the positive and moral aspects of economics are intertwined. I agree; *the positive and the moral aspects of economics are very much intertwined.* But honesty and clarity require that in talking about economics we try our hardest to separate them. The economist may be both a dentist and a priest, but there is altogether too much in history of dentists telling you, "You must vote in the following way." Why must you do it? "Because I know about teeth." The fakery of implying moral precepts under the guise of scientifically validated statements goes back a long way in history and is much to be avoided. I think one ought to recognize how closely these aspects are tied together, but that means it is all the more important when you make a statement, as an economist, to state clearly what kind of statement it is and what kind of validity you claim for it.

I am not making the argument that economics is separate from these broader considerations. I agree that it is not; and that's where I come down foursquare for clarity. I don't think that muddle is a desirable quality in economic analysis of any kind. I think of Paul Streeten's remark at the Conference upon which this volume is based about how valuable it is to have a book like *The General Theory* – how important to have self-contradictory opinions because such a book provides the impulse for people to pursue different lines of thought, different kinds of models. If I could reverse history for a moment: I regard Mahler's music as a muddle and I wouldn't accept it if someone were to say, "You don't understand the value of Mahler's music; Mozart appears as a reaction to Mahler." It's the Mozart I want, and the hell with Mahler. I feel the same way about prophets. Prophets will, of course, always be muddled. That's part of being a prophet. And to the extent that Smith and Keynes were prophets, they're muddled. But the value to me as an economist is the clear model that you extract. I teach my students that there abides these three: faith, hope, and clarity, and the greatest of these is clarity.

While the word "clarity" is not so easy to define, as Mr. Justice Stewart said of obscenity, "I may not be able to define it, but I know it when I see it." I am not arguing that many social concepts are not, in their nature, ambiguous. When there are concepts that are fundamentally ambiguous, there is no point in pretending that they are otherwise. But it is also a mistake to think that you're going to proceed very far with dentistry on that basis. I'm not a philosopher. I'm an economist. I'm trying to understand particular things. If I find that a concept like "love" or "power" is fundamentally ambiguous – I may be wrong, by the way; it might be very simple – then I try to accept that fact. I don't pretend that it's not.

On the methodological issue, I want to distinguish carefully between clarity of thought and precision of a model. I am not arguing that a precise model is the only, or even always the most useful, mode of thought. I *am* arguing that ambiguity and loose construction are never desirable characteristics in science, even in a weak science like economics. The phenomena themselves may be fuzzy or poorly understood; then one should be clear about that and how far it goes. The function of economics is to understand the world, not to imitate the world. I would not agree with whoever it was who told Colander that only formal models are worthwhile. (They may have a negative value, too. Sometimes if you make an unsatisfactory formal model, the experience teaches you what you don't really understand. I'd admit, however, that more often it misleads you into thinking you do understand.) The ambition to be like physics is very damaging to economics. It is very important, however, both on general intellectual grounds and from a political point of view if you're trying actually to have an effect on the practice of the tribe, not to suppose that the alternative to trying to be like physics is "anything goes." First of all, you'll never sell the brethren on that, nor should you. Biology is not catch-as-catch-can. Biology is just the chemistry of large molecules.

I once read a book entitled *Discovery Processes in Modern Biology.* It was a book which consisted of thirteen lectures by thirteen very distinguished biologists, each describing how he had come to do whatever it was he had become famous for. I was struck in reading this book by how different they were from your standard physical scientist, and, in particular, by how much of their success depended on observational acuteness – on seeing something that other people didn't see; on looking through the microscope and saying, "Aha! Those little bastards are doing THIS, not that!" And then following up in a very systematic way.

I don't know that that model can be applied to economics. But something a little more in that direction, away from axiomatic method, does strike me as the way to go. That's so easy to say and so hard to do.

Colander and Clower argue that modern-day economic theory has lost the role played by institutions. I agree with that. One of the big problems in modern economic practice is that it's unwilling, precisely because of this physicslike ambition, to suppose that historically grounded institutions can be really important. Your basic real economist would say: "If you think institutions are important, then we should have a theory which explains why there are these institutions and not other institutions." Just as a physicist would say: "You think the temperature at which this reaction is taking place in the universe matters; we just simply have to include the temperature as one of the endogenous variables." I think that's asking more than economics can possibly deliver, and the right thing to do is to try to understand social institutions as determinants of economic behavior. We should be clear, even if we cannot be precise, here too.

I agree with Colander about many economists' use of data. My problem is not at all that the economics profession does not frequently appeal to the data. It has appealed to the data all the time – in a way, too frequently. The problem is that if you limit the class of eligible observations to the standard time series or standard kinds of observations, there are many fewer degrees of freedom than one might at first think. There are many fewer statistical degrees of freedom from these highly intercorrelated time series than we get by normal count of observations. As a result, the profession, in trying to test extraordinarily refined hypotheses, gets this really very limited volume of data. It has simply refined its econometric methods, its statistical methods, beyond the capacity of the data.

From the point of view of the econometrician, I think there is really much less data available than is suggested. The only possible solution that I see is to enlarge the class of eligible facts, or class of observations, that one is willing to take account of. I think you have to include anecdotal facts, impressions, and direct observation. Most of the economists I know, including myself, don't have any talent for direct observation, nor, by the way, do we have any methods for dealing with it, which is not a reason not to deal with it.

The problem is much more subtle. It is certainly not true to say that the economics profession in its upper reaches today doesn't want to confront data all the time. It does! There isn't a Ph.D. thesis turned out in my department that doesn't have a chapter on empirical work – it's often just not believable empirical work. That's the problem. I do think that standards are, in a sense, lax, but it is not for want of priority. In fact, it's almost because the priority is so great. If you're told, "You really have to test this hypothesis or else we'll toss you out the window and you'll bounce," you'll test it. You'll test it whether you know how to test it, or whether it can be tested, or whether the data are capable of providing the test – you'll follow some recipe, and something will end up in the pot, and you'll say, "There! That's it."

CHAPTER 5

How ideas spread among economists: examples from international economics

CHARLES P. KINDLEBERGER

David Riesman's *The Lonely Crowd* (1950) distinguishes among people who are tradition-minded, inner-directed, and outer-directed. His metaphors for the last two are people with a gyroscope and a radar, respectively. In economics we can distinguish between students who get a mindset from their graduate training – monetarists from Chicago, Keynesians from Yale, and model-builder/testers from MIT, to borrow a scrap of conversation with Assar Lindbeck – and regard them as inner-directed economists who absorbed their ideas from outside for all time in their youth. The outer-directed may acquire a new Weltanschauung from the peer group when they move from graduate school to a teaching or research position elsewhere, or they may systematically scan the world of economics looking for interesting ideas. This paper seeks to explore how economists, largely in the field of international economics, sell their ideas as evangelists, or acquire them, to the extent that they maintain some receptivity, on the receiving end.

The information explosion in the last quarter of this century has gotten out of hand, as is widely recognized. A century ago an economist would have been in touch with the ideas of all his or her peers through reading their books, combing a limited number of journals, and conducting correspondence. As economic literature grew exponentially – texts, monographs, syntheses, specialized journals, symposia, Festschriften, and the like – new devices were put in place to assist economists to scan that literature: more book reviews, abstracts, indexes, and articles reviewing the specialized literature. In its early days, one could take *The Journal of Economic Literature,* read it from cover to

I shall cover such a wide range of ideas that it is impossible to adhere to the standards of scholarly rigor in citing sources numbering in the hundreds. Most of the references will be obvious to the beginner in international economics. I acknowledge, with thanks, a stimulating converstion with Professor Max Corden.

cover, and find out what was going on inside one's own specialty and throughout economics as a whole. As the explosion exfoliated, however, it quickly became impossible to keep up even with what was being written in one's specialty. A flood of less competitive journals sprang into being to accommodate the needs of the less prestigious universities and colleges which needed large numbers of teachers and adhered to the same rules as the major universities regarding publication as a requirement for promotion and/or tenure. Reading the literature has become a virtual impossibility, and in some cases scanning it systematically detracts seriously from teaching. At a minimum, one can write, or one can read, but not both. It is necessary to make choices, something for which the profession is especially fitted. This essay is partly devoted to scanning devices, and partly to examples of ideas in the field of international economics that have, or have not, made their way. The ideas are chosen arbitrarily and one-sidedly, mainly from international macro; the paper is not a survey article, and the pure theory of trade, with its links to welfare, is almost entirely neglected.

Scanning

My rule is to scan quickly the journals I take – *The American Economic Review, The Journal of Economic Literature, Economic Journal, Journal of Economic History, Economic History Review,* and *Journal of European Economic History* – reading one or two articles and book reviews and noting a few that I propose to get back to, though I rarely succeed in doing so. The periodicals and books I get free receive less attention. Books squarely in the field of current interest I have to buy since the lag of libraries in making them available is too long – unless I can get them as promotional gifts of a publisher or for reviewing. Beyond that I listen, and will read any articles and sometimes books remarked as interesting by two people whose judgment I respect. This is how I caught on years ago, for example, to Robert Mundell's paper on "Optimum Currency Areas" (*AER,* 1961) with its McKinnon follow-up (*AER,* 1963). At a Mundell and Alexander Swoboda conference on *Monetary Problems of the International Economy* (1969), Harry Johnson said that the optimum currency area was a dead end as an idea. Perhaps it was for him; not for me. I have gotten considerable mileage out of it, extending the concept to the optimum social area and the optimum political area. For a book, I have in mind Arjo Klamer's *Conversations with Economists* (1984), which was talked about a lot before the reviews appeared – the usual lag being one and a half to three years. What's talked about, of course, depends on what circle you move in. Moreover, if you have an interest in a problem it pays to ask the views of people who know about it. In a paper on libraries I once wrote that formal scanning devices for finding the relevant literature were less efficient, as I saw it, than asking someone who knows. This brought the anger of librarians down on my head; they have to guide searchers after every conceivable sort of information. They argue that the old-boy network is not open to new boys and girls. But teachers are available for questioning for leads to the literature outside the sources listed in syllabi or cited in footnotes or lists of recommended reading. If the new boys and girls have left the graduate school, they can ask their new colleagues.

In addition to the general journals and such specialized ones as *The Journal of International Economics,* there are working papers. Some come free and in specialized areas such as the output of the University of Michigan on trade, or of Reading in England on the multinational corporation. They get a glance, sometimes a reading, and in areas in which I am teaching, a filing. As shelves bulge and groan, the unwanted literature is discarded. MIT has two tables where excess literature is strewn available to the passerby. It is heavy with working papers. The discards at Brandeis are mainly textbooks given out by hopeful publishers but not adopted; they seem to hold little interest for the undergraduates.

The *National Bureau of Economic Research Reporter* lists scores of working papers with enticing titles each issue. I write for a few, but usually find them too replete with mathematical manipulation to suit my capacity on the one hand, and to satisfy my appetite for ideas on the other. Rigor is a salable commodity in today's market, but as in haberdasher stores where I can almost never get the style of clothing I want – "we haven't had that for twenty years" – it does not suit me. Working papers from high-class places such as the National Bureau or Brookings merit attention if the subject matter interests. But again, sparingly.

Then there are reprints. One reads those sent by friends to see what they are up to, and those in one's own field, sent because the writer thinks or hopes one would have an interest in the subject. Those that arrive because one has ended up on a list tend to go on the discard table available for the student with a possible interest.

Textbooks and syllabi teach students, and sometimes, in the first case, instructors who have become stale and need to be refreshed. New ideas in them are almost always lost. Paul Samuelson has warned about including "personal piffle" in textbooks. The one case I know where a textbook disseminated an interesting new idea was Stephen Hymer's view of foreign direct investment as belonging to the theory of industrial organization rather than international capital movements. In the third edition of *International Economics* (1963) I set this forth at length with attribution, since Hymer was having inexplicable difficulty in getting parts of the dissertation accepted for publication by the major journals. A number of instructors reading the text ordered Xerox copies of the 1960 thesis, which had a wide circulation before its belated posthumous publication in 1976. That this was not effective dissemination was testified to by the fact that in 1974 an expert in the field (Thomas Horst, *At Home Abroad*) thought that the concept had been original with Richard Caves in his widely noted article in *Economica* (1971). I chided Horst in a book review of that year in the *JEL*, and he recanted handsomely in a review symposium published in the *Journal of Development Economics* (1977).

How else do ideas get communicated? Max Corden, a frequent visitor to the United States from Australia, may read the culture here better than the natives, caught up in American mythology, do. He states that faculties do not talk economics to one another, at least not in the major American universities that he knows. They are too busy. One way for a foreigner to get an idea across is to present it in seminars at at least five, and preferably ten, universities. One may not have influence on one's age cohort; the faculty does not listen much to visitors. The significant audience is the rising generation of economists represented by graduate students on whom evangelical economists will want to make an impression. The other means of propagating economic notions is the conference. On these occasions scholars are normally away from home base – committees, telephone, mail, and so forth – and are prepared to listen, if not always during the formal presentations, at least at meal and coffee times.

In 1971 I was somewhat snippy on the subject of conferences. In a review of Mundell and Swoboda, eds., *Monetary Problems of the International Economy,* I stated:

One new industry of the 1960s is the holding of conferences on the international monetary system with an occasional admixture of central and commercial bankers. One need only mention in alphabetical order Algarve, Bald Peak, Bellagio, Bologna, Brookings, Burgenstock, Chicago, Claremont, Ditchley . . . to make the point. The rediscovery of money in international economics, somewhat belatedly perhaps, and of Gresham's law (by Triffin) sets monetary economists in motion to the airport, papers in hand. . . .

In the fall of 1976 I was asked to comment at a meeting at the University of Pennsylvania run by some sociologists whose names I cannot retrieve, on a paper by Harry Johnson on "The Role of Networks in International Monetary Reform." I do not believe the paper was ever published; it is missing from the bibliography of Johnson's work in the *JPE* for February 1985, and the conference proceedings do not appear in the usual outlet for Pennsylvania sociology, *Annals of the American Academy of Political Science*. I have lost my copy of his paper, but retain my comment, which in the circumstances is a little unfair to quote.[1] But Johnson made the point that there were two networks of economists working on international monetary reform, one an older group run by Fritz Machlup with the cooperation of Robert Triffin and W. J. Fellner, called the Bellagio group, which invited central bankers and treasury officials from whom they could learn and whom they hoped to influence. The other group was a younger stratum, led by Johnson, Mundell, Pascal Salin, and others. Johnson said that this group "intellectually enforced" the monetary approach to balance-of-payments adjustment. In a different meeting, he suggested that conferences can be divided into those resembling producer goods and those more like consumer goods. Consumer goods conferences bring answers to the immediate problems of practical people, while producer goods conferences concentrate on the production of basic knowledge (in Mundell and Swoboda, eds., 1969, p. 393). In "Networks" Johnson went beyond this metaphor to say that the type of conference he favored not only produced new ideas but enforced them.

This notion is reminiscent of Melvin Reder's *JEL* article on the Chicago school (1982) with its "strong prior" beliefs. Johnson said that if the monetary approach does not seem to fit the facts, it cannot be that the theory is wrong. I cannot quote from his text so I quote from mine. "All markets work and people are always rational. Keep the hypotheses but penetrate deeper to correct our understanding of how they are supposed to work." This comes close to Reder's description of the Chicago defense of its dogmas when the facts are not friendly: reexamine the data to see if they are correct, gather more, regard the aberrant result as a special case, and only as a last resort abandon the theory.

I happen to find the monetary approach to the balance of payments – and to domestic economic behavior, for that matter – counterintuitive. Instead of changing income (exports) and expenditure (imports) to bring the supply of money into line with the demand for it, I think of the function of money as balancing divergences in time between income and expenditure. And if more money is needed, it is not necessary to work harder or export more, spend less or reduce

---

[1] A search for this paper by the author and by the editors failed to turn it up, providing an example of how ideas can be lost.

imports – but just borrow. If there is too much money, don't slack off work or splurge – but lend.

In my comment on Johnson I made a number of points that relate to the present topic:

> Most intellectual views run in strong peer-group swings of fashion and climb aboard bandwagons going by such names as effective rates of protection, distortions, theory of the second best, optimum currency areas, and, most recently, rational expectations. . . . I permit myself the indulgence of thinking that markets mostly work but occasionally, like intellectuals, are caught up in the coils of fashion and euphoria. . . .
>
> Conferences of international monetary experts may do some of the things that Harry Johnson claims for the Chicago-Geneva-Siena-Dauphine-Manchester-Stockholm network. I do not know that network well except in its publications, which seem to me a more efficient way to disseminate its views. Far too much time at conferences is spent listening to familiar notions. New ideas can be disseminated otherwise, in lectures, papers, journals, reprints, symposia, and the like, which are typically cheaper. The foundations have chosen to support conferences and the first have the charm of tourism until one gets jaded. There is something to be said for scholars staying in their studies and classrooms, rather than jetting compulsively around the world, hastily scribbling an overdue paper on the plane, skimming the other papers the night before they are presented. . . .
>
> In the international field, enough is as good as a feast, as my old chairman used to say. No, it's better. There are strongly diminishing returns to conferring, and at the personal level they are frequently negative.

Apropos of seminars and faddism, Max Corden tells the story of going to Britain in some year that has slipped from my memory with two seminars prepared, one on two-sector growth models, and one on effective rates of protection. He gave the first at Cambridge before an enormous crowd, with standing room only, and the other at the L.S.E. with a mere handful of the faithful present. Growth models in international economics have long since lost appeal whereas effective rates of protection proved to be a seminal idea that launched hundreds of articles and dissertations.

One or two more remarks about media before turning to the ideas themselves. With the aging of one's scholarly cohort, one is asked more and more to contribute to *Festschriften*. The thoughts so offered up are for the most part lost, unless one gathers them into collections. There is almost no possibility of retrieving an article by X in a *Festschrift* for Y. It is true that the *Index of Economic Articles* now goes beyond the standard journals to include articles in *Festschriften* and symposia, but book reviewers, duty bound to say something pleasant about the honoree, have great difficulty in saying more than a sentence about the separate articles, and frequently single out one or two and list the names and titles for the rest. Moreover, the books are seldom read by others than the hero, reviewers, and possibly contributors, since the quality is so uneven. Many contributions, pulled from a desk drawer, represent papers rejected by refereed journals.

In the journals themselves, the editors' annual reports note the number of submissions and the percentage published. What is not known in the aggregate is the percentage of total articles written in some passable form that ultimately end up in print, perhaps after bouncing from the more to the less prestigious journals until they find an outlet. For a time I was the recipient of copies of correspondence and draft articles by a researcher in another social science who believed that refereeing in scholarly journals is outrageously biased, arbitrary, discriminatory (for example, against women), quixotic, and insider-dominated. There is some evidence for this view, but it is largely paranoid. Blind refereeing has been widely adopted, although it is usually easy to figure out who the writer is from the frequency with which given economists are cited. It is true, however, that editors and referees are subject, like the rest of us, to the winds of fashion.

It sometimes happens, no doubt, that two economists at different locations can affect one another's ideas through correspondence. I sometimes find myself conceding a point by letter, and, less often, winning assent from someone else. It may only appear more usual that argument by mail peters out with neither party changing his or her view. I have argued by mail on stabilizing and destabilizing speculation with Milton Friedman and William Poole, on purchasing power parities and good writing with Donald McCloskey, on flexible exchange rates with Egon Sohmen, on tariffs with Jaroslav Vanek, plus many more, but the arguments seem to dwindle into stalemates. Correspondence is more fruitful among friends who more or less know in advance that they think along similar lines, but are trying to understand better one or more points made by the other. Such exchanges I have had in abundance with Emile Despres and Walter Salant.

As for the flowering of ideas in economics, the ideas typically start in offhand remarks, are seen by others to be significant, and get picked up by a widening circle who provide rigor, test statistically, and add historical illustration (sometimes, primarily adding expositional clarity), as when Harry Johnson turned the diagram in Paul Samuelson's 1948 article on factor-price equalization on its side to win himself a prominent position in the literature. On occasion an idea will occur to a number of economists more or less at the same time, much as Darwin and Wallace came upon the notion of evolution simultaneously but independently.

The obverse of an idea starting small and building is the body of material that is worked over and over again, each time from a theoretical advance. The classic illustration is Jacob Viner's *Canada's Balance of International Indebtedness, 1900–1913* (1924) that "proved" the price-specie-flow mechanism as the means of transferring capital, only to have Coats raise the identification problem: Did the capital flow from Britain to Canada initiate the expansionary investment, or did the Canadian expansion give rise to the capital inflow? Gerald Meier suggested that the transfer mechanism worked less through changes in sectional price levels than by means of income changes and the foreign-trade multiplier. James Ingram went further to explain the aberrant behavior of Canadian exports in the other theories by adding a growth model. It is to F. W. Taussig's everlasting credit in working with the transfer problem that he confessed he could not understand how the real effect followed so quickly after the money transfer since the price-specie-flow mechanism was a time-consuming process.

Another classic historical episode that has been reworked a good deal, like the causes of the French Revolution, is the German hyperinflation of 1922–32 that attracted the interest of one contemporaneous group, Frank Graham, Constantino Bresciani-Turroni, James W. Angell, Moritz Bonn, and then died away in the literature until revived first by Nurkse and Laursen and Jørgen Pedersen at the end of World War II, and again following the refulgent inflation of the 1970s by Philip Cagan, Carl-Ludwig Holtfrerich, Jacob Frenkel, Peter Bernholz, Thomas Sargent, Rudiger Dornbusch, et al. The analytical tools were sharper on the latest round, and the material from German archives richer, although that was largely ignored by the economic theorists. It is hard to see, however, that the differences among the several points of view – especially between the monetarists and Bresciani-Turroni and Cagan, and the balance-of-payments adherents who trace inflation from balance-of-payments deficits to depreciation, price increase, and finally, money expansion – have narrowed, although a growing number of economists are becoming willing to change the model at turning points. Similar unresolved questions turn on whether the 1929 depression was worldwide in origin or American, was monetarist or Keynesian, or had room in its explanation for price behavior or not.

Seminal ideas

The general discussion thus far has touched on a large number of ideas in international economics – the transfer mechanism, foreign direct investment, factor-price equalization, optimum currency areas, the monetary approach to the balance of payments – and it has also left out some obvious ones such as the theory of comparative advantage. In the space that remains I propose to discuss the life profiles of a number of economic ideas. Among the profiles are:

1. *The simple idea, largely ignored or rejected by the profession, which refuses to disappear and keeps making its way,* as illustrated by John H. Williams' key-currency notion – an example of an idea that had difficulty in catching hold but finally won out, like Stephen Hymer's view of foreign direct investment.

2. *The powerful idea, buttressed by a wealth of metaphor and widely accepted, that is on the whole misleading.* I choose as my example flexible exchange rates thought to provide a country with automatic balance-of-payments adjustment and macroeconomic policy independence. One could just as well choose purchasing-power parity.

3. *A concept intuitively understood for years but slow in finding its way into standard analysis, which spreads rapidly once it has been formalized:* for example, effective rates of protection.

4. *The strongly held view, widely accepted, that is right for the wrong reason.* Here I refer to the condemnation of the gold-exchange standard.

5. *The temptation to choose a single horn of a dilemma and stick with it through thick and thin, when a more prudent analysis calls for frequent shifting of models.* Here I have in mind the choice among the elasticities, absorption, and money approaches to balance-of-payments adjustment.

1.   The ignored idea that will not go away

Classical economics derives largely from Newtonian mechanics with its notions of equilibrium, symmetry, reversibilities, and equalities, and is replete with elasticities, cycles, and stasis. Economists like Hyman Minsky who find in economic systems instability, irrationality (at any aggregate level), irreversibilities, and hierarchical structures have a hard time winning a hearing. One such idea is that of key currencies, advanced by John H. Williams in testimony before the Congress on Bretton Woods legislation, in articles in *Foreign Affairs,* and in other public statements. Rather than repair the entire world monetary system at one swoop, Williams favored proceeding one currency at a time, starting with "key currencies" on which other, less used currencies depended. An analogous distinction is made in development economics in the debate over balanced versus unbalanced growth.

(Balancers such as Ragnar Nurkse, Paul Rosenstein-Rodan, and the *Economist* wanted to revive the whole economy at once, so that income increases in one sector would furnish demands for increased output in others. Unbalanced-growth advocates, notably Albert Hirschman, believed in starting where the greatest productivity gains were available, leading to bottlenecks of supply or demand that would show where effort was next needed.)

The idea of key currencies had been in existence a long time without making headway. In the 1920s, Benjamin Strong, the governor of the Federal Reserve Bank of New York, opposed any plan that would "seek to stabilize all currencies simultaneously" (S.V.O. Clarke, Princeton *Studies in International Finance*, no. 33, 1973, p. 15). In reporting about the Preparatory Commission to the World Economic Conference of 1933, Williams referred to Great Britain and Germany as "key countries." The key-currency theory opposed Bretton Woods and favored an approach like that embodied in the Anglo-American Financial Agreement (the British Loan). Once sterling got repaired one could move to other currencies.

The key-currency notion was defeated with the success of the Bretton Woods institutions, after some delay, and the failure of the British Loan for reasons too complex to broach here, but the concept survives. It is implicit in the view that the gold standard was primarily a sterling standard, and that the Bretton Woods era was one dominated by the dollar. It is the core of the idea that currencies and financial centers are not arranged as equals but in hierarchies, with asymmetric relations and norms of behavior. The $N - 1$ aspect of money is implicit in it and in the Mundell conclusion, that one country must be responsible for price stabilization, but not its own balance of payments, while the rest of the world concentrates on its balance of payments, but ignores price stabilization. The G-10 agreement of 1960 recognizes that financially developed centers have different characteristics and different responsibilities than the ordinary run of national economy. Walter Bagehot's idea of a lender of last resort implicitly recognizes differences in responsibilities, especially when extrapolated from the national to the international level.

One extension of the key-currency notion is fallacious to my way of thinking. It is sometimes suggested, for example, by Mundell, that the world should be made up of blocs of fixed-exchange rate systems that should float against one another, perhaps a dollar area, a yen bloc, sterling, the mark, or, in today's world, the ECU. This has it backward, as I see it. The key currencies should be fixed in relation to one another, with freedom for the less focal monies to fix or flex against a particular key currency as they choose.

2.   *The powerful idea, widely accepted, and buttressed by*
      metaphor, that proves wrong

Economists have difficulty in distinguishing between partial and general equilibrium – when, that is, it is acceptable to deal with a problem with the *ceteris paribus* assumption, and when it is necessary to take account of the changes that reverberate throughout the system. Sometimes partial equilibrium analysis is converted to general-equilibrium analysis by the explicit use of heroic assumptions. Examples are furnished in the field of exchange rates by the analyses of John Burr Williams and of James Meade, with spending assumed to change in the background by the right amount and in the right direction so as to support the movements expected from a given change in the exchange rate.

Floating exchange rates have been strongly advocated not only by John Burr Williams and Meade, but also by Milton Friedman, Gottfried Haberler, Fritz Machlup, Harry Johnson, and, especially vociferously, Egon Sohmen, largely based on the analogy of a changing price clearing the market for a good under competition without feedbacks. Such a partial equilibrium model, however, is invalid when dealing with a price that affects so many facets of the typical economy and for which so many ancillary assumptions are needed. It was assumed by most economists, for example, that with free floating, capital movements would dry up. Such was not the case. It was argued that a variable exchange rate would add another instrumental variable to the set of equations describing the macroeconomy. With overshooting in both directions, the exchange rate often became a target.

I do not want to reargue the issue of fixed versus floating exchange rates here, but in a conference inspired by an interest in rhetoric it may be useful to gather together a few of the metaphors that the proponents of flexible exchange rates have used to make their case, to see how compelling they are, and to dig for equally cogent metaphors on the other side.

Machlup used to delight in calling attention to a European clown named Kroc who had an act in which he tried to move the grand piano to the stool instead of the stool to the piano. For "piano" read "prices and costs," for "stool" read "exchange rate." The metaphor is appropriate for piano solos. But suppose the music is Mozart's concerto for four pianos and an orchestra. The pianists must see one another and the conductor. In an intercommunicating system, it is advisable to set the stools where they need to be and move the pianos.

Sohmen has called the adjustable-peg exchange-rate system one of hiccoughs, and observed that in contrast, railroads ride on tracks that move up and down grades continuously, without abrupt changes. But there is a counter example: canals. Barges move on water on a level until it is time to go up or down; then they use locks.

In debating the issue, Friedman sought to win points by adducing daylight-saving time. Instead of changing habits as the days grow longer and shorter, change clocks. The comparison is moderately telling, but it must be noted that in an interconnected world it is important to have a fixed set of time zones, based on Greenwich, and a fixed calendar – the Gregorian New Style from 1752. Changes from standard to daylight time take place on the same dates in the United States, if not always between the United States and Europe. In the 1920s there was chaos when each town and state could choose for itself whether to accept or reject daylight time, and if accepting, when. *Campanilismo* in Italy, *à l'heure de son clocher* in France – each village on its own bells or time – refer to isolated, not connected, settlements.

Money has been compared to language, and monetary reform to language reform. Going back to gold, as Mundell, Milton Gilbert, and Peter Oppenheimer in economics and Jack Kemp and Lewis Lehrman in politics want, is to return to Latin. The adherents of the SDR or the ECU as a new synthetic money espouse a movement like that for worldwide adoption of Esperanto, a movement that makes progress slowly. Flexible exchange rates suggest that everyone should use only his or her own language in talking to people with a different mother tongue, and rely on translators and interpreters. A system in which the world uses one language – first Greek, then Latin, next Italian, for diplomacy French, and finally, to this point, English or perhaps American – is equivalent to a world that used the Venetian ducat, Dutch florin, then sterling, and lately dollars as international money. The system is asymmetrical and inequitable in that the strong country uses its own money and language, while others are forced to accept foreign-exchange risk and to learn a foreign language.

3.   The idea that needed formalization

Max Corden has written an account of the theory of the effective rate of protection in an appendix to his book on *The Theory of Protection* (1971). He hammers away at the point that the idea was obvious, turning up in Taussig's treatment of the tariff on woolens, as affected by the tariff on wool, and was expressed in rather vague terms as well by Haberler and Viner. Meade worked it out in *Trade and Welfare* (1971), but in prose rather than algebra, and failed to give it emphasis. The idea really took off with a bang after Clarence Barber's article on Canadian protection in 1955, so that Corden himself was consulted for the impact of tariffs on wage rates and hence on emigration, as he, Corden, was working on Australian tariffs and the impetus they gave to immigration. Barber's insight on the effective rate of protection was also picked up by Harry Johnson at about the same time, along with William Travis (1964), and then with empirical estimates by Bela Balassa. It spread rapidly as various economists undertook, in articles, in monographs, and in dissertations, to produce measurements of effective as contrasted with nominal rates of protection for a great many economies.

In Corden's account, the difference between the early notions and those of the 1960s was that the former were unsystematic, the latter systematic ". . . with clear arithmetic examples." That the idea was obvious and understood is evident in Italian economic history where it was well-known after 1860 that engineering goods experienced negative protection since the rates on iron and steel were higher than those on rails, locomotives, and machinery. Corden notes that H. B. Lary found a systematic statement of the idea by an Austrian economist in 1905.

The reason for the slowness in the universal adoption of the idea seems to have lain, apart from the general lack of systematization, in the general use of $2 \times 2 \times 2$ models in international trade, with both commodities final products and neither a component, and in the late adoption of input–output analysis, at least widely. William Travis pointed to a weakness in effective rates of protection in that the formula for their calculation assumes that the proportion of the intermediate product in the final product by value is fixed, just as input–output tables use fixed coefficients, whereas in his judgment these proportions should change as the tariff on the component, and its price, changes. In a letter to me, Johnson said he did not find this persuasive as an objection, but Corden believes that Johnson was strongly influenced by Travis. Perhaps he changed his mind on the issue; it would not be the only time. His original views on a number of issues – Hymer on foreign direct investment, Meade on the balance of payments, and Linder on *Trade and Transformation* (1961) – were originally strongly negative and ultimately became positive.

The $2 \times 2 \times 2$ model of international trade tends to lead economists and economic historians to neglect disaggregation and commodity inputs in other respects. W. W. Rostow and Travis, for example, have noted that the terms of trade should be calculated on the basis of national activities, or value added, at home and abroad, rather than for commodities, to net out the imported content of exports, both commodity and investment capital. Clark Reynolds calculated the Chilean terms of trade on the basis of "returned value," netting out of copper exports, for example, the profits retained abroad by American investors in Chilean copper mines. The same point may be made by calculating the terms of trade not on the trade balance but on the current account as a whole, with high export prices on the credit side not counting in full if they are offset in whole or part by higher profits on foreign investment that are remitted abroad (a debit).

I cannot forbear to lengthen an already long paper by adding some remarks about what Paul Krugman calls the "new international economics" (*Strategic Trade Policy and the New International Economics,* MIT paperback, 1986) and "new trade theory" (in "New Trade Theory and the Less Developed Countries," a paper submitted to the Carlos F. Diaz-Alejandro memorial conference held in Helsinki, August 23–5, 1986). The "new" theory rests on economies of scale. As I told Krugman at Helsinki, I find it a bizarre notion that increasing returns in international trade are new. I developed it at length in my 1953 textbook, based on the 1929 article of John Williams, reprinted in the AEA, "Readings in the Theory of International Trade." Jan Tinbergen developed it in his textbook, *International Economic Integration* (1954). I recall the joy in Cambridge, Massachusetts, when Kenneth Arrow made increasing returns respectable by formalizing Alfred Marshall's description of long-run decreasing costs historically with his paper on "Learning by Doing," a paper rapidly incorporated into international-trade theory by those who need formal models to understand the intuitively obvious. I confess to some irritation over Krugman's defense of his international-trade theory as new because it offers a well-worn truth in equation form.

4.   *The widely held view that is right for the wrong reason*

In 1959 Triffin wrote an attack on the gold-exchange standard that attracted wide attention and fairly general acceptance. It was an absurd system, he maintained, because it failed to put pressure on the country whose liabilities were accumulated as world reserves, and hence was inflationary. When the country came to see the necessity of correcting the import surpluses that the system encouraged, the world would find itself short of the appropriate amount of additional liquidity. To forestall the strain to be imposed by the United States – in the instant case, getting rid of its import surplus, as it would have to – it was necessary to create a new international reserve asset, such as the Special Drawing Right, agreed upon in 1965. Triffin wanted the asset not only as the main addition to reserves, but wanted it to replace existing dollars and gold.

The analysis rested on an erroneous view of the relationship between the U.S. balance of payments and world liquidity needs. Instead of an autonomous U.S. deficit arbitrarily creating reserves that were added to world liquidity, the "deficit," up to the late 1960s at least, was not autonomous but a response to the world's demand for liquidity. Under the definitions adopted by the United States at the end of the 1950s, increases in foreign holdings of dollars were regarded as a deficit, even when the U.S. current account was in surplus. The combination of a current-account surplus and increases in foreign dollar holdings came about, of course, because foreigners borrowed at long term in New York more than they spent for their import surpluses. Borrowing long and lending short, they were borrowing for liquidity, and the U.S. lending long and borrowing short was international financial intermediation, acting like a bank. A bank is not in deficit when its deposits and its assets rise.

The problem with the gold-exchange standard was not that it threatened a shortage of liquidity when the U.S. "deficit" was "corrected," so that a new source of liquidity would shortly be needed. The gold-exchange standard did not weaken the discipline of the United States, whose currency was used as world reserves: Presidents Eisenhower, Kennedy, and Johnson were all unduly worried about the balance-of-payments deficit. The problem of the gold-exchange standard lay in its subjection of Gresham's law. With two monies fixed in price, changes in expectations as to their values can lead to disruptive flows out of one into the other. The tendency holds not only for gold and silver under bimetallism, but for gold and a national currency. It can work in either direction as the "Golden Avalanche" of 1937 demonstrated, when the market and even central banks dumped gold for dollars.

Diagnosis of the weakness of the gold-exchange standard as subject to Gresham's law does not provide for therapy. Two monies may be inherently unstable unless firm expectations have been built in by two hundred years of stability – the pound sterling price of gold, fixed at 3 pounds, 17 shillings, ten and a half pence in 1717 and unchanged, apart from wartime interruptions, until 1931 – but more than one money is normally necessary. With metallic monies, retail transactions are too small for gold, and amounts in distant trade are too big for copper. In international trade, bills of exchange have been money alongside specie since at least 1200. The gold standard inevitably evolves into a gold-exchange standard to economize on the transactions costs involved in converting domestic into foreign money, which induces some domestic wealth-holders to keep part of their wealth in foreign exchange. Gresham's law can be defeated only by the adoption of a single world paper money used in all countries for domestic and international transactions. At the moment, the prospect is remote.

5.   The one-horned dilemma

International economics used to contribute ideas to the analysis of closed economies. In recent years, the flow of ideas has gone the other way. International economics has followed domestic macroeconomics in its progress from Walrasian markets with prices that bring demand and supply into equilibrium, to Keynesian models, to monetarism. The classical model emphasized price elasticities and the Marshall-Lerner condition, with changes in exchange rates, for example, producing large changes in exports and imports. Machlup was a primary expositor. Keynesian analysis relied on the foreign-trade multiplier to adjust exports and imports, and later developed the absorption model which emphasized that the balance of payments on current account was the mirror image of differences between income and expenditure (called absorption by Sidney Alexander): if changes in the exchange rate failed to alter the relationship between income and expenditure, they would fail to alter the balance of payments. A third alternative, the monetary approach to the balance of payments, "enforced" by the Chicago-Geneva-Siena-Dauphine-Manchester-Stockholm network, connects changes in the current account to changes in the relations between the domestic demand and the domestic supply of money. If desired demand exceeds the desired supply of money, the country cuts down on spending, or increases production, in order to reduce imports and/or expand exports so as to acquire money claims abroad. This last approach strikes me as implausible as a statement of the driving mechanism in balance-of-payments adjustment, though it may be a truism ex post. Economic agents typically vary money holdings to bring income and expenditure into balance, rather than vary income and/or expenditure to reach a target quantity of money. Money, that is, is an instrumental variable, not a target. Moreover, for agents with wealth or credit, a surplus or deficiency of money can be overcome by buying or selling a nonliquid asset, or lending or borrowing. The monetary approach thus appears to me as counterintuitive, which is a strong mark against it if one has some faith in a rhetorical approach to economics.

In the long run, ex post, the elasticities, absorption, and monetary approaches to the balance of payments converge. In the short run, however, one or another may lead. The economist who sticks to the classical approach through thick and thin, or the Keynesian, or the monetarist, is wrong a good part of the time. On occasion it is difficult to sort out which model is driving the economy. In 1984 when the dollar was strong, for example, and the current account weak, the deficit could be ascribed to the elasticities if one focused on the exchange rate or to absorption if one concentrated on the government deficit and the decline in personal savings. At other times, the proximate driving force is fairly clear. The large current-account surpluses of Saudi Arabia in 1974–6 and 1979–81, for example, can properly be ascribed to an elasticities model with the sum of the elasticities less than 1, whereas the Japanese surplus conforms more closely to the absorption model in which high personal and corporate savings, in excess of the government deficit, drive the paths of exports and imports. I cannot cite a plausible example in which an excess of money leads to an import surplus, or a deficiency to an export surplus, unless perhaps in pathologically inflationary or deflationary conditions.

Conclusion

There are many models that describe how economic ideas are propagated within the profession, once one breaks away from the pressures of graduate schools dominated by a powerful figure. In some, ideas spread slowly with two steps forward and one backward, and, like key currencies, never achieve universal acceptance. Some are adopted with too-great enthusiasm because of flawed analogies, like flexible exchange rates. Effective rates of protection were intuitively understood, but made rapid and wide progress only after systematization. The gold-exchange standard was denounced for wrong reasons; the intuition of the denouncers may have been sound though their rationalization missed the target. Moreover, denunciation based on Gresham's law would typically fail to note that in most circumstances, two or more monies are needed and hence are subject to inescapable instability. Finally, there is the temptation in debate to take only one horn of a dilemma, when in some cases it is hard to see which horn should be seized, and in others the separate horns work seriatim. I refer to the elasticities, the absorption, and the monetary approaches to the balance of payments.

Economics is a toolbox as Joan Robinson has said, and as Schumpeter was wont to repeat. Different problems require different modes of analysis. By the same token, economic ideas are disseminated in different degrees and in different fashions, and not universally in the same way.

CHAPTER 6

Journals, university presses, and the spread of ideas

COLIN DAY

I will first establish a simple framework for considering the information needs of various types of reader. Then in the rest of the paper I will use the framework to consider first the role that journals do and should play in the dissemination of economic ideas, and then the tasks that necessarily are left for books to perform. This program, of course, gives me many opportunities to criticize others and to exhort economists to write the books that I want to publish.

My topic is not dissemination of ideas to the intelligent lay reader, but dissemination within the discipline, that is, from the highbrow to the highbrow and from the highbrow to the "middlebrow."

1. What does your reader need to be told?

When we communicate with others we vary the form of the message to suit the nature of the recipient. With some a very terse, even telegraphic, message will suffice. With others a fuller but still demanding and terse statement will communicate effectively. Yet a third case requires that our message provide a substantial amount of background information if it is to be understood. The essential factor deciding which of these message types to use is the amount of relevant information that the recipient already has to help him understand the message. Given that most messages reporting research results are to be conveyed to a variety of recipients, more than one form of the message may well be needed. If one form only is to be provided, it needs to be designed to convey its information to the largest feasible part of its total potential audience. Identifying the audience, forming a picture of it, and guiding authors how best to communicate with it is a major part of the task of editors of both journals and books.

In thinking about this I have found it useful to work in terms of an analogy: giving directions to someone to get to a particular location.

To make it fully concrete, the location is a particular building in Manhattan, 32 East 79 St.

In the first case to look at, you live nearby and you are talking to a neighbor. You might say something like: "Over the florist's beside the deli." An informal statement and a brief one, but effective because of the common knowledge of the area that you and your neighbor have.

In the second case, your location has not changed but you are now talking to someone who is generally familiar with Manhattan but does not know the particular area. You switch to a formal statement and say: "32 East 79 St." You might elaborate a little and add, "Between Park and Madison." This is sufficient for your message recipient to travel to the building because he knows enough about the structure, transportation system, and address rules of New York.

In a third case, the person with whom we are speaking knows nothing of the shape or organization of New York. Clearly neither of the previous message forms will convey anything to this person. Much more basic information must be provided if the person is to find out how to reach the destination. The natural thing would be to get out a map. Then he can be shown the island of Manhattan, the structure of streets and avenues, the position of the address between Central Park and the East River, and the way to get there by subway.

Choosing the audience: This simple example shows the message being expanded with an increasing amount of contextual information to compensate for the diminishing amount of prior knowledge that the message recipient brings to the conversation. I have presented three cases but there are many intermediate ones. In conversation the content of the message will be carefully tuned to the need of the listener. The speaker will watch for signs of comprehension or lack thereof and provide more information or abbreviate what he is saying to fit precisely the listener's ability to understand. This is not possible when communication is via the printed word. The writer must make some assumptions about his readers' knowledge.

The choice of these assumptions is not a passive act. The writer must decide whom he wants to read his work, then make assumptions about what that category of reader needs to be told and what he can be assumed to know already. All kinds of readers may pick up what the author has written. His decisions will determine which of those readers will actually understand his message.

The decisions that academic authors make are, of course, standardized. The conventions are set by the traditions of the discipline and by the policies followed by the book and journal editors. The average economist does not reflect deeply upon whom he wishes to reach or how best to reach that audience. He settles down and writes a journal article carefully designed to follow the conventions so as to maximize the probability of acceptance for publication. Indeed he probably is thinking only of the referees and editors as he writes the article. He has just that handful of readers in mind. Acceptance for publication is such a formidable obstacle that in the vast majority of cases the individual author has to allow the journal editor to make the critical decisions about the needs of the target audience. Telling the editor of a distinguished journal in economic theory that you want to include more contextual information because you wish to reach a slightly broader audience is to invite a rather brisk answer.

It is probably because this issue is not within the control of the individual economist as he writes his articles, that economists are often lost and make peculiar decisions about level when they come to write a book. As an article writer the economist has not really had to think about his readers and their needs. When he enters the less regimented world of book publishing faces unfamiliar problems and decisions.

Defining the knowledge line: The fact that it is often editors rather than individual authors who decide on the audience to aim for and the needs of that audience does not alter the basic issues that should be considered in making those decisions. We may illustrate the situation by a knowledge line. Positions on the line indicate different levels of relevant prior knowledge. It is natural to think of moving along it from positions of considerable prior knowledge to positions of little prior knowledge. Readers are distributed along this line. We need to know the way they are distributed. There will be some clustering. How tight will the clusters be? With some idea of the shape of the distribution, positioning a piece of writing becomes a question of trading-off the increase in the number of potential readers that can be obtained by providing more information (although the likely multimodal shape of the distribution makes this quite complicated) against the cost of providing and printing that information.

Distribution along the knowledge line: The example of giving directions that I used earlier explored three cases. Although there is some simplification, it does seem likely that people would be distributed along the knowledge line in three quite tight clusters: those with detailed knowledge of the immediate locale, a larger group with a good knowledge of Manhattan, and the largest group with no such knowledge. Now if, instead of speaking with people, you are writing the copy

for an advertisement designed to bring people to this particular building, then you are faced with the question of which audience to aim for.
A dry cleaner advertising in a local paper might choose the "next to
the deli" style because he only wishes to attract a local clientele. A business aiming for a city-wide market would use the formal address, perhaps adding a reference to the nearest subway stop. A business (perhaps a hotel) aiming for a nation-wide clientele might provide a sketch
map or describe the location in words. In each case an audience is
selected and an appropriate amount of information to convey the message to that clientele is provided. The third case can be used to exemplify the choices that need to be made after the selection of the desired
audience: "On the upper East Side, a short walk from Central Park"
still presumes some prior knowledge. Because of the cost of advertising
space, the hotel must trade-off increasing the potential clientele by providing more information against the cost of buying the space to accommodate that extra information.

2.   *Journals and the trade-off between brevity and readership*

In communicating between economists, the pattern will be similar.
First there will be a small group who knows the researcher's work so
well that the ideas and results can be communicated informally and
briefly. At the next level there are those who can follow a technical
article reporting the work. Then beyond those is a bigger more variegated group who need some more information to comprehend the
work. This last group is very diverse. For example, some will need a
little more exposition of the mathematics, while others will need a
major explanation of where this piece of research fits into the discipline as a whole.

The distribution of economists cannot be established in a general
way to apply to all pieces of research. The pattern will vary greatly
among subfields. So in mathematical economic theory, there is a quite
homogeneous group who are accustomed to the standard style of article presentation. Relatively few are just beyond that group: not quite
comprehending. Most need substantial extra material if they are to
understand. By contrast, in reporting a piece of applied work, so much
knowledge is required that is specific to that project that only a handful
of people would understand a very terse formal statement; many readers will need background information. In the latter case, economists
will be much more evenly distributed along the knowledge line,
whereas in the mathematical theory case they are tightly and separately
clustered. The paper that expounds techniques taught in standard

graduate programs and draws on ideas of economics that are central to the discipline will probably have a readership of the tightly clustered kind, whereas one that draws on a wider range of influences will tend to have a more widely distributed readership. I suspect that the use of advanced mathematics, whether it be in theory or in econometrics, acts both to tighten the top cluster and to reduce drastically, if not eliminate, the population that lies on the knowledge line between the top cluster and the main body of economists. You either know it, or you don't. There are no intermediate positions. The problem of communication from the top cluster to the rest of the profession is thus a special problem for this type of work.

It is the mathematical theory papers that are the most terse and in form of presentation the most standardized, whereas empirical papers, history of thought papers, and so forth, tend to be longer and more varied in style and structure. And more difficult to get accepted. This now directs our attention to the trade-off between readership and level. Journal editors are notorious for requiring authors to cut out all expository material. The editor and the referees understand the paper without all that stuff. So it must go, because costs impose a page limit on the journal and a major consideration for the journal editor is maximizing the number of papers published. There may also be other considerations in the editor's mind such as projecting an image of high intellectual quality by eschewing material that is designed to help the reader.

In a field characterized by a tight top cluster, this strategy may suit the prior knowledge of the likely readers. It may be the right strategy since moderate amounts of extra information might bring few if any extra readers because there is little or no tail to the top cluster. However, this practice extended to types of papers and topics that are less mainstream can eliminate members of the more widely spread top cluster and certainly prevent the paper being comprehensible to those between clusters. The amount of extra material required to bring a substantial portion of those people into the readership may be quite small. The editor ruthlessly pursuing brevity may be sacrificing a substantially larger readership for the saving of very small amounts of page space.

However, even if the article is addressed to a readership that is quite tightly clustered, positioning relative to the readership is still a significant issue. The cluster will not have zero variance. Because it is the elite of the discipline who are rightly appointed to determine what deserves publication, it is the elite who also decide where to position papers relative to the distribution of readers. But by definition the elite are at the top end of the distribution and, if they use their own comprehension to guide decisions about what to include and exclude, then they are inevitably setting a level too high for a substantial part of the relevant cluster of readers. Journal editors do need, and I am sure that this is not news to most of them, to have a sense of the range of levels of knowledge within their target readership group.

I know of no experiments, but it is interesting to wonder whether journal subscribers would be prepared to pay a higher price to allow editors more pages and therefore longer pieces with more exposition that are easier to read.

Even were this unlikely experiment to be conducted, to succeed and to influence other journals, the expansion of readership would only be within the top cluster of people. The next cluster of economists – those whose training or specialism makes them inadequately equipped to read terse articles that assume much detailed knowledge of the topic and the relevant techniques – will still be left out. For these people, other forms of publication, whether it be book or review journal, are required.

Reading and understanding: Before I move on to the attractive subject of book publication, I want to say a little more about these top cluster readers. I have talked in terms of possessing sufficient prior knowledge to understand. And perhaps conveyed the sense of a checklist type of test: Do you know a, b, and c? Then you can understand a specific paper. But understanding is more subtle than that. Referring back to my simple analogy, although the formal address message conveyed sufficient information, the recipient was left without any clear sense of the street appearance or the type of building, for example, whereas the neighbor probably did have that extra depth to his understanding of which building was being specified. Similarly, understanding a paper really requires much more than reading it, knowing the terms in every statement, and grasping the logic by which each statement follows its predecessor. It requires a grasp of why the author is addressing this problem, how it fits into the discipline, and an insight into the deeper economic implications of the assumptions and conclusions of the paper. When we talk of understanding in this more mature sense and "measure" it along a line akin to the knowledge line, I will posit that the top cluster distribution is also quite widely spread. The culling of all "extraneous" material from the paper reduces the amount of help that the author (assuming that the author is able to help in this way) can offer the reader as assistance in fully understanding the paper.

In particular, it is the convention to write a paper in such a way that the actual thought sequences of the research process are carefully hidden. The paper is written as though the results sprang fully formed from the pen of the author like Athena from the head of Zeus. This practice seems to be designed to deprive the reader of much of the information that would permit him or her easily to comprehend the paper. This point is very nicely demonstrated in Roy Weintraub's book, *General Equilibrium Analysis*. In that book he reconstructs the sequence of conversations by which he and Dan Graham reached the results that they then wrote and published as a short paper in the *Review of Economic Studies*. The conversation is followed by a reprint of the article.[1] The juxtaposition demonstrates effectively how much is lost in the process of writing to conform with the sanitized conventions of the discipline.

It is my view that the standard way of writing journal articles means that many of the readers of the journals are being deprived of material that would substantially enhance their understanding of what they are reading. They follow the theorems and the lemmas but they do not mentally encompass the deeper economic insights that the author had, which motivated the choice of question and approach to it. Their limited grasp of what they read then feeds into their own research, which consequently becomes more mechanical than insightful. Of course this process in turn leads to many papers actually lacking deep insights and perhaps being fully represented by the standard style. And this of course is stronger justification for some rethinking of the conventions that journal editors apply than are mere issues of increasing readership: those conventions may well be lowering the quality of work in the discipline.[2]

Nonetheless, I doubt that my comments will change the world of journal editing one iota. To perform the intellectual tasks that I have been discussing for the top cluster and *a fortiori* for the second cluster, we must look to books.

3.   *The role of books:*

At this point I want to broaden my topic a little. Although there are some special aspects to the part university presses play in the dissemination of ideas, their role in economics is closely paralleled by a num-

---

[1] E. Roy Weintraub, *General Equilibrium Analysis: Studies in Appraisal* (New York: Cambridge University Press, 1985).
[2] I should not leave this section of my paper without saying that I am aware that some editors, especially Robert Clower during his editorships of *Economic Inquiry* and the *American Economic Review,* have encouraged creative diversity.

ber of commercial publishers who produce specialist books of high quality. So I will be including them as I consider the role of academic publishers more generally, that is, firms constituted in a variety of ways that publish books whose primary market is academics, others with a similar level of knowledge, and the libraries that serve them.

The research monograph: This is one kind of book that is quite close in nature to a long journal article. Some research work is very difficult to report at journal article length even when the conventions of the journal article are faithfully obeyed. Applied econometric work is a good example of this. By the time one has developed the model, discussed the data to be used, introduced and justified the estimation techniques to be used, and presented the results, fifteen printed pages tend to seem a trifle inadequate. A medium that permits very long pieces is needed. Yet the topic of such reports is usually of limited specialist interest only. We, like other academic publishers, persuade ourselves every so often that a particular topic is broad enough for book publication. And sadly, with about the same frequency, we find that we were overoptimistic. Or we print a very small number of copies, cut costs, and set a very high price. And that does not seem a very satisfactory approach. The fact is that a journal survives by presenting a portfolio of papers whose individually small readerships add up to a viable overall readership. The individual research monograph does not have a portfolio effect to help it. The discipline should be concerned at the difficulty of publishing such monographs. Again it is not just a practical issue: the lack of outlets for the kind of work that cannot be condensed to journal article length distorts the pattern of research in the discipline. Young economists wisely avoid types of research that cause publication problems.

Not all economists are equal: In talking about the distribution of economists along the knowledge line, I have implicitly taken it to be fact that not all economists are equal and that, in particular, many are not able to grasp the work that is presented in the terse style characteristic at least of the best journals in the discipline. This is probably true, but the same lessons can be drawn from the less controversial observation that economics is divided into many subfields and that most economists can only cope with that kind of article in their own subfield. Whichever way it is put, there is a barrier making it difficult for the majority of economists to grasp many of the ideas at the cutting edge of the discipline. This barrier harms the discipline. First, it means that teaching must lag seriously behind the development of the subject at all but a very few universities. If the teachers, however conscientious, cannot keep up with new developments, they certainly cannot pass them on to their students. Second, it slows down the development of the subject. While clearly those who would advance a particular research program had better be able to read the papers, the ideas of that research program will percolate more slowly through the rest of the discipline if the diligent but differently expert workers in other sub-fields cannot understand this new research. But I hope that I do not have to make the case too vigorously for the benefits of disseminating new ideas throughout the discipline.

I have argued that the crucial issue is providing sufficient contextual information. This may very well extend as far as introducing and explaining ideas and techniques that require considerable space to present. This consumes space and is thus costly to publish. It is not at all surprising that the journals avoid such material. Indeed I want to make clear that while I suspect that the line is often drawn by journal editors at a less than optimal point on the "knowledge line," journal articles are intended for the specialists in the subfield. Their function may well be more that of a medium of record than a communicator of ideas. The imprimatur that they put upon research by acceptance may be more important a function than reaching the wider audience that they could gain for that research.

Whether or not the journals see their task in such a light, at best they can disseminate to the top cluster of economists. And they can really only convey the results of one article at a time. This then leaves some clear and useful tasks for the book editors to perform, and necessary tasks for good economists to undertake.

The integrative book: A book provides enough scope for the author to present the results of many papers. Indeed very few articles provide enough meat for a whole book. The only example that I can think of is Nagel and Newman's *Godel's Proof.* Such books have, of necessity, an integrative function. Integration is not only a necessary character-istic of such books but also a central part of the work of scholars in advancing their subject. It is a neglected and underappreciated activity in economics. It should not be. Many economists are capable of read-ing each separate article, but understanding, as I have said before, takes much more. The ability to grasp the overall picture being created by a stream of articles is not a common faculty. It seems therefore to be part of the responsibility of researchers, at least if they believe in what they are doing, to present at some point the overall picture that they have been creating in the pointillism of technical papers. This is quite distinct from any popularization. I am arguing that such integrative writing is essential for the advancement of the general education of the members of the top cluster. The enthusiastic welcome for Andreu Mas-Colell's *Theory of General Economic Equilibrium* is evidence for this. It is still a difficult book that can be read only by the technically well-prepared, but its integrated presentation of a large body of work previously published only in separate highly technical papers has proved most valuable. Its readers are not the middlebrow economists for whom the math is still an insuperable obstacle. It is for members of the top cluster.[3]

In the curmudgeonly role that I have adopted in this paper, I must at this point lament how few economists follow a single research program through a number of articles. Rather, their creative work is butterflylike: articles randomly scattered through the discipline, usually butterflylike also in the way their drunkard's walk through the discipline keeps them in the sunlit patches of fashionable professional approval where the nectar of tractable problems can most easily be sucked.

Of course the integrative book can equally well, and even more usefully, synthesize a body of research from many authors. This type of writing is even more demanding on the skills of the author, but equally, certainly even more useful to the profession.

I would define one of the clear functions of academic book publishers in economics to be the publication of high level works that synthesize the results of important research programs. Sadly our task is not just to publish but to browbeat authors into writing such books.

Syntheses for the middlebrow: The larger task of the academic book publisher is to take ideas from the highbrow and communicate them to the middlebrow. By the middlebrow I mean those economists who are in the large second cluster along the knowledge line. Some might be described as permanent residents of that cluster. But with very few exceptions all economists fall into this cluster for work in some subfields of the discipline: outstanding econometricians will be defeated by the arcana of social choice theory, for example.

I feel that no more argument should really be needed to justify this type of book. But experience tells me otherwise. The development of a particular area of a discipline can be likened to rock climbing. The pioneers climb up into the unknown using all their skills and then at

---

[3]Andreu Mas-Colell, *The Theory of General Economic Equilibrium: A Differentiable Approach* (New York: Cambridge University Press, 1985).

intervals, when they themselves have reached a reasonably secure position, fix the rope and assist the following climbers to move up the rock. In this metaphor, the stage of rope-fixing and assisting is equivalent to the point at which the intellectual pioneers take time to write and communicate their ideas to the rest of the discipline. Such intellectual ropes are used to bring the rest of the discipline up toward the frontier. In economics, I feel that the pioneers are just climbing and climbing, and the rest of the discipline is being left further and further behind. But whether or not there is a trend in this, we can represent one of the roles of the academic book as being akin to the fixed ropes: the means by which the middlebrow of the profession are helped to learn the content of the latest work.

Such books, though, are not just for the middlebrow. Everyone's time is painfully limited. To decide to trace and read the journal article literature in a field other than one's own, even if one is fully capable of doing so, involves a massive investment of time. A clearly written book that presents the essential ideas, avoiding undue technicality and selecting the important from among the many contributions, can provide a means for relatively quickly updating one's knowledge away from one's own area of main interest. Commissioning and publishing such books is perhaps the most useful contribution that academic book publishers can contribute to the advancement of the discipline.

The integrative books on which I have placed great weight may, in many cases, be hard to distinguish from graduate textbooks, or at least books for graduate reading. The first type designed for the top cluster would be akin to advanced graduate books whereas the second type for the middlebrow would be suitable also for first year graduate students who, after all, are prepared to work harder than their elders, at least when the latter are just doing a little broadening reading. So without elaborating the case, I see the publication of graduate textbooks as being part of the task of the academic publishers, and one that grows naturally from, and cannot easily be separated from, the job of publishing integrative books.

Original work of book length: Apart from a brief digression on the problems of publishing long pieces of applied work, I have throughout this paper made the implicit assumption that new work in economics is primarily published first in the journals. This leaves the academic publishers with the responsibility of publishing various types of syntheses of articles. I cannot ignore the fact that a few economists – people who warm the hearts of us book publishers – work on large themes and topics and go directly into book form. They are a small minority

of the profession, not always, despite the way things work, senior tenured figures, who believe that their work has an integrity that requires
a broader canvas to present. Sadly, but unsurprisingly, that opinion is
not shared even by the wise and perceptive referees whom I consult in
many cases. But when the evaluations are positive then it is perhaps
an academic publisher's central role to bear with the unfavorable economics of such books and to produce those books and to try as ener-
getically as possible to tell the world about them.

Popularizing economic theory: Let me end this review of types of
books that are the appropriate function of academic publishers to disseminate with one category that overlaps with Donald Lamm's paper
(Chapter 9). There is one visible gap in the range of books by economists that disappoints me greatly. Whereas the physics profession
seems to produce a steady flow of books by outstanding scientists that
try to convey the excitement of their discipline to well-educated lay-
people, economists do not seem to find their subject exciting enough
to share with others. Of course, we have all those macro-policy-for-the-
layman and those panacea-for-our-woes books. But those are equivalent to books by applied physicists explaining how useful the transistor
is. We do not have the books that are equivalent to Einstein's *Relativity* (to start at the top), or those great books by Eddington and Jeans,
or *The First Three Minutes* by Weinberg, or (books that I have recently
discovered) Pagels' *The Cosmic Code* and *Perfect Symmetry.* Why is
this? Is it not a great intellectual achievement to generate models that
make sense and order from the chaos of human economic existence?
Are economists unsure of the worth of what they have done? Or has it
not dawned on them that funding comes through a political process
and that having an informed and appreciative public can be a significant help? Of course they do not ask for hundreds of millions of dollars
for accelerators and telescopes. But then I doubt that physicists would
write with the verve and excitement that the best of them manage if
their motives were purely opportunistic. They believe in their discipline and wish to share its excitement with others. I wonder why economists do not.

PART II

From economists to the lay public

CHAPTER 7

How economic ideas turn to mush

ROBERT M. SOLOW

Economic ideas – ranging from new but unelaborated concepts through isolated propositions about causality, all the way to full-blown theories – arise in the highbrow part of the economics profession and then diffuse first within the profession and then sometimes outside it to journalists, bureaucrats, politicians, and other citizens. Eventually they trickle away into the sand, or maybe – if the moon is in the seventh house – have some influence on events. There is also a backflow of ideas from the World Out There to the economics profession, but those are hardly ever economic ideas. They are rather social beliefs, priorities, or ideological conceptions. It is not only the Supreme Court that reads the election returns. More important, economists are responsive to the same currents of opinion that affect other people.

The vehicles by which diffusion takes place and the routes traveled by those vehicles can be the object of interesting studies. In this paper I consider one aspect of the diffusion process relevant to the spread of ideas from economists to the lay public.

The transmission of complicated ideas is imperfect. By the time an economic idea reaches its ultimate destination it has been changed, distorted in one way or another. This is surely the case when an idea diffuses outside the profession. The average person-in-the-street has probably never heard of monetarism – *even* monetarism! Among the subset who have, the picture in their heads is very likely quite different from what the median-difficulty elementary textbook conveys, and certainly not what any professional economist would understand, let alone what a specialist in monetary macroeconomics would teach to graduate students.

One's fear, of course, is that this distortion is often substantial and systematic. Economic ideas when they come to influence events – or only to reinforce the opinions and beef up the arguments of movers and shakers who have already made up their minds for quite other reasons – may bear little resemblance to the original ideas, the "real" ideas. In particular, it is almost certainly true that ideas get coarsened, even if not biased. Subtleties evaporate, including important subtleties, and qualifications disappear altogether. In the end ideas can be used to justify actions and policies that would not be supported by a correct statement. I imagine that everyone will agree with this description; I will try to give some examples later on.

What should we say about the proposition that whatever remains of an economic idea after the diffusion process is over is, by definition, the "real thing"? This is a sort of substructure/superstructure notion. Exposure to the World Out There wears away the extraneous decoration and leaves the true content bare. We would all scoff at that notion if it were applied to medicine or chemistry. If some researcher were to find that buffalo manure contains a substance that seems to shrink a certain class of tumors in a certain strain of mice, and the world were to conclude that buffalo-manure poultices are a sure cure for cancer, we would regard that as mass hysteria, not as a revelation of the true content of the research. Well, yes, but maybe that is too crude a description of what happens, or might happen, in the case of economics. Academic researchers devote nearly all of their time to refining basic ideas, touching up the picture here and there, generalizing in minor ways, and neatening proofs. That is how we get our kicks, and our promotions. If all that filigree work gets elided as the proposition works its way down to extra-academic discussion, maybe nothing of any significance is lost.

Nevertheless there are at least two ways in which that position is far too bland. The first is *bias* pure and simple. Economic ideas, instead of being merely coarsened, get distorted in one direction rather than another. The particular direction of bias might conceivably get selected by chance, but one really suspects that when it happens it happens usually for more systematic ideological reasons. The second point is even more bothersome. Simple coarsening can go so far that what is finally transmitted is merely false. If someone demonstrates that, under a long list of sharp assumptions, government bonds are not net wealth, and this reaches the World Out There as the proposition that government budget deficits have no effect on national saving, period, a genuine distortion has occurred. (The economic idea might have no real influence anyway, but that is another matter.)

This is pretty obvious, but it is often overlooked. Maybe we go along because economists enjoy the feeling that their discipline really matters to the World Out There, and we would rather think it is because of the austere beauty and depth of our science.

I am not talking only about esoteric bits of fancy theory, either. Here are some examples.

Take the Invisible Hand, for instance. Economists know, as a matter of logic, about the two fundamental theorems of welfare economics. Given a lot of favorable assumptions about the nature of technologies, the nature of consumer preferences, the existence of complete markets, the structure of all those markets, and the availability of information, every competitive general equilibrium is a Pareto-optimal state of the economy, and nearly every Pareto-optimal state of the economy can be represented as a competitive equilibrium for some pattern of endowments. Adam Smith would no doubt hardly recognize his brain-child. Nevertheless, whether he knew it or not, that is what he "knew." Every teacher of economic theory gets it right. Elementary texts omit the fine points, but presumably they cover the essentials if they cover anything.

I do not know what the readers of elementary texts understand themselves to have learned. The general educated and interested public thinks that economics has "proved" that "the free market is efficient," perhaps even the best of all possible worlds.

Not one reader in a thousand of the *Wall Street Journal* has any grasp of the qualifications without which the theorem, as a theorem, is simply false. That would hardly matter if the necessary assumptions were self-evidently true or even genuinely plausible to any open-minded observer. They are neither. Nor do even sophisticated economists have any real grasp of the robustness of the theorem: I do not know of any convincing story, either way, about whether an economy that differs from the abstract economy about as much as ours does comes even close to satisfying the conclusion of the Invisible Hand Theorem. There is some beginning research on this sort of issue but it has not got very far.

There is another widespread error that may be even worse in its consequences. Economists know that even under the best of conditions a competitive equilibrium is efficient only conditional on given endowments. A distorting intervention – tax or regulation – will generally do two things: it will destroy the property of efficiency and it will change the distribution of welfare. There is nothing in the Invisible Hand Theorem that justifies a claim that the second outcome is worse than the first. I feel foolish even reminding a professional audience of this elementary fact; but it must be perfectly obvious to us all that none of this penetrates to the more general public, which simply acquires the notion that the free market knows best.

This is the stuff of bull sessions and cheap shots. If the argument were to stop there, I could not bear to take up anyone's time with it. To my mind, the argument gets interesting only one level deeper. It is not at all clear to me that the effects of this coarsening are all bad. (Please note: my claim is only that the effects are "not all bad" and not that they are "not bad at all.")

What I have in mind is something like this. The fundamental theorems of welfare economics are on to something. They point to aspects of a market system that are not obvious, for example to the economy of information that is effected when prices perform their textbook function, and to the chains of substitutions and complementarities that transmit impulses from one spot in the economy to its far reaches. You can easily think of other such insights. One could make a plausible argument that, in the absence of misplaced confidence in the Invisible Hand, there would be too many interventions in the economy, or at least too many of the wrong ones. Let me put the point differently. I began by arguing that the World Out There believes that the economist's case for the market is stronger than it really is. Now I suggest the possibility that without that illusion the World Out There would not appreciate how strong the case really is.

You need only recollect the everlasting debates about free trade and protection, now newly revived, to see the force of this point. The classic arguments for free trade, by the time they reach the policy arena, elide a number of fine points, especially those having to do with the static character or the standard theory of comparative advantage. In their public form they are exceeded in crudity only by the standard arguments for protection. On the whole, I suspect most economists would argue that the case for open trade needs all the help it can get, and the loose use of the standard argument has done net good.

I could go on, because there is a lot here worth going on about. A close student of the rhetoric of economics could study the vocabularies and tactics used by those who want to take a technical and limited idea and make it have policy consequences. A historian of economic thought could study the extent to which and the ways in which events in the World Out There have an influence on the generation of ideas in the highbrow part of professional economics. A professional gossip might contemplate the role of particular personalities in mediating between the profession and the World Out There. My particular interest – what all this tells us about the nature of economics as a discipline – is best served by sketching another example.

It seems useful to turn to macroeconomics, which offers the added feature that competing schools of thought coexist within the highbrow profession. The first thing to say is that the same contrast is visible between the refinement of professional argument and the crudity of its residue in public debate. Just recently I watched a television interview with a member of Congress who has been a major player in the passage of the 1986 tax bill. He was asked what he thought about the proposition that the legislation might be mildly contractionary in the short run and adverse on investment in the longer run. It is an act of great charity to describe his answer as meaningless drivel. I would have felt better if I had thought he was uttering conscious nonsense in favor of a bill that he liked for other reasons; but I had the feeling that I was seeing the residue of economic ideas as perceived by a leading member of a committee with important economic responsibilities.

The underlying phenomenon is exactly as before. I have already offered the "Ricardian equivalence theorem" as a case in point. There is genuine and sharp disagreement within highbrow economics. Despite occasional bad manners, however, the conflict is over specific technical matters. How important is liquidity-constrained consumption expenditure? Do government securities offer services that are, in effect, unavailable from other sources? Are intergenerational bequests important in the long-term accumulation of capital, or are most generations very near a corner solution when it comes to saving for heirs? No feeling for any of this diffuses across the boundary into the World Out There. Some people think that "Deficits Don't Matter." Other people think that deficits represent "A Crisis of the Republic." There is even a substantial group that appears to think both things at the same time. Each group seems to believe that its view is warranted by some theory originating in academic economics. I don't think it really matters that this belief is occasionally pandered to by economists who ought to know better, do know better in fact, but cannot resist the temptation to be Somebody.

The same sort of thing is epidemic throughout macroeconomics and its public role. Academic ideas have resonances beyond their capacity logically to support. More often than not it is the logic that gives way.

Consider a less esoteric case than the intertemporal effects of deficit finance. I have ventured the guess that most ordinary people have never heard of or have barely heard of monetarism. What about those who have – readers of the daily financial press, for instance? I presume that they identify monetarism with the belief that variations in the money supply are important for something. For what? For variations in the price level, at a minimum. Now let us look more closely.

Do they think that monetarism is the belief that the price level moves proportionally to the money supply in the long run? Probably they do; but that belief is hardly peculiar to monetarism. Do they have the notion that the price level is proportional to the money supply even in the short run? Do they have any idea that the demand for money can shift, and that it is variation in the supply of money relative to the demand that should be said to move the price level (and perhaps other things as well)? You may be beginning to have your doubts, and we have just started.

Does the average reader of the *Wall Street Journal* have an opinion about the relation between changes in the nominal money stock and changes in the real money stock? Does he or she consider that changes in the real (and nominal) money supply may have effects on real (or nominal) rates of interest? If the answer to these questions is yes, one naturally turns to the further effects of money-supply variation on the level and composition of real output. Does the commuting public then revise its belief that the price level is proportional to the money supply in the short-to-medium run? If it does, then it must have formed some opinion about the interest-elasticity of the demand for money. Everyday monetarism, after all, depends on that elasticity being fairly small.

I am not even going to inquire into the person-in-the-street's views about the degree of endogeneity of the domestic money supply, or about the effects of the internationalization of capital markets on the demand and supply functions for money, because I hope you are getting the idea. By the time monetarism reaches the street, even Wall Street, it is a far cruder doctrine than the theory you teach to your students using any intermediate textbook on macroeconomics. It is so much cruder that it is only fair to say that it has become a different doctrine. Academic economists with a policy axe to grind may contribute to this process of losing in translation; that does not change what is happening.

Just to make it clear that I am not playing an ideological game, let me insist that you could ask similar questions about the diffusion of pop-Keynesian economics and find similar answers. There was a time when the reader of the financial press might have heard of the multiplier, might even have identified it with the notion that a dollar of government purchases or a dollar of tax reduction could be expected to generate more than a dollar of national income and the corresponding amount of employment. Was that a real or nominal stimulus and was it real or nominal national income? How does that response relate to the behavior of the price level after an injection of nominal demand? And, by the way, how is it related to the interest-elasticity of the demand for money and the slope of the LM curve? Some models show a multiplier effect that tapers off and then dies away, all or partly. Did that ever penetrate to the World Out There? No. Could it? That is the really hard question and I have to turn to it, though I do not pretend to know the answer.

There seem to be at least three sources for this debasement of economic ideas as they spread into the world at large from their natural habitat in professional discussion.

The first is inherent in the diffusion process itself. Economics is a complicated subject, whether we are talking about macroeconomics or microeconomics, theoretical economics or applied economics. It is unlikely that a meaningful answer to any serious question can be fairly stated in one or two short sentences. (A meaningful answer should include some statement about the conditions under which the answer is expected to be true, and about the circumstances that would make you suspicious about its truth.) Yet short answers are what the world wants; and by and large those are what it gets. I think – at least I hope – that is why the World Out There has got so accustomed to the spectacle of two – no, three – distinguished economists being quoted as saying two – no, three – quite contradictory things on any given day of the week.

Even the 900 words that seems to be the canonical length of a deep-think piece in the press are not adequate for anything much but dogma, and a 900-word opportunity is the exception. Most of the time the two short sentences are exactly what the economist gets. The two short sentences are not even his or her own; they are pieced together – often incoherently – from five sentences spoken into a telephone on the spur of the moment, and thus often incoherent to start with. Any improvement in the process must somehow change that.

I do not know if it can be done. Maybe nobody wants to hear more than two sentences about issues of economic life and economic policy. There appears to be no shortage of people prepared to express themselves in that form. I do not even know if the situation is better in other countries. I used to think that they do these things better in England; but I now suspect they merely have a fruitier way of pronouncing the words. It would be useful if others who know much more than I do about the mechanics of the diffusion process could suggest ways to provide opportunities for the serious discussion of serious ideas at a length and pace appropriate to them. I suppose no one can do anything about the person in the street's attention span.

It is tempting merely to express frustration on this subject; and I fear I tend to yield to the temptation. There are, however, real issues about the nature of daily and weekly publishing, and about the character of the audiences they serve. I do not try to go deeper, because I lack the necessary knowledge and experience.

The second aspect of the problem is inherent in the demands of the political process, and its relation to economic thought. Above I stated the commonplace: that good economics is bound to be complicated. Good economics is also bound to be uncertain. Even where the underlying principle is clear its application to particular circumstances is never direct. Too many other things are always happening at once. If there is anything that the politician does not need it is complexity and uncertainty. Just the opposite is called for. This demand for simplicity and confidence is strengthened by the fact that the political process is rarely interested in narrow economic policy for its own sake. What we think of as the heart of the matter is often seen by the players themselves as subsidiary to issues of distribution, party-politics, and image. You can hardly expect the President, the Senator, or the House Committee Chairman to tolerate distraction from the frying of his own fish by the complexities and uncertainties of economic analysis. That is why academic economists are so often scoffed at with jokes about "on the other hand."

Probably there is nothing to be done about this. It goes with the territory of democratic politics. Nevertheless there may be occasions for marginal improvements and they should be welcomed and followed up whenever they arise.

The third reason for the clipping of our intellectual coinage has its locus inside professional economics, and that is what interests me the most. The problem, I think, is this. Theory tends to outrun sound applied economics. Making fine distinctions is not a perversion of theory; it *is* theory. And so theory is always proposing hypotheses of such a degree of fineness that data cannot seriously test them, verify them, or improve them. We are unwilling to admit that to ourselves, for good reasons and bad, so one natural response is to refine econometric theory, too. We propose more and more elaborate ways to exploit the pitifully few real degrees of freedom history gives us. The result is that we pretend to answer questions far beyond the capacity of our observational material to provide credible and reliable evidence. Having gone so far, we find ourselves forced to pretend to believe the answers we get. We have ways of making the data talk, yes, but like any tortured soul they can be made to say whatever the torturer wants to hear.

The solution to this dilemma is certainly not to try to hold back the advance of theory. It cannot be done, anyway. Like all those bright and intense and good-looking Hewlett-Packard people in the commercials, economic theorists will keep saying: "What if . . . ?" Nor would I wish to discourage highbrow theory if that were possible. It can only do good to have bright minds exploring nooks and crannies, trying out new assumptions, and expanding the variety of model economies we know something about. Self-conscious pure theory is harmless. It is at the borderline of theoretical and applied economics and in applied economics itself that reform is required, if serious economics is to be taken seriously in the World Out There.

A complicated model plus a regression is not serious economics. There is hardly anything on the face of the earth so silly that a regression cannot be found to support it. Our standards of evidence are simply too lax. A statement about the real economy can earn its way either as a logical consequence of clearly valid assumptions or as the robust product of many pieces of evidence. I mean to emphasize two things here: robustness as the prime virtue and – consequently – the need to exploit all sorts of evidence including, but not limited to, formal statistical hypothesis-testing.

I am desperately anxious not to be misunderstood. I do indeed mean to suggest that subjective and anecdotal evidence can be valuable evidence. I do not mean to suggest that mere anecdotes, personal impressions, or *Fingerspitzengefuhl* is adequate evidence or better evidence than formal statistics. I wish I had a nickel for every time I have heard a "practical man" tell me how it really is, and tell me self-contradictory balderdash. Anna Rosenberg Hoffman, a lady who had been around, once said to me in a committee meeting: "What are you going to believe – 'the data' or your eyes?" Fortunately, we do not have to choose. If "the data" and your eyes tell you different things, something interesting is going on and further investigation is called for.

The fundamental point is that an honest economist will insist on robust results. Robustness can be confirmed only by consulting a wide range of evidence. Economics will then be more believable. And two further results will follow. There will be fewer of those occasions so beloved by the press when Economist A says that event E will cause X to rise, and Economist B, of equal eminence, says that event E will cause X to fall. We all know that A and B can easily find regression equations to back up their stories. More or less by definition they will find it harder to produce the kind of robust panoply of evidence that they should need for credibility.

The second result I would hope for is to whet the theorist's taste for simple strong models, the sort that have a prayer of accounting for those robust empirical regularities. Under those conditions, economic ideas might diffuse more accurately into the World Out There, both because they would be more transparently understandable, and because they would be more worth understanding. And if we could not produce that kind of theory and that kind of evidence, I would vote for a little more silence.

CHAPTER 8

The development of the ideas: strategic trade policy and competitiveness

DAVID WARSH

It is difficult to imagine a more unlikely trio than Barbara Spencer, David Halberstam, and Robert Reich. Spencer is quiet, shy, and wears glasses. She boasts no special knowledge of particular markets, companies, or investments. Yet Spencer just happens to be a distinguished young economist, a cofounder of a new branch of academic thinking about strategic trade policy, a woman near the top of her trade, but otherwise unknown, who has never published anything more accessible than an academic paper.

David Halberstam, on the other hand, is extremely well-known. He is among the best of a generation of fine newspaper reporters, the author of a remarkable career that has ranged from Mississippi to the Congo to Vietnam to Washington and Tokyo. For the last several years, he has been working the parallel stories of the automotive industries of the United States and Japan. Published in 1986 as *The Reckoning*, Halberstam's book probably will be widely compelling; certainly it will sell millions of copies, especially now that it is in paperback.

Robert Reich, of course, is a gifted controversialist, a lawyer who burst out of a junior policy position in the Carter Administration to become a leading advocate for a certain sort of government direction of industrial development. Perhaps more than any other advocate, with the possible exception of Harvard sociologist Ezra Vogel, the Cambridge lawyer is responsible for the widespread use of the phrase "industrial policy" that is at the center of today's political/economic debate. The United States has an industrial policy by default, he says; it should own up to its responsibility.

What these three have in common is that each is near the center of the controversy about whether the United States has been systematically snookered by its failure to understand the canny Japanese, or whether our recent trade deficits have some other cause. It may be fair to say there is no more pressing issue than this one when it comes to establishing, over the next few years, America's future place in the world economy.

The new international economics

Until recent years, one would have thought that no question was more thoroughly settled among economists than that free trade was an unmitigated good. From the time of the first economic modeler, David Ricardo, the principle of comparative advantage has been clearly formulated as meaning the special ability of one country to provide one set of particular products more cheaply than any other country. Ricardo's famous example was wine and cloth. Portugal was better at producing wine, England was better at making textiles, and both were better off trading with one another than either would be going it alone.

But in the early 1980s, the doctrine of comparative advantage as a sufficient explanation of the state of things began to come under increasing fire. This was partly a result of "progress" within economics; partly the result of changes in the world outside. As Paul Krugman has written, "Since World War II . . . a large and generally growing part of world trade has come to consist of exchanges that cannot be attributed so easily to underlying advantages of countries that export particular goods. Instead, trade seems to reflect arbitrary or temporary advantages resulting from economies of scale or shifting leads in close technological races."

The new international economics began in earnest, I am told, with the publication in 1984 of a monograph by Elhanan Helpman and Paul Krugman, *Market Structure and Foreign Trade: Increasing Returns, Imperfect Competition and the International Economy.* As the title suggests, Helpman and Krugman's work was another of those attempts to "get Chamberlin right," as economists sometimes put it among themselves; that is, to bend the analytic tools of theory to grapple with a world of big companies and imperfect information – this time in international trade. Much world trade was in industries with only a few big firms in each (oligopolies in economists' jargon) – airplanes, computers, pharmaceuticals, cars, farm machinery, and so on. These businesses were usually characterized by the need for enormous expenses for research and development, and great corresponding gains in efficiency derived from the experience of long production runs. There were, in other words, increasing returns to scale, and they were common enough to have major effects on the patterns of international trade.

This quickly gives rise to the question: Can nations engage in unfair trade practices? And this is where Barbara Spencer and her collaborator James A. Brander have come in, by introducing the notion of strategy into international trade. Strategic moves are those that are designed to affect a rival's behavior. You can't have strategy in atomistic competition, of course. But where only a few firms are involved, it may be possible to adopt a course that would affect a competitor's market share and profitability – especially if the rival is a foreign firm. Drawing on a tradition of the analysis of two-firm markets dating back to Augustin Cournot, using the latest in game theory, Spencer and Brander carefully reasoned through the circumstances in which it would pay for nations to play games with one another, subsidizing exports and protecting home markets. Their results suggested that there were indeed instances in which national policies could nurture industries that required big front-end investments, demanding to be amortized over long production runs.

It is crucial for the outsider to understand what economists themselves may take for granted: that this work is done in the rarified atmosphere of high theory. The key thing about Spencer and Brander's contribution is that they produced a model; they "wrote it down" in a way which mapped neatly into all the other models that, taken as a whole, comprise the present-day theory of international trade. There are many others in the "invisible college" of specialists who are concerned with international trade: perhaps a hundred persons in all are active in writing for and editing the journals that constitute the leading edge of the field. One or two may be more routinely forceful, intellectually speaking; a couple of others may be more intuitive; still others are more lithe and able to communicate easily with those outside the field. If any one of the band is to win a Nobel prize some day, it might well be Helpman, by common consent. But Spencer and Brander are near the top of their trade. They were in some significant way the first to raise the question of strategic trade policy, and in *Strategic Trade Policy,* the volume of essays edited by Krugman, their priority is recognized in the subtle etiquette of scholarship: Their essays are the ones that set the scene of the book.

So here we have the mother and father of strategic trade policy. They have successfully undermined the free trade dogma that is still taught in most universities, at least to some extent. (I should giddily add that many trade economists are still skeptical of the new arguments.) They have produced an argument with potentially great appeal to many business persons. And yet they are almost completely unknown outside their field. This is, I think, precisely the kind of influence that

Keynes was thinking of when he wrote that famous passage near the end of the *General Theory* extolling the eventual significance of economists' ideas. And yet perhaps he went too far in arguing that "the world is ruled by little else." Clearly, Spencer and Brander are just part of the scene.

Competitiveness

At the opposite end of the spectrum from the economist Spencer is the newpaperman David Halberstam. There could scarcely be two traditions more different from one another, or so it seems to me. Where Spencer went to graduate school for years to learn the specialized language of her science, Halberstam has no formal training except for his Harvard undergraduate education and the newspapers for which he's worked. Where Spencer talks only to other economists, Halberstam talks to everyone; he has no institutional ties to particular analytic communities and talks equally to bankers, manufacturers, CIA agents, Wall Street analysts, and economists. Where Spencer writes only on those topics where she can hope to be nearly absolutely certain, Halberstam must forever "tell the story whole," seeking at least provisional answers to all the obvious and not-so-obvious questions on his readers' minds. He's done so in a series of books: two on Vietnam, one on the media, one on the rise of modern professional basketball, another on Olympic rowing, and still another on the United States and Japanese economies since before World War II, that is, his *Reckoning.*

Halberstam says he set out to write *The Reckoning,* his car book, in the autumn of 1980. "In the wake of the fall of the Shah of Iran it was clear that the entire American industrial core was vulnerable to relentless challenge from a confident, disciplined Japan. How and why that had happened seemed to me a story worth telling. While there were a number of experts on both sides of the Pacific, it struck me that there was no book that tried to tell the parallel stories of the Japanese ascent and the American *malaise,* and that it was a perfect opportunity for a writer willing to spend the five years or so it would take to report the critical events closely."

In digesting a prodigious amount of material, what Halberstam produced is what he has called "soft drama," a narrative of "something profound that has taken place so quietly, in such small increments, that it is barely visible to the naked eye." The narrative device he employed to tell his story was to contrast the decline of the Ford Motor Company with the rise of Nissan motors. Like his earlier *Breaks of the Game,* the book has a heavy moralistic component: as Mark Feeney put it, writing in the *Boston Globe*, the saga is "A Big Three Gotter-damerung with Grosse Point as Valhalla and Henry Ford II as a bib-ulous Wotan." In this version, which bears a resemblance to the anal-ysis of the short-term orientation of American managers associated with Robert Hayes and the late William Abernathy, the struggle for the soul of Detroit is won by "bean counters," battalions of finance-trained whiz-kids that were led by Robert S. McNamara. The Japanese, for all their foibles, produce the "good car men" of the 1980s.

Halberstam is simply not very interested in the kind of strategic con-siderations that preoccupy Spencer and the other new international economists. "For all Japan's flaws, its own exclusive tendencies," he writes, "it was hardly Japan's sins that had made Detroit vulnerable. Certainly Detroit had made only the most half-hearted gestures to open the Japanese market to its products; it had never lobbied very hard to open it, and it never bothered to ship right-hand-drive cars, which the Japanese use, instead of left-hand-drive cars, which Ameri-cans drove." In *The Reckoning,* the car wars are really a complicated agon, comparable to, say, the *Iliad,* in which great heroes of two nations act out their fates in a kind of ritual combat.

Is there any reason to think that Halberstam talked much to econ-omists in framing his tale? Not really. Mainly he seems to have relied on William Niskanen, who for a time as chief economist at Ford fought the leadership efforts of his company to get the government to intervene in the auto industry's behalf – a case of free trade dogmatism if ever there was one. Indeed, Halberstam's whole reconnaissance could be said to be a rear-guard action against experts, and to the extent it leads him to neglect the analytic setting in which his tale unfolds, that is too bad. The reputations that were casualties of the spectacular Japanese success included those of John Kenneth Gal-braith, the analyst who powerfully argued in the 1960s that competi-tion was pretty much a thing of the past, and Henry Ford. But Gal-braith is not mentioned in the book.

One of the ironies is that Ford began to perform especially well in the marketplace just as Halberstam's book appeared. Its Taurus and Sable lines are clearcut hits; its new and relatively anonymous man-agers are getting high marks even from competitors. Indeed, Robert H. Waterman, the McKinsey consultant who co-wrote *In Search of Excel-lence* (with Thomas J. Peters), has written Ford up as a shining exam-ple of corporate renewal. But this simply illustrates the perils of jour-nalism. Just as economics, in its urge to get things right, forever risks leaving something important out of the model, so journalism, in its urge to provide a timely diagnosis, risks getting things wrong. Halberstam's book has probably not succeeded in framing the story as well as his earlier book, *The Best and the Brightest,* framed the story of the Vietnam War. But even so, it confirms Halberstam's reputation as one of the most remarkable journalists of his generation. He was there when the story broke and he filed on it.

Alliance with the policymaker

Somewhere in between Barbara Spencer and David Halberstam is Robert Reich, the peripatetic analyst of international trade based at the Kennedy School of Government of Harvard University. A Yale Law School graduate, Reich spent some time as director of policy planning at the Federal Trade Commission during the Carter Administration, then burst forth as the author of a pair of lucid polemics that sought to become much of the platform of the Democratic Party in 1984. In *Minding America's Business,* Reich teamed up with a former Boston Consulting Group consultant named Ira Magaziner to offer a prescription for picking "sunrise" and "sunset" industries. Then in *The Next American Frontier* he extended the analysis, laying out a simplified schema of American economic history, with the Era of Mobilization (1870 to 1920) giving way to the Era of Management (1920 to 1970) and then to the present-day era of the flexible production system. Reich operates with an entrepreneurial flair in a tradition going back to Thurman Arnold, another federal "trustbuster," who preferred a business planning system to the high degree of decentralization that existed in the 1930s.

On the surface, Reich's analysis looks quite a lot like the more boldly assertive versions of strategic trade policies. Japanese industrial planners target particular markets, skillfully rig incentives, and clobber American firms, who respond with demands for protectionist measures. First it was steel, then it was automobiles, now it is semiconductor memory chips. "There are only two alternatives to this sad tale. Either the government refrains from intervening in semiconductor trade altogether – letting the chips fall where they may, as it were – or the government helps the American semiconductor industry stay in the race by subsidizing the next generations of chip technology. The first alternative, favored by those who believe that world trade follows the dictates of 18th and 19th century economists, is attractive in its simplicity. If the Japanese can make cheaper and better chips, let 'em. We'll buy them and be better off for the deal." What is needed to stay ahead in high tech, says Reich, "is a partnership between government and business, aimed at embracing the future rather than preserving the past."

Surely it is tantalizing to consider the pronounced resemblance of some of Reich's ideas to concepts that have had wide currency in the twilight technological zone of business strategic planning. The fact is, a kind of industrial analogue to strategic trade planning has been developing in the corporate world since the mid-1950s. Then the focal point was the strategic planning department of the General Electric Company. It was there that Martin Shubik and Sidney Schoeffler identified market structure as a key determinant of profitability, and a number of separate strands have grown out of that particular Athens. The best-known of these strands was surely the Boston Consulting Group in its heyday. But perhaps the most interesting is the Profit Impact of Market Strategy begun by Schoeffler, first under the auspices of the Harvard Business School, and later at the Strategic Planning Institute. As described in *The PIMS Principles: Linking Strategy to Performance* (Free Press, forthcoming), these notions sound more than a little like game-theoretic Reichian analysis – yet they are grounded in deep economic theory.

But business consultancy is not the realm in which Reich prefers to operate. His is the realm of discourse that Mike Pertchuk calls the domain of "the Giant Killers." What claim to the mantle of authority does Reich make? Certainly, it is not to economics, except in the most cursory way. Reich's appeal is to his readers' "common sense"; his venue of choice is on the Op-Ed page of the nation's leading newspapers. It is instructive to think of the list of people who have achieved remarkable success in this fashion: it includes Jane Jacobs, Rachel Carson, David Halberstam (in his pieces on Vietnam), Jude Wanniski, and perhaps George Gilder with respect to the tax act. Maybe it is too early to know whether Reich belongs on this list, but it is not unreasonable to think that he does.

The key angle here is alliance with the policymaker. The vizier is nothing without his sultan. It is an extremely rare economist who admires Reich, I think, even including the strategic trade types; and most journalists are mistrustful of his zeal. His natural allies are other policy advisers on the fringes of economics: sociologists, business school professors, consultants, trade group officials, and the like. But as long as there are politicians who are interested in his advice, he remains a powerful player on the grid that I have been describing, and only the rash will omit him from their line-up cards.

Independent generators of ideas

I have sketched the paths by which three persons from widely different walks of life have arrived at their opinions about "the targeting game."

So what can be said about diffusion of economic ideas in this complicated landscape? Well, the most obvious remark is that there are at least three areas where relatively independent generators of ideas may operate more or less autonomously. It is not that there aren't frequent collisions among them: journalists listen to economists and economists listen to journalists, and it is only the most blatant ideologue who doesn't make an occasional petition to professional authority, in the style of Wanniski appealing to "the Mundell-Laffer hypothesis." But ideas exist within each hierarchy, and the denizens of each realm don't have much reason to muck around in the others.

The second observation is that all three of these circles give signs of being organized in leagues. That "invisible colleges" are the fundamental unit of organization in scientific communities is well-established in the literatures of the sociology and history of science. It wouldn't take much to extend the analysis to economics, and somebody ought to do it. Yet on closer examination, Halberstam, too, is a constituent of the community. He is a senior member of the generation of correspondents for whom Vietnam was the galvanizing story. He is a member also of a coterie of journalists who are seeking to explain contemporary economic changes, a group that includes younger writers such as Robert Samuelson, James Fallows, Joel Kotkin, and Daniel Burstein. These communities follow tacit rules, share interests in certain topics, and recognize dominating successes in many of the same ways as their scientific counterparts.

What distinguishes the economist from the reporter from the controversialist? Surely this question is the basic one in beginning to understand the rules that govern the patterns of diffusion of ideas from one part of society to another. The institutional settings aside, I'd say that the real difference among these types of analyst has to do with the sense of each of what constitutes an explanation. They are arranged, in my mind at least, according to the degree of their skepticism. At one end of the scale is the scientist, whose ideal of intellectual integrity has been described by Richard Feynman as "a kind of utter honesty, a kind of leaning-over-backwards. . . . The first principle is that you must not fool yourself and you are the easiest person to fool. So you have to be very careful about that." At the other end of the scale is the enthusiast. His mind is made up; he has no truck with disinterest. Somewhere in between is the reporter. He's trying to get the story right, but he's trying to get it done, too. Like the businessman and the voter whom he serves as proxy, he can't afford to wait for science; science is very often too slow.

Toward the end of *The Reckoning*, David Halberstam cites with approval the story of how Chalmers Johnson teased Naohiro Amaya about there being only two Ph.D. economists at MITI. "Amaya answered that this was true, for running MITI was too important to be left to economists. Then he cited a study that showed the more Nobel laureates in economics a country had, the more likely its economy was to go downhill." If it is true that economists have only recently discovered the basis for the strategic trade policy that the Japanese have been pursuing to their great advantage for more than a century, it only underscores Amaya's point. The key observation again belongs to Richard Feynman (it serves as the motto of John Ziman's splendid little essay, "Public Knowledge"): "A great deal more truth can become known than can be proved."

CHAPTER 9

Economics and the common reader

DONALD S. LAMM

As one of Lord Keynes's "practical men," I must accept my lot before this learned assemblage as the "slave of some defunct economist." This servitude, I hasten to add, is involuntary. As a dropout from Econ 10, Yale's principles of economics course in my day, I'd prefer to deny that any defunct economist, or, for that matter, any funct economist, has me in thrall.

Sadly, the denial will not wash. I have been reading manuscripts and books in economics for nearly three decades. Some of the wisdom and folly therein no doubt governs my day-to-day decisions as a business-man. I must confess, however, without a trace of chagrin, to one devi-ation from rational economic behavior. Attempting to purvey the ideas of economists to the general reader or, as I prefer, the common reader, is an activity that flies in the face of profit-making behavior. Most of the remarks that follow will underscore that proposition. Still, there are satisfactions in publishing that cannot be inferred from even close scrutiny of profit-and-loss statements. One of them for me is to seek out economists willing to endure the slings and arrows of scornful colleagues by writing in a form intelligible to the nonspecialist.

The task is not an easy one. As far back as 1963, I learned that from Arthur Okun, who had recently returned to teaching from a stint as a staff member on the Council of Economic Advisers. The early 1960s were, of course, the heyday of the new economics, and an American president, tutored in economics by Walter Heller and others, had inveighed in an eloquent address against some stubborn misconcep-tions in the area of fiscal policy and the public debt. "The myth per-sists," said President Kennedy, "that federal deficits create inflation and budget surpluses prevent it. Yet sizable budget surpluses after the war did not prevent inflation, and persistent deficits for the last several years have not upset our basic price stability." A few weeks later, this same myth-stalking president had to do some remedial homework in macroeconomic policy. On a Sunday afternoon, Professor Okun received a telephone call at home from a perplexed chief executive who needed a short course in the distinction between monetary and fiscal policy. Okun did his level best. But at the end of twenty minutes, the president interrupted. "I think I've got it. M stands for money; it also stands for monetary policy, which is chiefly concerned with the supply of money; and that means M stands for Martin." Making the connection between the money supply and William McChesney Martin, the chairman of the Federal Reserve, may have been a useful insight at a time when one had to cope with only M-1 and M-2. The task has become far more formidable with measures of the money supply running at least to M-10, with a few compounds such as M-1A and M-1B, and other Ms undoubtedly waiting in reserve.

The afternoon exchange with President Kennedy failed to produce an Okun's Law. Had one surfaced, it might have run along these lines: to be grasped by the laymen the ideas of economists must be explained in terms of actors and events in the real world. Adam Smith knew that. In *The Wealth of Nations,* his famous example of the pin factory, what would now be called an application, is but one of hundreds of instances where Smith resorted to concrete illustration. His theoretical argument is honeycombed with historical allusions, as when he speaks of the metals bartered in Sparta and Rome, the low wages of China, and the enforced inherited occupations of ancient Egypt. He includes case studies, citing the Cottagers of Scotland and the people of the Highlands, not to mention his frequent references to weavers and smiths and butchers and bakers.

1985: A year like any other?

1776 was obviously a good year for economics and the common reader. But what is the situation in our own time? In approved empirical fashion, I have dug into available data on activity in the publishing of books on economics. Since I possess neither the skill nor the patience for detailed time series analysis, I have limited my investigations to a single year, 1985. It appears to be a representative year if numbers of titles published in economics is a reasonable indicator. To get that number (2,084), I have had to penetrate a mystifying and strangely alluring entry in an annual accounting of books published in the United States. The accounting appears in tabular form in *Publishers' Weekly,* the journal of the book industry, and it breaks down new title publication by categories. In most years the category leading in number of titles is "Economics, Sociology," varying between eight and ten percent of the total.

Information from the R. R. Bowker Company, the parent firm of *Publishers' Weekly,* refines that figure considerably. Under the heading "Economics, Sociology" are subsumed all the Dewey Decimal classifications from 300 to 399; economics coexists not only with sociology but also with such subjects as social sciences in general, statistics, political science, law, education, and even "customs, etiquette, and folklore." Some might be tempted to observe that the last item, folklore, bears a distinct resemblance to economics, or vice versa. Kinder observers will note simply that a field that has spread its investigations to virtually all aspects of human interaction from the board room to the bedroom gets a bit fuzzy around the edges.

When categories other than economics are eliminated from the count, the results begin to fall in line with one's expectation. In the general category "economics" (330 in the Dewey Decimal system), 249 titles are tallied; this figure covers everything from monographs, for example, *The Fertility Revolution: A Supply-Demand Analysis,* to books for the great unwashed, for example, *Economics in Plain English, Updated and Expanded.* But if subjected to close analysis, the broad category "economics" will be seen to harbor mostly textbooks. Principles texts, new and revised, lurk there; so do intermediate and upper division theory texts, with the notable exception of texts in macroeconomics. When Mr. Dewey devised his classification scheme economics was largely the word according to Alfred Marshall and admitted no distinctions along macro and micro lines; now there is a subcategory, 339, "macroeconomics and related topics," with 60 titles enumerated for 1985.

Much more heavily represented are three other subcategories. The most surprising is labor economics with 294 titles, surprising, that is, considering the slippage in academic attention to the field since the New Deal and its afterglow. But the classification includes a wide variety of titles, from *The Devil Makes Work: Leisure in Capitalist Britain* to *Keeping America at Work: Strategies for Employing the New Technologies.* Bigger still is 332, financial economics. This is where the crop of fast-buck manuals is found, with titles such as *Money Dynamics for a New Economy, Crisis Investing,* and *Make Money in Real Estate with Government Loans.* Such inspirational tracts, I might note, appear side-by-side with Keynes's *General Theory,* the latter presumably shelved with financial economics because the term "macroeconomics" was not in use at the time of its publication. (Diehard monetarists please take note.)

Largest of the subcategories, with over twice the number of titles in "economics" itself, is 338, production, represented in 1985 by 670 titles. This one is even more of a catchall; it includes the current tidal wave of books on entrepreneurship or corporate derring-do such as Mary Cunningham's *Power Play: What Really Happened at Bendix* (a descendant of the old kiss-and-tell story) and still has room left over for such heavyweights as *Management of Values: The Ethical Difference in Corporate Policy and Performance.* The output in other subcategories – in public finance (65 titles), in socialism and related systems (65 titles), and in international economics (56 titles) – falls into more predictable alignment with the general category of economics. But these numbers, too, may be deceptive if one thinks of the concerns of academic economists. *All You Need to Know about the IRS,* for instance, does not appear on reading lists for public finance courses alongside such standard works as Stiglitz's, *Economics of the Public Sector.* Yet they fall in the same Dewey Decimal category.

What does this numerical tour tell us about the role of books in the transmission of economic ideas? Mostly that bibliographical systems, designed to simplify storage and retrieval of books, give the misleading impression that one out of thirty books published in 1985 was written by or about economics. Only the most innocent investigator would mistake titles tinged with some economic content for the genuine article, a book that takes the theory and practice of economics seriously.

Reviews, reviewers, and all that

It is a commonplace of trade, or general, publishing that browsing and word-of-mouth do more for book sales than any measures under the publisher's control such as advertising expenditure. Not far behind browsing and word-of-mouth is another influence that money cannot – or should not – buy: reviews. In arbitrating the choice of titles to be covered in their columns, the editors of *The New York Times Book Review, Book World,* and the *New York Review of Books* wield considerable power over the life and death of trade books. Few regular readers of those periodicals will be surprised to discover that economics, the Dewey Decimal categories aside, fares poorly in the struggle for limited review space. *The New York Times,* for example, gives space, including "in brief" reviews, to fewer than 2,500 titles a year out of some 30,000 books ostensibly written for the common reader. A former editor of the *Times Book Review* once confessed that he broke out in hives when he opened a book larded with graphs and tables. That malady, if prevalent among the *Times* readership, never had a chance to surface during that editor's tenure. The change since his departure is not very great; a skimming of reviews of books on economics or even remotely connected with it turns up a few in the first half of 1985;

the number increased in the second half but only because a single issue
(October 20) contained a special feature devoted entirely to books on
economics and business. It started off with a long review of a brief
book, Kenneth Boulding on Robert Heilbroner's *The Nature and
Logic of Capitalism,* a work undeniably by an economist but with an
aspect that transcended the discipline. Found in the same issue were
Lester Thurow's *The Zero-Sum Solution* and *The Fatal Equilibrium*
by the renowned Marshall Jevons (for those unacquainted with the
author, a pseudonym for William Breit and Kenneth Elzinga, who constitute the economists' version of Ellery Queen). Aside from those
titles, the reviews veered sharply away from economics per se, cover-
ing works on such subjects as John Delorean, the collapse of the Penn
Square Bank, and another Joseph Granville prophecy of doom, *The
Warning: The Coming Great Crash in the Stock Market.*

What can one deduce from this low turnout of serious books on economics in the review media? First, the pool from which reviewable
books is culled has an extremely shallow bottom. The number of these
books directly confronting economic ideas on issues in 1985 most
likely was less than 100; many of those dealt with policy questions and
were issued by nonselective publishers whose imprints command
slight respect among the reviewers.

A second deduction might be in the nature of an informed hunch:
Book review editors, mindful of circulation figures, have concluded
that economics titles do not figure prominently in the interest profiles
of their readership. Whether free-standing sections or merely a handful
of pages in the arts and leisure sections of major metropolitan newspapers, the book reviews are expected to pay their way and contribute
to overhead and profits as well. They are constantly under pressure
from the newspaper's publisher to justify their existence and must
compete for space with other features that customarily draw higher
advertising dollars. Inevitably, this means that a book review editor,
like a theater or music critic, must avoid subjects so arcane that the
very title of the book will cause readers to turn the page without paus-
ing to catch even the "lead" line of a review.

There is a third factor that may inhibit reviews of economics books.
It happens also to bedevil publishers seeking to influence impulse, or
even premeditated, book purchases with prepublication endorsements
("blurbs") on book jackets. Bluntly stated, only a handful of economists are known to the public at large. John Kenneth Galbraith and
Robert Heilbroner head the list; both are swamped with galleys and
review copies sent by publishers hoping for the phrase that may launch
a thousand shipments. Trailing behind are Lester Thurow, James

100   **Donald S. Lamm**

Tobin, Paul Samuelson, and, in the case of books with pronounced political or ideological coloration, Robert Lekachman and Milton Friedman (reading from left to right). Combing the roster of Nobel Prize winners in economic science produces few names with wide recognition value; (the same, of course, might be said about Nobelists in other fields). Quotes may also be solicited from prominent former chairmen of the Council of Economic Advisers – Walter Heller was the usual lead choice followed at some distance by Gardner Ackley and Herbert Stein – and also from the small band of economic journalists – Alfred Malabre, Herbert Rowen, Leonard Silk, and David Warsh among them – whose articles appear with some regularity in newspapers and magazines.

What the paucity of reviews suggests, above all, is a variant of those vicious circles, so often cited by development economists; the sparse offering of economics books addressed to the layman encourages reviewer neglect which, in turn, assures low visibility for the books that are published, and ultimately discourages economists from setting down their ideas at lengths beyond the journal article. All writing is hard work; writing books compounds a difficult task.

In lieu of conclusion: lessons from experience

It would be the height of arrogance to draw firm conclusions from the limited series of observations presented in this paper. I have chosen instead to cite a few lessons from experience, using the casual empiricism of the preceding pages to bolster my observations. There is some danger in claiming too much from these lessons, for the fascination of book publishing for its practitioners derives to a considerable extent from the futility of generalization. The wisdom of P. T. Barnum – "another sucker is born every minute" – has guided much enterprise in our society. It does not quite apply to book publishing. Just when a publisher is confident that he has ordered his choices into a set of surefire formulas, what appear to be constants turn into variables. The six lessons I advance may therefore have a shelf life of fewer than twenty-four hours.

Lesson #1. Economists are prone to burn their intellectual bridges behind them

In this respect, economists affirm their bonds with other social scientists. For just as psychologists pay mere lip service to the founders of their discipline – Wilhelm Wundt and William James – so economists as a group show little interest in the works of the worldly philosophers. Until a few years ago, there was but one edition of *The Wealth of Nations* easily available in the United States. With difficulty today one can obtain a copy of Ricardo's *Principles of Political Economy and Taxation,* and Mill's *Principles of Political Economy,* all one thousand pages of it, can be purchased in paperback at a price befitting a hardcover. The prospects are considerably better in the case of Malthus' *Essay on the Principle of Population* with an even half-dozen paperbound editions in print. If the experience of my firm with the Norton Critical Edition of Malthus is any indication, the users are to be found more often in intellectual history and environmental studies than in economics courses.

Only one nineteenth-century economist survives and prospers, to judge from the availability of inexpensive editions, library and bookstore holdings, and frequency of appearance on college course reading lists: Karl Marx. Yet, as in the case of Malthus, far greater demand for Marx's works exists outside than within economics departments. It is perhaps no accident that the two leading college anthologies of Marx's writings – Robert Tucker's *Marx-Engels Reader* and David McLellan's *Karl Marx: Selected Writings* – are both edited by political scientists.

Perhaps most startling is the sales history of a book that economists generally acknowledge as the leading twentieth-century masterwork in their discipline: Keynes's *General Theory of Employment, Interest and Money.* In the aggregate the figures do not look all that bad: 53,000, since publication in 1936, of the hardcover and 110,000 of the paperback, first issued in 1968. But when contrasted with other monuments of twentieth-century thought, the total of 163,000 seems rather pallid. Freud's *Civilization and Its Discontents,* a more accessible work, to be sure, has sold 950,000 cloth and paper editions since its publication here in 1960. Even Freud's rigorous *Introductory Lectures on Psychoanalysis,* in print in paper only since 1977, will overtake Keynes's *General Theory* at their present rates of sale early in the next decade. Closer to home, any successful *intermediate* macroeconomics textbook, published in the 1980s, should exceed the level of sales of *The General Theory* within six years of publication.

A discipline might well bog down if its practitioners buried themselves in its classic works. But the neglect of the great books in economics, manifested, too, in the scant enrollment in history of economic thought, leaves the ideas of the classical economist at the mercy of textbook writers and other interpreters. A stream is usually clearer at its source; so, too, tend to be the ideas that flow through a field of inquiry.

Lesson #2. Books written for the common reader often pander to econophobia

One could mount a parade of titles that demonstrate that economists and noneconomists (abetted perhaps by their publishers) write defensively about their subject. Consider these for starters: Paarlberg's *Great Myths of Economics,* Mishan's *21 Popular Fallacies in Economics,* Lekachman's *Economists at Bay: Why the Experts Will Never Solve Your Problems,* Schumacher's *Small Is Beautiful: Economics as if People Mattered,* and, for the ultimate put-down, Pool and Rose's *The Instant Economist.* Beyond the title, economists often feel it necessary to apologize for the language and methods of their field. Lester Thurow, in the Introduction to *Dangerous Currents,* no doubt meant to disarm his readers when he wrote:

I want to be as precise as I can without succumbing totally to the language of the trade. . . . If we are to expose what is unproved and in general try to demystify the language of economists, we must to some extent fight them on their own technical ground, where they seem to hold sway completely. Occupying the high technical ground with a boldness and confidence that to me is not justified, economists have been able to cow the public, press, policy makers and politicians in ways not usually open to academics and technical people. Paradoxically, this happens even while economists are not held in especially high repute.[1]

The effect of this passage, I'd maintain, is just opposite to what Thurow intended. My resistance runs high from the start.

Keynes took a different tack, one that provokes rather than deflates intellectual curiosity, in the Preface to *The General Theory:*

This book is chiefly addressed to my fellow economists. I hope it will be intelligible to others. . . . I cannot achieve my objective of persuading economists to re-examine critically certain of their basic assumptions except by a highly abstract argument and also by much controversy. At this stage of the debate, the general public, though welcome at the debate, are only eavesdroppers at an attempt by an economist to bring to an issue the deep divergences of opinion between fellow economists which have for the time being almost destroyed the

[1] Lester C. Thurow, *Dangerous Currents; The State of Economics* (New York: Random House, 1984), p. xvi.

practical influence of economic theory and will, until they are resolved, continue to do so.[2]

Lesson #3. In their preference for mathematical models over prose arguments by description and analogy, economists shortchange the humanistic side of their discipline

This is so obvious a point it bears no belaboring. The reward structure of the profession favors technical brilliance. Offers of chairs and other gilded appointments flock to the economist who builds a better model, although it often appears that celebrated economists are far more adept at abstracting from the real world than at returning to terra firma from the outer space of theory.

Lesson #4. Most economists leave the big issues to others, whether inside or outside the academy

In a sense this is a corollary to Lesson #3. One is hard pressed to find many books in economics that have changed our thinking on exigent matters of public policy, on life in contemporary society, or on human nature itself. Ironically, the economics bestsellers tend to get a bad press from the profession. Galbraith's *The Affluent Society* and especially his *New Industrial State* received withering crossfire from supposedly friendly lines whereas, on the opposite flank, Friedman's *Free to Choose* and to a lesser extent, *Capitalism and Freedom,* were treated as ideological tracts to be approached with extreme caution. Controversy, of course, is good for the body politic, and good for the sale of books. It is a shame that economists rarely air their disagreements with each other at book length.

One imprecise but useful index to the impact economics has within, one assumes, a highly intelligent academic community can be found in the recently published *Harvard Guide to Influential Books.* By my count, out of roughly 550 titles listed, a mere 19 are either by economists or, as with John Rawls' *Theory of Justice,* about matters that have a place on the economist's main agenda.

Lesson #5. Journal articles and monographs aside, the natural market for most ideas in economics – including old

[2]John Maynard Keynes, *The General Theory of Employment, Interest, and Money* (New York: Harcourt Brace, 1936).

*ideas that have not fared well in the test of time and new
ideas that haven't yet stood any test at all – is the textbook*

At the peak of their sales, both Paul Samuelson's *Economics* and
Campbell McConnell's *Economics* exceeded in a single year the life-
time sales to date of Keynes's *General Theory*. Every year, six or seven
introductory textbooks achieve sales of 60,000 copies or more. The
market, variously estimated at a million and a half to two million students per annum, is immense. It is also captive.

*Lesson #6. Publishers have done a poor job of inciting
economists to express their opinions at book length*

While much in this paper supports the generally held view that economists write either muddy or inaccessible prose, a strong argument
might be mounted that economists who have shown themselves mas-
ters of the essay – Robert Solow comes readily to mind – have not been
persuaded to go the extra mile to write a book. Often the germ of a
book may be lurking in an article that goes unremarked by publishers.
Or publishers, aware that economists are skilled at calculating opportunity costs, fear that the asking price for a book might be too high for
its likely yield.

A personal confession might be appropriate at this point. In 1969,
barely six months after he had left the chairmanship of the Council of
Economic Advisers, Arthur Okun was musing over the fact that *The
Economic Report of the President* in vintage years, such as 1962, contained trenchant statements that, despite the *Report's* large circulation,
had but casual impact on the man in the street. That provided me with
an opening, and I asked him whether he was ready to try his hand at
a book. Several topics such as the growth/no-growth debate were mentioned and dropped. One stuck: the idea of a book on what Okun
called "the big tradeoff," equality versus efficiency. Since Okun suf-
fered from the allergy common among many economists to writing a
book from scratch, it was proposed that he treat the subject in lecture
form. A string or two was pulled, and the next year, he was chosen to
deliver the Godkin lectures at Harvard. When it came to the question
of publishing the lectures, Joseph Pechman, the director of economic
studies at Brookings, put so high a price on the manuscript that I
flinched. It turned out, of course, that the book became the all-time
bestseller from Brookings. It would have received far wider notice in
the major review media (and greater sales) if a certain commercial
publisher had had the courage to pursue what he had initiated.

Perhaps it is the lesson of that experience that impels me now to urge budding editors to seek out economists with ideas and the literary grace to express them. The results are not guaranteed. Thomas Schelling's *Micromotives and Macrobehavior,* for example, may have just missed in a bid for general readership. But this is true for similar efforts by academics in other fields. Stephen Jay Gould, the Harvard paleontologist, did not achieve his present visibility with his first trade book (or more accurately, collection of essays), *Ever Since Darwin.* But his reputation and readership in the public at large grew from that work to a great size.

I may be too much of an optimist.

In the nineteenth century, a wag once contrasted the state-building efforts of two would-be great powers in the heart of Europe. For Germany, he concluded the situation was serious but not hopeless; for its neighbor Austria-Hungary, however, the situation was hopeless but not serious.

Like citizens of the Hapsburg Empire, economists speak in several languages, indulge in border squabbles, alternate between overpraising and belittling their achievements, and refuse to discard imperial ambitions. As long as economists insist on placing the highest value on exchanges with other economists, the common reader will remain an outsider, convinced that in contemporary economics the situation is hopeless but not serious.

PART III

From economist to policymaker

CHAPTER 10

Economic ideas and economists in government: accomplishments and frustrations

A. W. COATS

From time immemorial, as the saying goes, governments have had to tackle economic problems, and long before the emergence of a recognizable corpus of economic ideas or a recognized group of individuals claiming expertise in economic affairs, there was an ample supply of economic advice, however unwelcome. The suppliers were a motley company, including: royal favorites and sycophants; consultant administrators (Schumpeter's apt term)[1]; various species of "practical" men – especially merchants, financiers, and businessmen, who were often spokesmen for some vested interest; and a miscellaneous category of journalists, purveyors of popular nostrums, and ardent amateurs. In this century – most notably since the early 1930s and, more especially, during and since World War II – both the supply and the demand for economic information and advice have expanded enormously at all levels – local, regional, national, and international – and there has been a concomitant transformation of economics as an intellectual discipline and a policy profession.

In line with the other contributions to the volume, this chapter is mainly concerned with present and immediate-past United States experiences. Yet here, as elsewhere, the current situation and prospects can best be understood from a longer and broader historical and comparative perspective. Despite the professional economists' perennial preoccupation with economic policy, and the substantial and growing literature on the role of economic ideas and techniques and economists in government, little systematic research has been undertaken.[2] Con-

[1]Joseph A. Schumpeter, *History of Economic Analysis* (New York: Oxford University Press, 1954), Part II, Chapter 3.
[2]See the discussion of these matters in A. W. Coats, ed., *Economists in Government: An International Comparative Study* (Durham, NC: Duke University Press, 1981), and the sources cited therein. This volume covers ten countries in the post–1945 period: Great Britain, Australia, India, Norway, the United States, Israel, Hungary, Japan, Italy, and Brazil. It also appeared as a complete issue of *History of Political Economy,* 13 (Fall 1981).

sequently, the available knowledge is patchy and unsystematic, and only indirectly relevant to the spread of ideas.

Much economic writing has focused on policy recommendations and goals; much less on the economists' contributions as experts or specialists to the formulation, making, and implementation of policies. Where addressed at all, such topics have too often been treated either in personal or anecdotal terms, or on a high level of generality, with insufficient consideration of the practical difficulties encountered in organizational and policymaking contexts. Disproportionate attention has been paid to the discussion of disembodied ideas or doctrinal systems – such as neoclassical economics, Keynesianism, or monetarism – and far too little to the detailed practical utilization of economic ideas and techniques in specific times and places.[3] Where detailed studies of particular policy issues and episodes have been undertaken, usually by economic historians, the role of economic ideas and the professional economists' contributions have generally been slighted or ignored. Thus there is a wide-open field for constructive research.

The title of this paper deliberately distinguishes between economic ideas and economists. It is not just that some economists may have no ideas at all, or at least no ideas unfamiliar to persons untrained in the discipline, for there is no hard and fast line between professional economists and intelligent laymen, some of whom (for instance, civil servants) have acquired considerable expertise on the job. Nor is it appropriate here to evaluate the effects, whether transitory or lasting, of training in economics on its victims.[4] (Some critics and humorists have indeed argued that such training is actively harmful and debilitating, but this claim has not been seriously investigated.) Of much greater significance is the fact that many economic ideas supplied to governments emanate from noneconomists, and that many, perhaps most, of the economics graduates employed in official bureaucracies are not idea-merchants in any sense of that term. Much of their contribution is noneconomic, and much of the official economic work is routine data collection, presentation, and analysis calling for only a limited use of economic ideas or expertise. Moreover, as economics has become more quantitative, and as efforts have been made to satisfy governments' virtually insatiable appetite for economic and social statistics, a variety of other quantitative academic disciplines have been increasingly called upon for this purpose, such as statistics, mathe-

[3] Ibid., for examples.
[4] For an important recent study of that training, see David C. Colander and Arjo Klamer, "The Making of an Economist," *Journal of Economic Perspectives,* 1 (Fall 1987), pp. 95–111.

matics, operations research, accounting, and so forth. It is the economist's combination of quantitative skills, mathematical techniques, and basic economic concepts (at least some of them inescapably qualitative) that constitutes his or her distinctive contribution to government. Excessive concentration on the quantitative aspects of the subject undermines the economist's professional product differential. However, as economics is a vocationally nonspecific discipline it is no easy task to identify those functions and roles that economists are uniquely equipped to perform.

Comparatively little of the research on the role of economists in government has been concerned with the routine tasks already mentioned. Understandably enough, far more attention has been directed at the more glamorous activities of top level economic advisors, such as the President's Council of Economic Advisers,[5] heads of government departments, or senior officials in international agencies.[6] Yet between these exalted characters and the routine toilers are several layers of intermediaries who also deserve some consideration, for they include many essential receivers and purveyors of economic ideas and utilizers of economic skills. Policy is not simply formulated at the "top of the office" or at Cabinet level. Much originates way down within the bureaucratic system and is modified, refined, and reshaped repeatedly as it moves up to the highest decision-making levels. Also, once adopted, policy has to be implemented, often by interpreting and adapting it to fit changing particular situations, some of which were unforeseen by the original framers and key policymakers. Economic ideas, both professionally acceptable ones and popular nostrums anathema to the professionals, are operative at all levels and stages of the administrative and executive process,[7] many of which are unrecognized or unknown to academic economists lacking wide experience.

Restrictions of space preclude more than a brief sketch of the

[5]Even in this case, attention has usually been focused exclusively on the chairman's role. See, for example, Edward S. Flash, Jr., *Economic Advice and Presidential Leadership: The Council of Economic Advisers* (New York: Columbia University Press, 1956); and Erwin C. Hargrove and Samuel A. Morley, *The President and the Council of Economic Advisers* (London: Westview, 1984). A useful bibliography is provided in William J. Barber, "The United States: Economists in a Pluralistic Polity," in Coats (1981), pp. 207–9; also see Robert H. Nelson, "The Economics Profession and the Making of Public Policy," *Journal of Economic Literature,* 25 (March 1987), pp. 49–91.

[6]*Cf.* the essays in A. W. Coats, ed., *Economists in International Agencies: An Exploratory Study* (New York: Praeger, 1986).

[7]David Henderson, a British economist with considerable government experience, has launched a sustained attack on this "do-it-yourself economics" in *The BBC Reith Lectures: Innocence and Design: The Influence of Economic Ideas on Policy* (Oxford: Blackwell, 1986).

remarkably diverse conditions under which economic ideas are brought to bear on governmental affairs, whether they originate within or outside the bureaucratic or policymaking context. Fortunately, despite the severe limitations of our knowledge, some useful provisional generalizations can be offered.

To begin with, it is clear that economists (however that category is defined) have seldom been unwilling to offer advice or make policy recommendations. Thus despite the classical and neoclassical writers' predominantly anti-interventionist bias, they were, generally speaking, neither passive observers nor nonparticipants in government business. Adam Smith, for instance, defined political economy as "a branch of the science of a statesman or legislator,"[8] and despite his attachment to free trade he spent a late period of his life as Commissioner of the Customs in Scotland, and performed his duties assiduously. Smith's approach was compatible with that of his European contemporaries, for whom political economy was but one of the sciences of the state *(staatswissenschaften)*. Contrary to the laissez-faire mythology, a long line of nineteenth- and early twentieth-century British economists participated actively in policy debates and served their government either as ministers, consultants, or public officials.[9] This was long before the post–1930 growth of government employment for economists, a movement that became explosive during World War II and the subsequent era of Keynesian hegemony. And, as has been recently observed, the subsequent reaction against interventionism has not been followed by a significant decline in the demand for economists (although perhaps the time lag is long). On the contrary, economists have been influential in defining and implementing deregulation policies in the United States.[10]

Nor are Britain and America peculiar in their use of economists. All over the world since 1945, in regimes of every conceivable political complexion and at every level of economic development, professional economists have been found useful – nay, indispensable – to those with the power to generate an effective demand for their services. They

---

[8]Adam Smith, *An Inquiry into the Nature and Causes of the Wealth of Nations*, R. H. Campbell and A. S. Skinner, eds. (Oxford: Clarendon Press, 1976), Introduction to Book IV. See also Donald Winch, "Science and the Legislator: Adam Smith and After," *Economic Journal*, 93 (September 1983), pp. 510–20; and Gary M. Anderson, William F. Shughart II, and Robert Tollison, "Adam Smith in the Customhouse," *Journal of Political Economy*, 93 (August 1985), pp. 740–59.

[9]The list includes John Ramsay McCulloch, Nassau Senior, James and John Stuart Mill, Henry Fawcett, William Stanley Jevons, Leonard Courtney, Herbert Somerton Foxwell, Alfred Marshall, William James Ashley, William Albert Samuel Hewins, Sydney John Chapman, and Ralph Hawtrey.

[10]Nelson, *op. cit.*

have become an identifiable and influential subgroup within the political culture – whether as heads of state, cabinet ministers, members of legislatures, civil servants, journalists, or scholarly activists.

Needless to say, the numbers, functions, and effectiveness of economists in government have varied considerably over time and place according to the local political climate, the nature and range of the administration's economic and social objectives and responsibilities, and the character and efficiency of the bureaucratic machine.[11] Nevertheless, these variations are not infinite, for there have been discernible international tendencies toward homogeneity resulting from the growth of international economic cooperation and interdependence fostered by deliberate policy actions and facilitated by the emergence of an influential network of international agencies concerned with economic affairs. The consequences for the economics profession have been striking, as a result of the global demand for economic expertise and the remarkable development of improved communication of all kinds.

The principal elements in this process are widely recognized, but their combined impact has not been fully grasped. They include: the widespread dissemination of relatively standardized textbooks; the growth and homogenizing tendencies in advanced graduate training; the worldwide readership of the leading professional journals; the increasing mathematization and quantification of the discipline, which has helped to overcome language barriers; and the vastly expanded global mobility of students (many of whom have training abroad), professors, and an army of nonacademic professionals and experts. In this context the role of the leading international economic agencies has been both directly significant and of symbolic importance. Especially through transnational organizations there is now an international network of officials sharing a common body of economic knowledge and/ or a broadly similar outlook toward the solution of current and prospective economic problems. Economists have become significant actors in the network of intergovernmental contacts, exchanges of information, plans, and negotiations that have helped to shape world trade, monetary affairs, investment, and economic development during the past four decades.

Of course there are many impediments to the spread of economic ideas, such as ignorance, prejudice, and vested interest, and both transmitters and receivers operate in a highly selective fashion. On the most general level, the prevailing social and cultural attitudes toward intellectuals, professionals, and technocrats in any society necessarily influ-

[11]*Cf.* Coats, 1981, for comparative studies.

ence the readiness to listen to and act upon advice from so-called experts, and though a deficiency in the local supply of suitable, appropriately trained personnel can be overcome by importing foreign economic advisers, this solution carries with it certain unavoidable difficulties.[12] Cynics contend that the variety of opinions on policy issues within the economics profession is such that a policymaker can always find some economist who will endorse any proposal he favors, and this explains why some heads of state surround themselves with a mixed bag of economists. The individual and professional implications of playing this game are obvious, but on the other hand an adviser who insists on advocating ideas and policies that directly conflict with the government's declared aims and doctrines is certain to be ineffective and likely to be dismissed. Within the constraints of his job the adviser should set out the various policy objections fully and honestly and offer his recommendations.[13] If his advice is rejected he should accept defeat, lick his wounds, and live to fight another day. But if he repeatedly accepts defeat passively in the hope of future victories, he will run the risk of reducing his effectiveness to the point where he becomes not merely neutral but neuter.

The adviser has responsibilities to his profession and the general public, as well as to his employer, and this can be a source of conflict. His position may require him to explain the government's actions and aims to the public, and in so doing he will find it difficult to draw the line between partisan advocacy and merely instructing or informing his audience. At times he can preserve his integrity only by remaining silent when he strongly disapproves of official policies, and if his silence proves embarrassing or unacceptable to his employers, he should resign. But whether, and if so, when, to resign, and whether to do so silently or loudly in a blaze of publicity, are matters for his professional conscience. Resignation, however conducted, is a once-and-for-all decision, a confession of failure, and a gesture unlikely to have any impact on policy. And his successor may be much more compliant and lacking in professional integrity and qualifications.

Resistance to economic advice, especially if couched in theoretical

---

[12]Dudley Seers, "Why Visiting Economists Fail," *Journal of Political Economy*, 70 (Aug. 1962), pp. 325-8; George C. Abbott, "Why Visiting Economists Fail: An Alternative Interpretation," *Public Administration* (Australia), 54 (Spring 1976), pp. 31-43; George Rosen, *Western Economists and Eastern Societies: Agents of Change in South Asia, 1950-1970* (Baltimore: Johns Hopkins University Press, 1985).

[13]The remainder of this and the following paragraph is based on the useful discussion in Walter W. Heller, *New Dimensions of Political Economy* (Cambridge, MA: Harvard University Press, 1966), Chapter 1, and my unpublished "Report of Discussions" at the Royaumont Conference on the Role of the Economist in Government, April 1974, sponsored by the Ford Foundation.

terms, may exist for a number of reasons, including the recipient's inability to understand or unwillingness to respond appropriately. On this matter the reminiscences of successive chairmen of the President's Council of Economic Advisers (CEA) are revealing. Before Reagan, the post–1945 Presidents most eager and willing to listen to economic analysis and be guided by expert opinion were Kennedy and Ford.[14] Johnson evidently responded positively only when clear political issues were at stake, whereas Nixon, who certainly possessed the requisite intellectual capacity, was bored by economic discussion. President Reagan seems to have been unusually uninterested in, and incapable of dealing with, economic problems, to judge by David Stockman's highly colored account of his traumatic experiences as Budget Director,[15] and matters may have been even worse in the 1920s, under Warren Harding.[16]

Herbert Stein, CEA Chairman under Nixon, has emphasized the importance of the President's views and capacity in economic affairs, remarking that he should be seen as

the dominant decision maker in economic policy, as the judge of economics and economists, and as the major figure attempting to set the psychological tone of the economy. In those senses he is the nation's chief economist.[17]

Of course, impediments to economic ideas do not arise only at the peak of the governmental structure. Gardner Ackley, another CEA Chairman, commenting on "the intellect and desire to learn of the

---

[14]Hargrove and Morley, *op. cit.*

[15]*The Triumph of Politics: The Inside Story of the Reagan Revolution* (New York: Avon, 1987), especially pp. 50, 54, 99, 310, 315, 373.

[16]After listening to his advisers arguing over a tax issue, Harding is reported as protesting: ". . . I can't make a damn thing out of this tax problem. I listen to one side and they seem right, and then – God – I talk to the other side and they seem just as right, and here I am where I started. I know somewhere there is a book that will give me the truth, but, hell, I couldn't read the book. I know somewhere there is an economist who knows the truth, but I don't know where to find him, and haven't the sense to know him and trust him when I find him. God! What a job." Cited by Harold Orlands, "Academic Social Scientists and the Presidency: From Wilson to Nixon," *Minerva* 3 (Summer-Autumn 1986), p. 174.
The most effective channels of communication may be indirect. On one occasion a senior British economist, after an exhaustive unsuccessful attempt to persuade an obstinate Chancellor of the Exchequer, considered that his time might have been better spent writing an anonymous article for *The Economist,* a periodical carefully read by the Chancellor's staff.

[17]Herbert Stein, "The Chief Executive as Chief Economist," in W. Fellner, ed., *Essays in Contemporary Economic Problems: Demand, Productivity and Population* (Washington, D.C.: American Enterprise Institute, 1981), p. 57. See also his *Presidential Economics: The Making of Economic Policy from Roosevelt to Reagan and Beyond* (New York: Simon and Schuster, 1984). For a valuable treatment of the problems of dealing with ministers, see Patrick Weller and Michele Grattan, *Can Ministers Cope? Australian Federal Ministers at Work* (Richmond, Victoria, Australia: Hutchinson, 1981).

intended recipient" of economic advice, added, wryly, that unfortunately "public officials are mostly just our students grown older; many of them still can't and won't learn."[18]

Quite apart from the serious indictment of the educational process in a society where large numbers of students take at least one college or university course in economics, this remark raises questions about the economist's status and credibility as an expert. In a prestigious bureaucracy staffed by intelligent amateurs or educated laymen, such as the British civil service, self-assured officials may regard economics as little more than common sense disguised in repulsive jargon, and may accordingly be unwilling to listen because they think they already know it all. This seems to have been a fairly common attitude in Whitehall during and for some years after World War II. As Lord Robbins, Director of the influential Economic Section of the War Cabinet Offices, recalled in his *Autobiography,* the economists' success depended on their readiness "to become part of the machine and accept its logic rather than pretend to some special status."[19] Had they sought to emphasize the authority of their expertise they would simply have undermined their effectiveness by reinforcing existing official prejudices.

A fundamental issue that cannot be explored here is the widespread skepticism toward economists in general and academic economists in particular, not least among experienced public officials who themselves acquired graduate qualifications in economics in their youth.

According to a leading sociologist of science, research scientists (including economists) are engaged in novelty production, and an individual producer's status in the "reputational system" is directly dependent on the extent to which his innovative contributions are utilized by other scientists.[20] By contrast, as a leading international agency economist has noted,[21] in large-scale organizations independent originality, intellectual brilliance, and research productivity are less valuable than teamwork, ability to be decisive when action is required, communication skills (especially in jargon-free language that can be understood by senior policymakers), and skill in obtaining, assessing,

[18]Gardner Ackley, "Providing Economic Advice to Government," in Joseph A. Pechman and N. J. Simler, eds., *Economics in the Public Service: Papers in Honour of Walter W. Heller* (New York: Norton, 1982), p. 202.

[19]Lionel (Lord) Robbins, *The Autobiography of an Economist* (London: Macmillan, 1971), p. 186. For a more extended treatment of the British experience, see A. W. Coats, "Britain: The Rise of the Specialists," in Coats (1981), *op. cit.,* pp. 27–66.

[20]Richard Whitley, *The Social and Intellectual Organization of the Sciences* (Oxford: Oxford University Press, 1984).

[21]George Baldwin, in "Report of Discussion," Coats (1986), *op. cit.,* pp. 116–17. Similar views could be cited from economists in national governments.

and applying empirical data. Thus a World Bank economist's career, for example,

> is almost totally affected by his or her technical competence, how well he or she writes, how articulate he or she is in meetings, how well he or she is able to function in small multidisciplinary groups (missions), and how well he or she gets on with officials in developing countries. Bureaucratic skills are far more important than in academic life,[22]

and this includes the capacity to make effective use of economic ideas. In the OECD, for example, the role of persuasion is vital because the organization has virtually no decision-making functions.

> At a rough guess, from the middle grades up, an economist working in an international organization spends only half the time using professional skills to decide upon the right answer to a problem; the other half will be devoted to trying to find the best way to persuade people that it is the right answer. And as the individual rises in the hierarchy the art of persuasion becomes steadily more important.
> Economists' training does not necessarily fit them very well for this selling job. Good academic writing, based on logical reasoning, with assumptions and qualifications carefully laid out, and examples and corroboration relegated to numerous footnotes, is too long and pedantic for the busy policy-maker. Econometrics is much worse. Historical or country examples are likely to be much more telling. Numbers should be used sparingly, tables should be kept small, charts should tell a story. Intellectual qualms and professional conscience must, at least on occasions, be overruled so as to permit oversimplification in order to advance what is hopefully a good cause. Anyone who is not prepared to spend a good deal of their working life drafting, redrafting, and re-redrafting – and then trying to sell the product to national officials – should not make a career in an international organization.[23]

The lessons of economists' experiences in national governments are broadly similar. Though professional skill (that is, knowledge of and ability to use economic ideas and techniques) is a necessary condition for success in an official bureaucracy, whether at the top or some way down within the hierarchical structure, it is by no means a sufficient condition. The list of desirable qualities required by an ideal government economist is indeed daunting. It includes

> tact; patience; adaptability; the capacity to work quickly under pressure; the ability to communicate with non-specialists in a variety of circumstances and at different levels of audience comprehension; skill in the arts of persuasion; a sense of timing; grasp of bureaucratic procedures and conventions – i.e., the capacity to 'play the machine'; appreciation of the problems of administrative

---

[22]George Baldwin, "Economics and Economists at the World Bank," in ibid., p. 89.
[23]Stephen Marris, "The Role of Economists in the OECD," in ibid., p. 103.

feasibility and political practicality; recognition of the limits of one's profes-sional expertise; and sheer stamina.[24]

Obviously such a combination of virtues is rarely found in any single individual, and this helps to explain why exceptional ability in this work is so unusual. How far the typical professional economist's training prepares him or her for work in the public service is a highly pertinent question, for the better the preparation the more likely it is that professional economic ideas will exert a healthy impact on official policymaking and its implementation.

The nature and effectiveness of current academic training in economics is obviously too large and controversial a topic to be examined here. Suffice it to say that the present situation in this "age of technique" gives serious cause for concern. If so little weight is attached to interest in and ability at empirical research, a broad knowledge of economic literature, and a thorough knowledge of the contemporary economy, as has recently been suggested,[25] then new entrants to the profession may not merely be ill-equipped, they may even be crippled. Much of the literature on the work of economists in government stresses that it involves more art than science, judgment in such matters as a "feel" for the real world, knowledge of what governments can or cannot do, sensitivity to the problems of drafting and administering legislation, and, for the individual performer,

judgment on how close to get to the political process, on when political costs outweigh economic ones, and on when the battle is lost so that one should keep quiet even if one believes one knows better than the politicians what can be done to achieve objectives.[26]

Economists often tell jokes involving an element of self-aggrandizement, emphasizing the damage they can do. In practice, however, their most valuable contribution more often involves "damage minimization,"[27] by modifying, refining, or even blocking the ill-considered policy proposals made by laymen – for example, by emphasizing the opportunity costs of a given action or, more broadly, the system-wide implications of a specific policy. In the use of economics, in the spread of economic ideas in the world of affairs, we should heed the words of a famous living therapist: "First let us do no harm"; and, with a rider: let us also endeavor to encourage others to do likewise.

[24]These desiderata are culled from the literature cited in Coats, 1981.
[25]Cf. Colander and Klamer, op. cit.
[26]J. W. Neville, ed., Economics, Economists and Policy Formulation, CAER Paper No. 13 (Australia: Centre for Applied Economic Research, September 1981), p. 9.
[27]This term was coined by Alan T. Peacock.

CHAPTER 11

The spread of economic ideas between academia and government: a two-way street

WILLIAM J. BARBER

Discussions of the flow of ideas between academic economists and government officials have tended to focus on the academic's role in shaping public policy. It is quite understandable that this should be the case. Academics have discretionary time to write papers on the topic. And it is probably reasonable to assume that their thought processes are conditioned in some measure by Keynes's oft-quoted comments about the power of ideas as a force for good or evil. In his account, the academic scribblers hold the upper hand, while the practical men are depicted as being enslaved by some "defunct economist." This characterization, to be sure, is flattering to those who operate primarily from the ivory tower. Small wonder that academics should find it appealing!

But does this characterization do justice to the reality? The process through which new ideas are generated and ultimately translated into policies and programs that shape the flow of history may be too complex to be reduced to a simple and unidirectional schema. And perhaps as well there is an element of exaggeration in the claims made for the primacy of the academic scribblers. Certainly one can think of an abundance of cases in which fundamental changes in economic policy have taken on a life of their own quite independent of inspiration from mainstream professional journals. The Tax Reform Act of 1986, as Joseph Minarik effectively demonstrates in this book, is one such instance: the forces coalescing to produce this result had a political momentum that generated an outcome different from the one the theorists working on optimal policies in public finance would have prescribed.[1]

One suspects as well that the historian of the next generation who attempts to explain the redirection of American economic policy in

---

[1] See the essay in this volume by Joseph J. Minarik, "How Tax Reform Came About."

1981 will discern that arguments derived from political opportunism will carry the weightiest explanatory power. Nor is this phenomenon unique to the 1980s. The historical record is filled with policy initiatives which have been distinctly out-of-step with received expert opinion at the time. When this has occurred, a handful of academically based mavericks can usually be found who are prepared to be public advocates of positions that political leaders are prepared to embrace. At the same time, the mainstream professionals have typically distanced themselves from the more heterodox within their ranks. Cornell's George Warren, for example, presumably enjoyed his moment of notoriety in 1933 when his panacea for depression – that is, an increase in the price of gold – won official favor with Franklin D. Roosevelt. Most of his academic colleagues, however, reacted to his position in much the same way that a later generation responded to Professor Arthur Laffer's formulation of "supply-side" economics.

Even though the academic establishment does not always get the hearing in official circles that it believes it deserves, the opportunities open to economists to spread their ideas within government have certainly increased over the past half century. One of the arresting features of the recent history of the United States government is the expansion in the size of the "Washington Economics Industry." There may be quibbles about the precise magnitudes involved, but two facts are beyond dispute: (1) that the growth in numbers of economists in Federal employ has expanded at a faster rate than the overall expansion in Federal employment of professionals; and (2) that economists have been increasingly spread over an ever-widening range of agencies, bureaus, and Congressional staffs.[2] These outcomes may, in part, be attributed to the way the language of economics has been absorbed into official discourse. Any branch of the bureaucracy is likely to be disadvantaged in its appeals for favorable treatment of its budget

---

[2] Attempts to pinpoint the number of economists on the payroll of the federal government are frustrated by ambiguities in the official assignment of the title "economist." Many of the Federal employees so described are heavily engaged in statistical and administrative – as opposed to analytic – work, whereas the economists who serve as senior policy strategists with Presidential appointments are omitted from the classifications. Over the period 1958 through 1978, the number of government employees classified as "economists" by the Civil Service Commission and its successor (the Office of Personnel Management) expanded by 91 percent, whereas aggregate Federal employment of white-collar professionals grew at a significantly slower rate – 45 percent. Unfortunately, the Reagan administration has not sustained the practice of timely publication of the series entitled *Occupations of Federal White-Collar Workers* from which the data cited above are derived. The National Science Foundation, however, has reported that the number of economists in the Federal government grew by about 60 per cent from 1980 to 1983 (as cited by Herbert Stein, "The Washington Economics Industry," *The American Economic Review,* 76 (May 1986), p. 6).

requests and in its lobbying for pet programs without the aid of those who can write and speak economics. As Herbert Stein has noted, "It was almost as if someone had suddenly decreed that the language of the government would be Latin. There would be a great demand for people who could speak Latin."[3]

Does this infiltration imply that a pipeline is now in place to speed the flow of new thinking from the academy to the policy practitioners? The evidence to date bearing on this issue is inconclusive. It would appear that some who make a career in the bureaucracy may, in fact, be rather insulated from new intellectual influences. In the first place, the time pressures involved in analyzing day-to-day problems leave few hours to spare for building new intellectual capital. This is a recurring theme in the testimony gathered, for example, by William Allen in his sample of some sixty interviewees who recounted their experience in government.[4] Second, the content of the journals themselves – from the perspective of those engaged in the conduct of ordinary bureaucratic business – may seem to be of little direct value for practical purposes. In the judgment of one practicing economist-bureaucrat:

Most of the journal articles and much of the other formal products of the profession's research today are too refined and complex to be absorbed when policy is being formed. Indeed, the worlds of applied policy economics and of academic economics have been diverging for some time. Fifty years ago most of the articles published in journals such as the *American Economic Review* could pass for government studies, and vice versa. However, the journal articles of today bear little resemblance to the typical work product of the government economist.[5]

To be sure, earlier academic training in the discipline's style of thinking continues to be relevant: indeed, many regard that contribution from the academy to be adequate for on-the-job requirements. Even so, the enlarged presence of economists in the regular official establishment provides no guarantee that the transmission belt for new ideas will be well-lubricated.

Idea brokerage between the ivory tower and the corridors of power – at least potentially – can be more significant when academic economists migrate to Washington for shorter terms of duty in senior

[3]Herbert Stein, "The Washington Economics Industry," *The American Economic Review*, 76 (May 1986), p. 5.
[4]William R. Allen, "Economics, Economists, and Economic Policy: Modern American Experience," *History of Political Economy*, 9 (Spring 1977), pp. 48–88.
[5]Robert H. Nelson, "The Economics Profession and the Making of Public Policy," *Journal of Economic Literature*, 25 (March 1987), p. 85.

official positions. The Council of Economic Advisers, of course, is a primary institutional mechanism for this type of contact. Since its creation in 1946, the bulk of its members have been recruited from universities and research institutes to which most of them have later returned. From the four decades of experience with this institution, it is clear that it takes a special chemistry between the idea-producing economists and the idea-consuming politicians to generate significant reorientations in economic policy. Alfred North Whitehead may have overstated the issue in his remark to the effect that no birth is so painful as the birth of a new idea. But it is surely true that a lot of pangs are typically associated with the acceptance of a new idea when, in the nature of the case, it requires rejection of an established way of thinking. To the economic adviser, the challenge is particularly formidable. Few of the policy initiatives that promise to have significant social impact can be backed with hard evidence. They are more likely to take the form of counterfactuals – statements of what can be expected to happen under a regime which is not yet observable. To persuade political leadership to buy propositions that are as yet untested calls for skills in salesmanship that not all economic advisers possess, however impressive their analytic credentials may be.

Perhaps the most noteworthy example of successful policy-advocacy on the part of academic economists transplanted to the Council of Economic Advisers occurred during the Kennedy Administration. The Heller Council brought with it a solid conviction in the correctness of its model for fiscal stimulation led by a demand-side tax cut. It first sold its perspective to a President who was initially reluctant to accept it. (Among other things, Kennedy was uncertain how to reconcile his resounding call for "sacrifice" in his Inaugural Address with nonaustere proposals to spur spending; this hurdle was negotiated with language asserting that the unemployed were the last on whom burdens should be imposed.) It then sold its case to a Congress in which the old ideas about the sanctity of budget-balancing were alive and well. (A new vocabulary contributed to this achievement: the CEA avoided attacking balanced budgets head-on by asserting its support for a balanced budget when properly specified – i.e., at full employment.) But the analytic force of an idea was certainly not sufficient to carry the day. The political skills of its sponsors made an important contribution to the outcome.[6] On certain issues, however, even the most

[6]For a more extended treatment of the political tactics of the Heller Council, see William J. Barber, "The Kennedy Years: Purposeful Pedagogy," in *Exhortation and Controls: The Search for a Wage-Price Policy, 1945–1971,* ed. Craufurd D. Goodwin (Washington: The Brookings Institution, 1975).

accomplished idea-promoter can expect to be frustrated by sales resistance at the top. One suspects that an advocate of floating exchange rates would have made no headway during the Johnson administration. Similarly, the mere mention of CEA Chairman Martin Feldstein's analysis of high-employment structural deficits seemed to trigger bouts of amnesia at the Reagan White House in 1984.

The potential for impact of academically generated ideas is perhaps particularly promising when an academic economist is appointed to head one of the operating agencies of government. Surely the story of airline deregulation would have been different had Alfred Kahn not been selected by the Carter Administration to lead the Civil Aeronautics Board. He too brought a model with him based on his academic research on the theory and practice of regulation – and he brought the missionary zeal to see his ideas put to work.[7] Moves toward deregulation in the trucking and railroad industries also owe much to the positioning of two professional economists as members of the Interstate Commerce Commission.

Posts that carry operational responsibilities obviously enhance the "clout" that economists can deploy to spread their ideas. But, to borrow from the terminology of development economics, spread effects usually have "backwash effects" as well – that is, new products or processes may threaten the space of established producers. Attention to one or two recent success stories should not obscure the constraints on the effective spread of ideas that can be introduced by those likely to be caught up in the backwash. Bureaucrats like to protect their own turf, and new ideas – whatever their recommendations in principle – are not likely to receive a warm welcome if their adoption involves redefinitions of bureaucratic status and function. On its intellectual merits, the negative income tax as an alternative to an administered welfare system may have considerable persuasive power. But those who have attempted to translate variations on that theme into policy have been forcefully reminded of the capacity of the "welfare bureaucracy" – which perceives a threat to its jobs – to frustrate such reform. By the same token, one might bet with some confidence that the Federal Reserve System will never commit itself to thoroughgoing Friedmanite monetarism. If growth in the money supply were, in fact, to be governed by a fixed rule, most central bankers would be victims of

---

[7]Alfred Kahn's achievements as a bureaucratic in-fighter have been admiringly treated in Thomas K. McCraw, *Prophets of Regulation: Charles Francis Adams, Louis D. Brandeis, James M. Landis and Alfred E. Kahn* (Cambridge: Harvard University Press, 1984), and in Martha Derthick and Paul J. Quirk, *The Politics of Deregulation* (Washington: The Brookings Institution, 1985).

technological unemployment. Placement of economists at or near the centers of policymaking thus provides no assurance that new economic ideas will be effectively spread.

Has a spread effect operated in the reverse direction – that is, has experience in government altered the thinking of economists who have later returned to academic life? After the First World War – when academic economists were first engaged on a significant scale in the operations of government – the view was widely entertained that this experience would revitalize, if not revolutionize, the development of the discipline within the halls of academe. Irving Fisher, for example, in his presidential address to the American Economic Association in December 1918, regarded the wartime collaboration between economists and public officials as a potential turning point. Those who had had hands-on contact with the pulse of events would not thereafter be content to organize their teaching and research around abstract formalisms. A new era was potentially at hand in which economists would be refreshed by a new perspective on the relevant problems and on the ways to approach their solution.[8]

By one reckoning, the feedback from government to the mainstream of academic discussion might appear to have declined over time. Herbert Stein, for example, has calculated that economists in government account for only about 3 or 4 percent of the articles appearing in major journals, despite the fact that their numbers are about two-thirds as large as those of their academic colleagues, and that the percentage of the contributions of officials to the professional literature is now lower than it was at the turn of the century.[9] This outcome, of course, might be interpreted as reinforcing the view that the character of the journal literature (with its increased mathematical sophistication) has indeed widened the gap between what the editors of scholarly journals are interested in and what interests the practitioners within government. But this can only be a part of the story.

Though economists in government are not paid to contribute to the enlargement of theory, they do have prior access to information which can be the grist for theoretical puzzles. Given the preemptive claims on their time for the discharge of official duties, it may often be the case that they have little energy available to pursue independent lines of inquiry. But it has not always been so. One can think of instances in the past in which inventive analytic formulations were generated by

[8]Irving Fisher, "Economists in Public Service," *The American Economic Review*, 9 (March 1919), pp. 5–21.
[9]Stein, *loc. cit.*, p. 6.

official economists. Cases in point would be Mordecai Ezekiel's "cobweb theorem" (a by-product of his observations of data available to him in the Department of Agriculture) or the "balanced budget multiplier" concept produced by William A. Salant in the form of a memorandum while employed on Lauchlin Currie's White House staff in 1942.[10] Nor can there be any doubt about the fertility of the interaction between economist-bureaucrats and Alvin Hansen's Fiscal Policy Seminar at Harvard in generating an Americanized understanding of Keynesian aggregate demand management in the late 1930s. The conception of the "net contribution of government to spending" in the attempt to account for the recession of 1937–8 was novel at the time and it is unlikely that this contribution to the assimilation of the Keynesian message could have been put in place without the stimulus supplied by economists working in government.[11]

These examples demonstrate that economic ideas can certainly be spread in more than one direction and that insights developed within the bureaucratic establishment can be ahead of the textbooks. The most prominent instances of this phenomenon, however, appear to have occurred in the 1930s and 1940s. That period may have been exceptionally congenial for such developments. In those years, many of the analytic talents that might otherwise have been directed into academic careers were attracted to government service – partly because the latter then provided the bulk of the new professional opportunities. In an instance or two – the ill-starred career of Lauchlin Currie at Harvard is a case in point – contributors to analytic invention took refuge in Washington when the academy denied them tenured status.

But perhaps the more significant test of the feedback of governmental service on the development of the discipline is not the contributions that economists make to the journals while in official employ, but the imprint of governmental experience on the professional work of former employees who return to the universities and research institutes. No measurement of this aspect of the spread of ideas is readily available. The questions posed in Allen's interviews, for example, were couched in the form of "How did you contribute to governmental

[10]Mordecai Ezekiel, "The Cobweb Theorem," *Quarterly Journal of Economics,* 52 (February 1938), pp. 255–80, and Walter S. Salant, "Introduction to William A. Salant's 'Taxes, the Multiplier and the Inflationary Gap,'" *History of Political Economy,* 7 (Spring 1975), pp. 3–18.

[11]For an elaboration of this point, see William J. Barber, "The Career of Alvin H. Hansen, in the 1920s and 1930s: A Study in Intellectual Transformation," *History of Political Economy,* 19 (Summer 1987), pp. 191–205.

thinking?", not as "How has government service contributed to your own thinking?" This issue might well merit the attention of the next round of interviewers.

Even in the absence of systematic direct testimony from the principals, there would appear to be adequate grounds for the view that the thought processes of at least some academic veterans of bureaucratic infighting have indeed been conditioned by official work. Something does seem to differentiate the style of many ex-officials from that of the average academic economist who has remained innocent of governmental employment. Many in the former category have absorbed a point of view that is more highly sensitized to the limitations of formal model-building for its own sake and to the inescapability of frictions in the translation of theoretical insights into policy application. This point of view, in turn, enriches their subsequent contributions to academic research and teaching. And it is certainly no accident that ex-officials dominate the contributions of economists to popular education on the "Op-Ed" pages. They can speak with some authority about what is relevant in public debate.

When the late Arthur Okun left his post as chairman of the Johnson administration's Council of Economic Advisers to take up a fellowship at the Brookings Institution, he was asked to comment on his impressions about this transition. He likened his status to that of a retired professional football player who had moved to the TV booth on autumn Sunday afternoons: "You no longer risk getting hurt and you get a better view of the game." Certainly the view of the game must be more sophisticated for the ex-insider than it is to the bulk of economists who have never strayed from the ivory tower. That added dimension of sophistication, in turn, enriches work within the academy. The traffic in economic ideas between academia and government flows on a two-way street.

CHAPTER 12

The exchange of favors in the market for commitments

JAMES K. GALBRAITH

Introduction

Policy ideas sprout among economists from time to time, often as a by-product of academic work. Yet sometimes, some of the same ideas can be found, far from home, in politics. As with coconuts on a far shore, questions arise. How did they get there? How, once there, did they survive?

The simple exchange model which economists are fond of is not well suited to describe this spread of ideas from academic to political life. Academicians "transmit" and politicians "receive," but in what coin do politicians make payment? Prestigious jobs are rare: there are, after all, only three seats on the Council of Economic Advisers and seven on the Federal Reserve Board. The satisfaction of influence can be gained more reliably from students, and for money. "National reputation"? Surely most economists believe that reputation is not built of invitations to testify before Congress. It is not personal gain but duty, motivated perhaps by conviction, that calls participating academics to drop their coconuts on the waves. And the model that explains such a sense of duty is, of course, evolutionary, and was not cast in the mold of the market.

At its point of genesis, the policy idea is a pastime, an idle pursuit. But once on the far shore, in dealings among politicians, the matter becomes more serious. For politicians policy ideas are "plans of action." And plans of action are the coin of the political realm. Good or bad, they are necessarily political; those responsible must evaluate them with political benefits and consequences firmly in mind. The cast-off coconut is soon lost to the mother tree, but to the natives on the far shore it is food.

Among politicians, then, the concept of "spread" as "exchange" takes on a more readily appreciated meaning. A policy idea is, or is not, adopted. This implies an element of choice and the exclusion of other, conflicting choices. Policy ideas have not "spread" simply when they have had a hearing. To live, they must have *adherents*. This fact associates the idea with the commitment to it, which, unlike the idea itself, possesses the crucial characteristic of an economic commodity. Commitments can be bought and sold. It is in achieving commitment to policy ideas that straightforward elements of exchange enter the political picture.

There is no mystery, of course, in the exchange of political favors among politicans. But, to qualify *as an idea* a plan of action must also serve some purpose beyond immediate politics, beyond short-run constituency service and public relations. It must have a broader substantive content than, say, a convention center or an airport. An idea, as such, must serve in the pursuit of an ideal. The coconut must be prized for its beauty, over and above the milk and meat within.

And here is a problem, for such "ideological" content is what public choice theory, the conventional application of economic methods and rational actor market models to workaday political life, seems to exclude. If "ideas" and "politics" are necessarily in conflict, then there can be no allowance in politics for ideas unless politicians, irrationally, pursue extrapolitical purposes. Ideologies are incompatible with the incorrigible short-sightedness and self-dealing of the politician who only maximizes votes. Adherents of public choice theory sometimes follow such reasoning to the conclusion that the political system cannot function for the public good because the pursuit of votes conflicts with the spread of ideas.

This paper makes explicit provision for the observed presence and spread within the (unconstrained) political system of bona fide policy ideas. Yet at the same time economists try to respect the rational-actor canons that make the public choice framework useful.

As it turns out, the conditions for the rise and spread of ideas among rational politicians are quite simple. The market model must be extended to cover two concepts that are the historical weak points in Walrasian models generally and in their public choice analogs in particular. The first such concept is *production,* that policy ideas are an (intermediate) input to the production of policy. The second is *accumulation:* the policy process leads to the development of stores of political capital, which can in turn be used to advance policy ideas.

These concepts usefully clarify the nature of the exchange. Let us compare the market for policy ideas with a *forward market,* which proceeds in conjunction with the production of policy. The medium of this market is, as in any forward market, the contract or (telling word) commitment: the promise to deliver or to receive something – in this case, often, a legislative vote – at a given time for a given price. And so we may think of the policymaking institutions as an exchange, in which complex contracts are traded between political players with different objectives, different liquidity positions, different degrees of risk aversion, different time horizons, and different estimates of what the future holds.

To understand the functioning of such a market and thereby understand the spread of ideas from economists to politicians, we need to assess two main features. First are the attributes of the traders: What motives animate them and what resources do they dispose of? Second are the attributes of the institution: What constraints and incentives does it impose? When we have these features in mind, we can ask: What is the basis of the exchange for which the market exists? In our specific case, what is the basis for an exchange of commitments, or "spread of (policy) ideas"? We shall see that the possibilities for the accumulation of political capital, and hence for the development and spread of policy ideas, depend in crucial ways on specific institutional characteristics of the political system.

Market participants

What are the politicians' motives? Legislators, in real life, have many, and the crude notion that "politicians maximize votes" to the exclusion of other activities is clearly false. Constituency service – and vote-getting – is surely paramount much of the time. But legislators may also wish to curry favor with their colleagues, their leadership, or with the Administration. They may wish to repay a debt or to exact revenge. They may wish to play the game for its own sake, for the pleasure of winning. They may wish to establish a reputation, in preparation perhaps for a run at higher office, perhaps for a more remunerative retirement in the consulting sector. They may wish to consume the benefits of office directly. Or they may wish to take a stand, "on principle."

Some rational actions may cost votes. Currying favor with a Speaker from Texas can be costly in Massachusetts (and vice versa); too much moral principle has a price in water projects; a fondness for playing to the galleries can damage internal and occasionally even external reputation. These choices may diminish the probability of reelection. But they are nevertheless not necessarily irrational – they may still enhance utility if their marginal utility exceeds the utility value of their marginal cost (in declining reelection probability). For the politician, the question is, "Can I afford it?"

An appropriate economic metaphor is of an endowment: call it political capital, or the ex ante, subjectively perceived probability of reelection. Each legislator at each moment has a certain amount, determined by all of the accidents of personal and institutional history: on what committees he serves, on what issues his views are respected, what parliamentary office he holds, the quality of his constituency service, what he has or has not accomplished in the course of a career. The amount may be known with tolerable accuracy, from past election experience, current polling, and other sources. As in the endowment metaphor, the politician chooses a portfolio of positions, designed to maximize the expected return (a flow of utility not strictly limited to raising political capital), subject (usually) to the constraint that the discounted probability of bankruptcy (defeat at the next election) remains tolerably low.

A simple and useful empirical distinction here suggests itself: between legislators who know they can "afford it" on a range of issues, and those who either know they cannot or don't know at all. Some politicians face the bankruptcy constraint and have to beat it. Others reach a position where they have some political capital to burn. Since political capital is, to some extent, transferable, this creates at least part of the precondition for exchange. That is, those with more political capital than they need immediately have something that the others want, and may also want something – usually support in some form – that others are in principle able to provide.

Still, it is not obvious that the others, those with little capital and tightly constrained by the prospect of defeat at the next election, are in a position to trade. Can a vulnerable politician modify his actions so as to consummate a deal? Clearly, with full information no one will pay a politician to do anything he would in any event find himself obliged to do (nor will two equally and perfectly informed investors trade stocks). A rational politician on the margin of electoral survival cannot offer to take a potentially damaging political risk out of love.

But he can be induced to take such action if the risk can be more than offset, or hedged, for example, by a political favor. Such trades are feasible because there exists in the system a stabilizing speculator – someone willing to absorb short-term political risk in return for longer-term programmatic gain. There must exist some politicians who can afford to dip into their capital – to drop their own near-term reelection probability trivially from .97 to .96, say – in exchange for something else that they value, perhaps an asset yielding returns over a longer horizon. Then the latter can, if they choose, maintain the former on their political indifference curves, while channeling votes to a constructive use. And this, in essence, is how "policy ideas" spread within the political sphere: through an exchange of favors for commitments, between those with political capital to spare and those without.

Institutional restraints

Institutional characteristics strongly condition all forms of political exchange. These are, however, highly specific, as may be seen by comparing key characteristics of the two Houses of the United States Congress.

In the House of Representatives, there is always an impending election. House members serve for nonoverlapping renewable two-year terms. Over a long career, a surviving incumbent will face the voters a dozen times or more. This situation strongly affects the distribution of accumulated political capital across members.

To a newly elected House member, matters appear much as they do in the institutionally unstructured public-choice model. The next election is a milestone beyond which the planning period does not extend. And the next election is, of course, always less than two years away. As any model might predict, junior House members are notoriously short-sighted.

As time passes, though, perceptions and behavior change. The best business analog – simpler and better than the discount rate – is the payback period. Certain investors take a short view, and eschew all projects that involve long periods of illiquidity and uncontrolled risk. Others take the long view: higher risk, higher return. Obviously, one can take the long view only if one has enough capital to ride out short-term fluctuations in particular asset values that may occur before one's ship comes in.

Retirees aside, each succeeding election eliminates mainly those members whose ex ante probability of reelection was low,[1] while providing survivors with both better information about their standing at home and greater confidence in it. In more than a few cases, members come to face perennial opponents, about whose behavior and prospects they acquire a reasonably sure feel. There is also synergy on the electorate's side: nothing so reinforces voters' confidence in their own judgment as being on the winning side. Finally, any member serving

[1]They are replaced of course, by other junior members with, at first, relatively low ex ante reelection prospects, so the mix in the aggregate may not change. But this does not affect the critical aging of the survivors.

over the turn of a decade will also – as never happens with Senators – face a redistricting, the effects of which usually consolidate senior members in their districts.[2]

Senior members thus become secure, and their payback periods lengthen. Those at the top – subcommittee chairmen nearing seniority levels sufficient to bring them major chairmanships or leadership positions – tend to develop payback periods that extend at least to the expected end of their senior colleagues' careers.[3] Except in rare political climates when the effective Democratic majority in the House is lost or under threat (as it was for a year or so in 1981–2), these officials have, easily, the longest time perspectives of any officials in government, solely excepting judges appointed for life.

Thus the House sustains, effectively, two classes of members. A majority are trapped in the tidal eddies of a short and powerless career. A few escape to calmer lagoons, in which their political fortunes can grow (like carp) steadily for decades. The former, in our market, are the hedgers, the farmers facing a fall harvest in a volatile market, preoccupied with shifting their risks. The latter are the speculators, liquid enough to assume risk, up to a point, in the interest of larger gains over a longer period of time.

The U.S. Senate is a far less orderly place. Senators serve for overlapping renewable six-year terms, and rarely face their constituencies more than four times over a long senatorial career. Moreover they seldom confront the same opponent twice. Turnover in the Senate is quite high as a proportion of the membership exposed in each election, and defeat of incumbents is as common as it is rare in the House.

Accordingly, to a Senator each election is a major milestone. No matter how senior, Senators do not consider themselves secure in their seats; each election must be faced as though it carried a serious risk of defeat. Much depends, too, on the periodic vagaries of the Presidential election cycle, which strongly affect the fate of incumbent Senators even as they barely ruffle feathers in the House. Against this, victory brings with it the assurance of a substantial gain in seniority and insti-

---

[2]This is true even when the other party controls the redistricting process, since consolidation of one party's voters into a single safe district improves the other party's chances in the remainder.

[3]Speaker O'Neill made reference to this in an interview given just before his retirement: "When I was on the rise, I used to say, 'How long is old Carl Albert or old Sam Rayburn going to stay around? You know, anybody going to get a break?'" The Speaker's next comments were even more revealing: "I just said to myself one day. . . . 'You know, it's high time for you to step aside and show some loyalty to some people who've been loyal to you.'"

tutional position, since two more elections must roll by, with all of the turnover (including of more senior members) that they entail, before any particular Senator just past an election is exposed to the voters again.

For these reasons, contrary to the conventional view of the Senate as a place of long perspectives, Senators' payback periods may be expected to vary directly with the time to the end of their terms, and only in rare cases to extend beyond that. To the staff, the consequence is a cycle of radically changing personalities that comes to seem characteristic of the rhythm of the place. After each election, a new crop of forward-looking statesmen, one-third of the Senate, newly elected or reelected, takes office. At the same time, a hapless cohort of thirty-three or thirty-four soon-to-be-exposed incumbents turns, single-mindedly, to the fund-raising and crowd-pleasing of the impending campaign.[4]

Patterns of leadership

As is well-known, resolution of the Arrow problem tends to require the concentration of decision making in the hands of a single rational actor, with voting processes reduced (or at least revised) from a decision making to a ratifying, legitimating role. The remarkable accomplishment of the U.S. House of Representatives lies precisely in effecting this transition. Senior leadership, relying on loyal legislative specialists in the drafting committees, has shown itself able to concentrate legislative talent to rational effect on quite a wide range of issues, and then to bring politics to bear so that (with crucial assists from the executive branch) the sans-culottes majority comes to ratify the result.

The mechanisms whereby this was achieved have their origins in the constitutional structure of the House. There are other prerequisites as well, the most important being effective leadership. This the House has enjoyed since 1975. In addition, through institutional changes, the Speaker obtained, for the first time in memory, effective control of the House Committee on Rules, making possible the use of the Speaker's latent powers in a single-minded way. Control of the rules, implemented in conjunction with committee chairmen, also makes it possible to deny fractious House committee members the opportunity to

---

[4]A simple demonstration of this could probably be had by comparing Americans for Democratic Action (ADA) and other interest group ratings of Senators and Congressmen. The theory would predict a six-year cycle in Senatorial ratings not present in the House.

put forward amendments on the floor that did not pass in committee, and so promotes loyalty from committee members to their own chairmen. These accomplishments have been of historic importance for U.S. government in the period since Watergate, and now seem to have survived the transition of Speakers from O'Neill to Wright.

One might expect the intertemporal deal, the long-term loan of political capital, to be a potent force in the Senate, because of the fact that each electoral victory insures incumbency for a full additional six years and so provides a safe contracting period. But rules and circumstances disrupt this market; for many desired deals the relevant agents are in the wrong positions. Because, mainly, of the capriciousness of the Senate's election cycle, those in the speculating (leadership) role are generally no safer (more liquid), on average, than the hedgers. Stores of political capital do not accumulate automatically with seniority in the Senate; indeed, often less senior members have it (for example, if they have just been reelected) while more senior members do not. And the Senator in the key position politically is often not the one with the highest seniority in the right committee. This forces deal-making to occur on an ad hoc and shifting basis, which complicates patterns of trading and raises transactions costs.

The spread of ideas between leaders and followers is thus more difficult in the Senate, especially across elections, than in the House. This has been especially true since 1980, when the question of which party controls the Senate came to be an issue in each election, creating the possibility of a shift in control that would upset the power even of Senators not personally at risk for their seats. Such institutional instability cut sharply into the clout of the President with Senators of his own party in 1981–6, since one could not enforce discipline on any Senator whose seat might prove indispensable to the fragile Republican majority.

Thus no effective procedural mechanism for rational leadership control blesses the operations of the Senate. Senate leadership is politically unstable, and therefore is unable to make deals with members on the necessary scale. Partly for the same reasons, Senate leadership is also institutionally weak, and in particular does not control the rules of the legislative game as it is played within the Senate. Senate committee chairmen have no great need to be loyal to their leaders, and are not. Senate committee members have correspondingly less need to be loyal to their chairmen, since they cannot be denied a second chance on the floor if they lose in a committee vote. The Senate thus remains mired in the Arrow problem, as the reports of several recent commissions (Stevenson 1976, Pearson-Ribicoff 1984) attest.

The patterns of exchange

These elements of structure tell us something about the spread of ideas in the House and Senate. As corporate institutions they both operate with short time horizons, reflecting the outlook of the marginal member. Yet the House possesses what the Senate lacks: an institutional subculture with a radically longer payback period.[5] Hence, the relevant political market in the House, particularly on economic issues, often involves the exchange of political goods with differing time streams of benefits and costs. The leadership offers the followers opportunities to make short-term political points, in return for which the followers support the leaders on complex and potentially damaging programmatic questions.

Pork barrel in the House is, typically, not a set of spot-market transactions among members of equal standing. It is, instead, but one instance in the general exercise of leadership power. Members of the Ways and Means Committee, under a strong chairman, get their pork (in the form of "transition rules" in tax legislation) for cooperation with the chairman on his agenda, whatever it might be. Score-keeping over time is possible because only one agent – the chairman – has to do it, and the chairman has staff who function, in part, to keep track of precisely what the chairman needs and of who has earned his favor.

Members of the Senate Finance Committee get their pork more or less simply for sitting on the committee and acquiescing in the pork of everyone else. Pure political exchanges of this pork-for-pork type have the character, both in the public-choice parable and, where they exist, in real life, of sequential small-change spot-market transations: my convention center for your ship channel in this bill, my airport for your research lab in the next. This favors-for-favors market is institutionally Walrasian: recontracting but no transactions occur until the market clears, at which point all transactions are effected at once. Senators on the Finance Committee thus load their pet projects onto a single legislative vehicle – usually toward the end of a session – and so concentrate their logrolling transactions into a few short bursts of legislative time. Score is kept in a rough way by assuring that every relevant Senator gets some piece of every logrolling bill. There is very little

---

[5]Of course certain individual Senators do operate with long horizons, corresponding to great security or high ambition. But the means for amplifying the power of such behavior in the Senate is extremely weak (witness the isolation of a Proxmire). The House leadership showed its long time horizon repeatedly during the Reagan Administration, including through its opposition to Gramm-Rudman, and has made that horizon the effective force in policymaking on many recent occasions.

in such circumstances that a chairman can do to impart an ideological thrust to events; indeed, there is almost nothing he can do at all except preside over an annual sequence of "Christmas trees."

The House's two-class nature also makes possible a three-way deal whenever the Administration is in a position of asking the House leadership for help. The Administration has mainly short-run favors to dispense: high-level stroking if the President is of the same party as the House majority, simple promises of nonaggression otherwise. These the House leadership does not need for itself. But the Administration can offer such favors *through* the leadership *to* the followership, promoting passage of legislation on which it has reached a substantive compromise with the leadership by augmenting the latter's political clout with its own followers.

It is this potential for structured trading which has provided the grounds for recent deals between the House leadership and the Administration on matters as diverse as the Tax Equity and Fiscal Responsibility Act (TEFRA 1982), reform of Social Security financing (1983), the International Monetary Fund quota increase (1984), and comprehensive tax reform (1985–6). On such matters, the leadership of the House acted in the service of ideas, for shared national purposes that bore no relationship to constituency service. Indeed, raising taxes and foreign aid had net short-term political costs to individual members of the leadership, but these played little role in the decisions.

The Administration's side of the deal, in such cases, was directed toward members with less seniority and short time horizons. One pattern in the Reagan years was for the President to provide rank-and-file Democrats with indemnity from political attack from their future Republican opponents on the specific issue on which they had supported the joint leadership–Administration position. The International Monetary Fund case, in which the President was required to write a letter to rank-and-file Democrats stating that their joint position was in "the national interest," provides a graphic illustration of such a deal.

Tax reform – never a crowd-pleaser – occurred in 1986 partly for similar reasons, including a crucial pledge from the White House not to criticize the work of the Ways and Means Committee while the bill was being drafted. Here, too, the President's role included corralling members of his own Party in the House into support of their opposition's leadership against their own constituents (see Joe Minarik's paper in this volume) when the chips were down.

It is highly instructive that a radical-conservative Administration found it easier to bargain with a liberal House than with a moderately conservative Senate on tax reform. The two-class structure of the House, once again, provides the reason. The Administration could deal with the House because the House leadership could deliver its members, whereas the Senate leadership could not.

This difference showed up starkly in the drafting phases of the tax reform bill. The House Committee produced a rational bill, with just enough favors disbursed to produce the requisite number of votes. In the Senate, the drafting process broke down, and only after the initial effort (and its collateral, universal logrolling) had collapsed was Chairman Packwood able to create a temporary, remarkable climate of mutual restraint (and, as Minarik says, mutual shame) in which the Senate could enact a relatively clean bill. The greater efficiency of the House process showed up, too, in an apparently more hazardous road to final passage (as Minarik describes), whereas the Senate produced an all-or-nothing proposition to which in the end only three Senators declared themselves opposed. That the Senate bill contained a more thorough tax reform also shows an ironic, felicitous serendipity of the Senate's modus operandi. The Senate, but not the House, could have as easily produced no tax reform at all, but the Senate could also produce, where the House could not, a more nearly perfect final bill.

In sum, basic institutional characteristics, laid down for the most part by the Constitution itself, structure the relations of exchange within the House and Senate. These relations govern the spread of commitments to policy action – the spread of ideas – over a wide range of issues. They constitute the normal means of trafficking in legislative affairs.

Implications for policy design

The coconut palm cannot control the tides. Nor can it reshape and restructure the bounty it produces. But can knowledge of conditions on the far shore be put to evolutionary advantage? Perhaps trading practices can be improved. Perhaps simply knowing how the coconuts are traded can tell us something, if we care to learn it, about the sort of palms to plant.

Much is made, these days, of the evil of pork-barrel politics. There is an extensive academic movement for simple, extrapolitical rules to govern fiscal policy, as there has been an academic demand for simple rules to drive out discretion in monetary affairs. The purpose of such rules, it is averred, is to get the political process under control. Don't shoot the crocodiles, say the constitutional amendment enthusiasts: drain the swamp.

For economists with ideas to spread, the first and most important implication of the analysis above is to steer away from such schemes. Those schemes would destroy (and are perhaps intended to destroy), the precise mechanisms of control whereby a legislative leadership can translate ideas into law. Without pork-barrel nothing substantive would happen in the House. Moreover, the extent of pork-barrel is under most conditions strictly regulated in the House, both by the overall scarcity of resources and by the need to preserve the political value of favors to their recipients. The problem lies not with pork-barrel politics as practiced in the House but with anarchic logrolling, which lacks both defined limits and structured purpose, and is by far more characteristic of the Senate.

A second clear implication concerns the channels of regular, effective propagation for legislative ideas. There are two: through the President and the Administration, and through the leadership of the House. The leadership of the Senate, specifically, does not count. Nor do junior members or the minority in the House. Individual Senators with ideas work their will, like all other mortals, through the President and through the House, and seldom directly through their own institution.

The case of tax reform is again instructive. Tax reform's intellectual leader was, as Minarik notes, Senator Bill Bradley, a figure both respected and well placed (though in the minority and quite junior at the time) on the Senate Finance Committee. But Bradley's tax reform did not happen in the Senate. It happened only because of an agreement to make it happen between the President and the leadership in the House. Senate action came late and serendipitously; Bradley earned his historic role outside his authorized legislative channels. One cannot imagine Chairman Dan Rostenkowski working outside the framework of his committee in the way that Bradley did. Nor can one imagine tax reform progressing as far as it did had Rostenkowski been as cold to it as was, at the outset, Senate Finance Chairman Bob Packwood. But still less can one imagine a junior member of Ways and Means (in the minority, yet!) upstaging and ultimately converting a chairman in the way that Bradley upstaged and converted Packwood.

Much is made, too, these days, of the need for simplification in political life. Yet, when worked through the normal and effective channels, a legislative idea does not have to be simple. Institutional resources for coping with complexity, even the extreme complexity of tax and welfare laws and of the budget, exist. But, because such resources are scarce and their use is expensive, control of access to them becomes the critical element in designing complex policy. This the Administration and the House leadership alone can provide.

In this decade the House leadership and the Presidency have fallen at opposite ends of the political spectrum. And so a curiously bipartisan government has existed, providing possibilities for political input and legislative success to skilled actors from left, right, and center. But what if the channels to effective influence are blocked? This is a problem that Republican members of the House (like Jack Kemp when he was still in the House) and mavericks in the Senate (Phil Gramm) confront regularly. Their characteristic solution tells of the power, and the limitations, of the simple idea.

The key to broad-based appeal for an insurgent legislative program is apparent simplicity – the substitute of choice where the reputation and established power of the initiator will not suffice. This has been especially true in the tax area, where no proposal is truly simple, but all compete to appear so: the ten percent "across-the-board" reductions of Kemp-Roth, the "10-5-3" depreciation reforms of Jones-Conable, the original tax reform proposals (Bradley-Gephardt and Kemp-Kasten), and a minimum corporate tax. It is also true of periodic protectionist insurgencies (minimum content in 1984, the Gephardt amendment in 1988). The apparent comprehensibility of such systems makes them tractable in public debate, even if there would be nothing truly simple about their operation in practice.

For ideo-legislative insurgency, a coalition of the disempowered is required. But the glue of binding, effective, intertemporal exchange of favors is lacking – the powerless have too few favors to offer. Nor, deprived of staff and senior leadership, can insurrections rely on the reputations and prestige of their leaders. Ties of ideology alone can partly substitute, but are not sufficient: ideological coalitions are too small. Outside pressures must therefore be brought to bear. These can be mobilized, but only if the mobilizing principle (a balanced budget, a ban on abortions, an "across-the-board" tax cut, or, 1988's Republican favorite, a spending freeze) is both widely appealing and apparently simple. In such cases "heat" from the press, the interest groups, and the guerrillas and panic-artists of the think tank and syndicated column industries can be made felt in Congress – and especially in the Senate, where weak leadership opens doors to simplistic ideas.[6]

[6]The problem of insurgency has been dissected in some recent works on supply-side economics, including Roberts (1984). The principles that made supply-side viable also apply to monetarism, to tax simplification, to Gramm-Rudman, and to a host of other ideas that at least started their legislative odyssey as antiestablishment rebellion.

For the economist, living in academic tranquillity by the seashore, the lessons are few, and simple. Ideas can have political power. Some ideas can be designed to suit the channels of effective leadership power. Others can serve as instruments of insurrection. In most cases this is a stark choice: Phil Gramm's budgetary tactics are as useless to Jim Wright as Daniel Patrick Moynihan's proposed welfare reforms would have been in the hands of Jack Kemp. But a few ideas, and perhaps the most successful, can, like Bradley's tax reform itself, start out with the characteristics of insurrection and then be converted, when the complexity of the process requires it, into vehicles for Presidential and leadership action. The lessons boil down to this: Know your audience. Write the name and address on that coconut before you cast it adrift.

CHAPTER 13

How tax reform came about

JOSEPH J. MINARIK

The adoption of the Tax Reform Act of 1986 is full of uniqueness and irony. The new tax law violated all the rules of conventional wisdom built up by the tax policy fraternity. It was guided through the legislative process by personalities reversing their own past patterns of behavior, and in some cases, it might be argued, the political law of gravity. It is not clear to me whether tax reform can be a case study for similar efforts in other policy areas, or just a shooting star to savor (or, depending on one's point of view, to curse).

The goal of this paper is to explain the Tax Reform Act of 1986 and how it happened, and to give some insights into this experience and the spread of economic ideas. The first section explains where the bill fits into the spectrum of tax policy alternatives. The second section discusses how the policymakers chose this particular economic option. The third and final section describes the even more remarkable political choice: the decision to act on such a far-reaching scale.

The 1986 Tax Reform Act

There are two important aspects of the Tax Reform Act of 1986 that must be kept in mind. The first is that the law was by no means a strictly partisan effort. Among the bill's active supporters were such prominent liberals as Senator Bill Bradley (D-NJ) and such undeniable conservatives as President Ronald Reagan. The vocal opponents of the law included such dyed-in-the-wool liberals as Senator Carl Levin (D-MI) and solid conservatives such as Senator Malcolm Wallop (R-WY). General Motors, a massive industrial giant, supported the bill; USX (formerly U.S. Steel), massive in its own right, opposed it.

Opinions expressed are those of the author and do not necessarily represent the views of The Urban Institute or its sponsors.

141

This bipartisan split was perfectly predictable (though its legislative outcome was hardly so). Each party was torn between conflicting interests. For the Democrats, the bill was a big tax cut for the poor (a significant plus), and a big tax increase for big real estate (a crushing minus). Even big labor wasn't too sure of where it stood on the bill (on final passage, the AFL-CIO took no position), which left the Democrats hanging. For the Republicans, things were no clearer. Individual corporate executives were thrilled, at least at the end of the process, by the prospect of much lower statutory tax rates; but their corporations, in many instances, nevertheless faced higher taxes. Capital-intensive businesses lost the investment tax credit and much of the benefit of accelerated depreciation, and venture capitalists were horrified that they would have to pay at the same tax rate as everyone else.

This political confusion muddied the waters considerably. The bill was not a simple presidential proposal, passed through Congress by a strong majority of his party with a smattering of opposition support. Of course, with one House in opposition control, that script would not work in any event. Even after the President climbed on board, there was always the issue of counting noses on both sides of the aisle in both Houses, and especially within the tax-writing committees.

The second aspect of the law, especially important in a consideration of the spread of economic ideas, is the economic nature of the bill. The Tax Reform Act of 1986 was by no means a state-of-the-art academic creation. It was, rather, a "low-tech," low-budget approach to our tax policy problems – which is still, at least in my opinion, the right approach.

Much of recent academic thought has centered on taxes on consumption rather than taxes on income. The notion of a personal expenditure tax, computed by households on an annual basis, has gathered solid support from the economics profession in the United States as well as in Europe. This idea was taken up by some "new ideas" liberals (such as Gary Hart), as well as by many of the traditional conservatives who have advocated a national value-added tax (VAT) or other such indirect tax on consumption. Other strains of current thought include optimal-tax-type fine tuning of incentives toward investment and other meritorious economic activities, prominently including research and development.

Instead, the 1986 tax law is a fairly long stride toward the old-line economic ideal of a comprehensive income tax. It downgrades, though it does not completely reject, the consumption tax principle of deferring tax on the income from capital until it is finally consumed. Furthermore, the law leans toward the age-old principle of imposing equal taxes on all forms of economic activity, rather than attempting to approach an optimal tax solution of selective tax preferences for particular enterprises. This last position reaches its logical conclusion in an aggregate tax increase on corporations (though the impact on individual firms varies considerably).

Why income tax reform?

This section describes the policymakers' choice among the fundamental tax policy alternatives: income taxation, expenditure taxation upon households, and consumption taxation upon transactions. It weighs the options from the policymakers' point of view, and explains why they chose as they did.

Economists have long argued for comprehensive income tax reform, defined as broadening the definition of income for tax purposes to match more closely the underlying economic concept. Working from the pre–World War II writings of Robert Murray Haig, Henry C. Simons, and others, Joseph A. Pechman put forward some of the earliest arguments, in the 1950s and 1960s. Pechman's major contribution was to quantify the effects of departures from a uniform tax base, in terms of the amount of federal revenue lost and its distribution by income class. With this information spread among the economics profession, and popularized by Philip M. Stern, there arose a greater sense of the trade-offs between selective tax preferences and lower tax rates. Of course, this realization among the economics profession and the attentive public did not prevent lower tax rates from being traded away for selective tax preferences almost continuously.

At about the same time, Stanley S. Surrey, a lawyer, contributed a new view of the selective tax preferences in the law. He likened the tax savings from a preference for a particular purpose (for example, encouraging investment in physical capital) to a government outlay for the same purpose. Thus was coined the term "tax expenditures." This concept was institutionalized on an illustrative basis in the federal budget in the mid-1960s and has had a powerful influence on virtually all deliberations on the federal income tax ever since. On the other hand, proposals to operationalize the tax expenditure concept in the congressional budget process, usually by imposing a limit on tax expenditures like the ceiling on outlays, have consistently failed.

An outgrowth of the tax expenditure idea was another Surrey concept, the "upside-down subsidy." Surrey pointed out that tax expenditures delivered through exclusions or deductions (such as the deduction for medical expenses) reduced tax liabilities for upper-bracket individuals more than for lower-income persons; thus, at late-1960s tax rates, a dollar of medical expense deduction reduced the taxes of a top-bracket taxpayer by 70 cents, but for a bottom-bracket person by only 14 cents. This outcome struck Surrey as inequitable and motivated him to argue on principle against tax expenditures (at least in the form of deductions) as a means of pursuing public purposes.

The concerns of Surrey and Pechman might well be pigeonholed as 1960s arguments: largely based on fairness in general, and on vertical equity in particular. Although tax reform's reductions of marginal tax rates could possibly stimulate the supply of factors of production to some degree, this was a secondary argument at most. Likewise, the improvement in resource allocation that could be achieved through equalizing the tax treatment of different economic activities was seen as a side effect. The reason was, quite simply, that the nation already had robust economic growth, and the major concern was to spread the fruits more equitably. Thus, when researchers computed the reduction of tax rates that was possible through broadening of the tax base, the emphasis was on which taxpayers got the largest tax cuts; and the default position was to set the rates so as to make the tax burden distribution as progressive as possible, subject to a constraint that the top marginal rate not be too high.

Of course, by the mid-1970s, with stagflation in full swing, national concerns were changing. At first, this raised some subsidiary income tax issues. Economists argued that inflation was distorting the measurement of income from capital in the income tax base – overstating the income of lenders and understating the income of borrowers, eroding the depreciation deductions of investors in physical capital, and creating and inflating phantom capital gains. These effects created all the wrong incentives: borrow to increase consumption, or to finance with debt instead of equity; and consume existing wealth, rather than reinvesting it in overtaxed physical or financial assets. Some economists saw in these effects the seeds of a long-term economic decline through reduced capital formation. The prescription was indexation of the tax base to reflect real rather than nominal magnitudes of interest income and expense, depreciation, and capital gains.

A second subsidiary income tax issue, reflective of another strain of tax policy, was concern about the double taxation of corporate source income – profits taxed first at the corporate level and then at the individual level when distributed as dividends. Again, the fear was that investment in incorporated enterprises would suffer, both absolutely and relative to investment in unincorporated businesses.

Other economists were thinking more radically – hitting the inflation and double taxation issues precisely, and with one blow. Many were taking off from Nicholas Kaldor's proposal that the tax base be converted from income to consumption. Kaldor's concern had been one of capital formation, or perhaps deformation – he saw the rich in England consuming their wealth rather than reinvesting it. When viewed anew and with the perspective of more recent developments, this personal expenditure tax – allowing a deduction for saving, and taxing dissaving in full – eliminated the inflation problem (because consumption is always in current dollars) and the double taxation problem (corporations would not be taxed, because they do not consume). A lawyer, William D. Andrews, filled in many important operational details. David F. Bradford put the Treasury on the case in 1977 with *Blueprints for Basic Tax Reform,* followed closely by the Meade Commission report in England, and a similar report in Sweden written by Sven-Olof Lodin.

Still other economists concerned with capital formation were thinking somewhat more conventionally. Rather than instituting the world's only personal expenditure tax (this tax had been tried but dropped by India and Sri Lanka), they recommended following the mainstream of Europe with a value-added tax (VAT). The major differences between the personal expenditure tax and the VAT, apart from the novelty of the former, were administrative (the VAT would be an additional tax while the personal expenditure tax would replace the income tax) and distributional (the personal expenditure tax could have its own exemptions and deductions for low-income relief, whereas the VAT would require some outside mechanism to lift its own tax burden from the poor). Major advocates of the VAT included Washington superlobbyist Charls Walker and other spokesmen for business.

It is probably fair to say that the personal expenditure tax had captured the imagination of the greater part of the economics profession by the early 1980s. The exactness of this tax's solutions to the inflation and double taxation problems was the key to this appeal. The question was whether, if fundamental tax issues should reach the top of the nation's policy agenda, the personal expenditure tax could translate into politics as neatly as it had into economics.

As it happened, tax reform leapt to the top of the agenda following the massive tax cuts of 1981. This was counterintuitive for at least two reasons. First, the 1981 law might have cooled public dissatisfaction with the income tax (perceived in opinion polls as the most unfair tax) merely by reducing taxes. Such was not the case; in fact, the "safe harbor leasing" provision in the law was offensive to many people. It combined a negative corporate income tax, the buying and selling of tax breaks, and the subsidization of corporate "losers" – notions with some policy rationale, but repugnant to most noneconomists – all in one package. Only a year later, safe harbor leasing was repealed. Yet the generosity of the 1981 law toward business, which motivated safe harbor leasing in the first place, continued to undermine support for the income tax by allowing major, profitable corporations to pay no tax. A largely labor-funded organization called Citizens for Tax Justice began to issue periodic press releases that listed profitable corporations with no tax liability. Before long, members of Congress were being continually hammered in their public appearances about corporate taxes. Even the most pro-business members soon decided that this had to stop.

Second, all past experience indicated that the 1981 tax cut had cost so much revenue that further changes in the law would be impossible until years of inflation and growth could restore the tax base. In fact, the revenue cost was even greater than that; several rounds of emergency tax increases soon proved essential. Furthermore, the tax rate cuts had become so much a part of the economic policy baseline, not to mention the president's agenda, that raising revenue required plugging loopholes in the tax base. This process exposed many obsolete and unjustifiable tax preferences; it provoked a great deal of unseemly dissembling on the part of affected interests; and it demonstrated to many members of Congress that tax preferences could be repealed without causing the sky to fall in.

The 1981 law's reduction of the revenue baseline had another, subtler effect. Like it or not, tax reform packages have always been graded according to the maximum individual income tax rate that they could attain with no loss of revenue. A crucial factor in the determination of that maximum individual rate is the handling of long-term capital gains. It became evident during the debate on the 1981 law that an equal-yield, equal-progressivity reformed income tax with no preference for long-term gains could achieve a maximum individual income tax rate of 28 percent – simply because the 1981 law cut taxes so much. The 28 percent rate was a policy milestone, in that the maximum effective tax rate on long-term gains was set at 28 percent by the 1978 law that was so beloved by the capital formation lobby. If a reformed tax with a 28 percent top rate would silence (though it certainly would not convert) the capital formation crowd, it was reasoned, the traditional allies of tax reform might be able to build a coalition large enough to pass a bill. This was the foot in the door for tax reform. And as is fairly widely recognized by now, that foot was wearing a basketball sneaker.

Senator Bill Bradley was the first member of Congress to confront the choices in a fundamental restructuring of the income tax law. He considered the expenditure tax option for some time, but eventually rejected it, despite its popularity among the economics profession. There were several reasons for this decision. One was the probable public perception of unfairness in a tax on what people spent rather than on their economic capacity, and the extreme unfairness that would result unless gifts and bequests were included in the tax base as if spent – an unlikely policy outcome. A second was the danger that the expenditure tax base could become even more leaky than the income tax base in the legislative process. A third was the difficulty of transition, especially in providing adequate relief to older persons (who had already paid income tax on their accumulations of wealth) without depleting the tax base. A fourth was doubt over whether and to what degree a complete lifting of the tax burden on capital and a shifting of it to labor would be an economic plus. A fifth was the simple uniqueness of the tax; given that no other nation is committed to a personal expenditure tax, there is a nontrivial possibility of extremely difficult or even insurmountable administrative problems.

A final reason, easy to trivialize but impossible to ignore, is the complexity of the expenditure tax concept to a public raised on an income tax. A former superior of mine, a lawyer who worked for a number of years on congressional staffs, used to say that his first rule in dealing with members of Congress was not to bring up present values. This rule is probably a bit too harsh, given that the economic sophistication of members has been increasing steadily. But this policy adviser's second rule is perhaps even more to the point: A policy position must be explained to a member not just so that he can understand it, but so that he can explain it to his constituents. My own experience in explaining the expenditure tax to groups of members of Congress, in company with other economists both favoring and opposing the concept, is that the room quickly goes dead from two separate reactions: the first, eyes glazing over in lack of comprehension; and the second, boredom in the realization that this concept could never be explained in a town meeting to a cross section of their constituents. And this latter reaction should not be trivialized; economists who bank on significant behavioral responses to an expenditure tax had better be able to argue that such behavioral responses will materialize even if the bulk of the taxpayers do not understand the tax.

So Bradley settled on reform of the existing income tax as a journey on familiar territory. His judgment was confirmed by no less an advocate of capital formation than the president himself. The administration approached the 1984 election, after two years of exposure for Bradley's "Fair Tax," concerned that the bill could be a lethal weapon in the campaign. So President Reagan, in his January 1984 State of the Union address, assigned the Treasury to formulate recommendations for the comprehensive reform of the tax system. This same Treasury that had touted the expenditure tax in *Blueprints for Basic Tax Reform* now rejected it on grounds identical to Bradley's. The Treasury also considered the VAT as an add-on to the current system, substituting for some income tax revenues, but rejected it as an unnecessary additional complexity and as potentially unfair – and probably as a hard political sell against an opponent touting income tax reform. (Every tax expert in Washington remembers that Al Ullman, chairman of the House Ways and Means committee, lost what was thought a safe seat in Oregon at least in part because of his espousal of a value-added tax.)

Thus, from well before legislative consideration began, there was no doubt that the target was a fundamental reform of the existing income tax. One might rather cynically conclude from this result – after decades of failure by economists to sell the comprehensive income tax, followed by the conversion of much of the profession to consumption taxation – that the way to spread an economic idea is to abandon it. (I hope that this observation is not remembered as the major contribution of this paper.)

Several other decisions in the formulation of the Bradley-Gephardt bill (Rep. Richard Gephardt joined as House cosponsor) helped to steer the debate and to push it toward a conclusion. The key principles of the bill were achieving workability ahead of academic purity and isolating the essence of tax reform from subsidiary issues. The former principle led to the rejection of the consumption tax option, and also to the omission of the indexation of capital income from the bill. It was concluded that indexing the tax base would cause prohibitive administrative and political difficulties, which later developments proved to be correct. When the Treasury's initial study proposed indexation of interest, depreciation, and capital gains, experts in accounting in the financial sector uncovered serious practical problems, and the interests who were ostensibly to be benefited by indexation professed themselves to be dissatisfied. These provisions were dropped or scaled back in the Treasury's revised plan, and they disappeared by the end of the process.

The latter principle dictated that the Bradley-Gephardt bill be both revenue and distribution neutral (that is, that it raise the same total revenue as the then current law, and that each individual income class, and corporations taken as a group, pay the same tax as under that law). Thus, Bradley-Gephardt could not be attacked on the ground that it was a redistributionist scheme, or that it would debilitate the corporate sector. Though the importance of this choice can never be known for certain, Bradley-Gephardt, contrary to some pundits' initial assessments, maintained its credibility and kept tax reform on the national agenda. The price of this decision was that Bradley-Gephardt could not offer a dramatic tax cut for low-income persons (though it did increase personal exemptions and standard deductions sufficiently to lift the poor from the tax rolls), and that it could not use a corporate tax increase to avoid the last, painful choices to attain revenue neutrality among individuals.

Bradley-Gephardt was perhaps most radical in its handling of the corporate tax. The first Bradley-Gephardt bill included changes only to the individual income tax; revisions to the corporate income tax were promised later. The second bill included these corporate reforms (as well as further individual revenue-raisers equal in yield to those in the Tax Equity and Fiscal Responsibility Act of 1982). The Bradley-Gephardt corporate tax was a U-turn from the changes of 1981; it eliminates numerous subsidies, including the investment tax credit and most of the benefit of accelerated depreciation, and reduced the corporate rate to a flat 30 percent (equal to the highest individual rate in the second version of the bill). The depreciation system was designed to impose equally effective tax rates on all investments in physical capital. This entire approach bespoke a radically different philosophy from the existing corporate tax; it turned away from government intervention in resource allocation and sought the lowest possible uniform tax burden on corporate income from whatever source.

This feature of Bradley-Gephardt helped to spawn the aspect of the Treasury plan that caused the most controversy and contributed most to the ultimate passage of tax reform: a $25 billion per year increase in corporate income taxes, which financed a $25 billion per year cut in individual taxes. Some observers argued that it was a simple sweetener for individuals, who vote, out of the deep pockets of corporations, who do not. But inside sources suggested that the numbers dictated the result. After defining the individual and corporate tax bases as they thought proper, the Treasury simply found that the corporate tax raised too much revenue at the 35 percent top rate that they originally contemplated. They lowered the corporate rate 2 percentage points below the top individual rate, but hesitated to go further because of a possible inducement for hitherto unincorporated businesses to incorporate to cut taxes at the margin. With the repeal of the prominent tax preferences plus this tax increase on corporations, Treasury I completed the U-turn from the 1981 business tax policy.

It was here that this particular president, and his particular party affiliation, probably had more to do with the ultimate success of tax reform than in any other connection. For one thing, Ronald Reagan's approach to tax policy was rather unidimensional: the level of the top individual tax rate was far and away his most important consideration. Long-time Reagan watchers relate that the president was deeply offended when his career took off at the end of World War II and he discovered that he was paying 91 percent of his marginal income to the federal government. When he became president, the supply-side ideology had reinforced his aversion to high tax rates. The Treasury's proposed 35 percent maximum rate took on a highly symbolic meaning to the president; he realized that if the proposal passed intact, he could claim that the maximum individual income tax rate was cut in half during his term of office. This potential achievement compensated for a multitude of sins, not the least of which would be the knifing of virtually every traditional Republican party constituency with not just the repeal of most major tax preferences, but a net $25 billion per year corporate tax increase to boot.

Thus, the "Nixon visits China" scenario was replayed. The president unquestionably carried a large number of reluctant Republican votes in both Houses of the Congress. Had Walter Mondale been elected in 1984, those votes would have been unobtainable. The Democrats would have had to pass the bill on a straight party-line basis, against charges of unrestrained redistributionism and corporation bashing, with no votes to spare, and under the most intense pressure from their own allied interests. It is hard to imagine how tax reform could have succeeded under those circumstances.

Once on the table, the corporate tax increase was impossible to sweep away. The extra $25 billion of corporate revenue saved the Treasury from making those last hard choices on the individual side that a distribution-neutral bill required. With the tax cut, the Treasury could give more relief to the near-poor, which did not buy many votes directly but to some extent wrapped the bill in the flag. With less revenue to raise from individuals, the plan could yield more winners and fewer losers; the president could say emphatically that the typical taxpayer would get a tax cut. And perhaps most decisively, once such a tax cut was offered to the voters, it would be political folly to step forward and propose to take it away.

With the president firmly on board, tax reform had a shot at passing in Congress. The obstacles to legislation of this sort are well known in political science: A minority of taxpayers with a lot to lose lobby vigorously, while the majority with less to gain are silent. In this instance, the odds were even worse. Although 75 percent of the taxpayers would receive a tax cut under the final law, a poll found that only 25 percent of the taxpayers realized this. Half of the taxpaying population would get a tax cut but did not know it. The majority was not just silent; legislators reported receiving angry calls of protest from constituents who, after only rudimentary examination, were found actually to benefit from the bill.

What tax reform had going for it, from a political point of view, was the potential to present an airtight case for the general interest. If the law could be written to reach all income, with the burden thus spread as thinly as possible, no taxpayer's share would be excessive. Then, any taxpayer who wanted his preference restored would have to justify special treatment in a system whose burden was already low. Bradley, in an elegant phrase, referred to this as "the power of the idea." Someone else, in a phrase somewhat more earthy, said that the right bill would "shame them into voting for it."

With hindsight, even though the passage through each House of Congress was different, there is a basic similarity to the two experiences. Each tax-writing committee had to go through a collective metamorphosis before it could really get down to work. In each instance, there was enough influence by affected interests that the chairman lost several important early votes. In the House, the last painful defeat came on a bank provision, where the committee chose to liberalize the existing law and actually decrease rather than increase revenue. Anecdotal accounts have it that an indiscreet industry lobbyist cried, "We won! We won!" outside the committee room after the vote, which so humiliated and angered the members that they reversed the vote and proceeded with new resolve. An important subsequent procedural assist came when Chairman Rostenkowski enforced a revenue neutrality requirement on all amendments – if a member wanted to restore a tax preference, he had to propose a base broadener or a rate increase to make up for it.

The bill passed through committee with some unexpected vulnerabilities. In the final deliberations, with the last few billion dollars to raise to achieve revenue neutrality, the chairman found it easier to work in caucus with his own party members; and so the Republicans on the committee felt slighted. That problem, coupled with the natural Republican discomfort with the substance of the bill, added up to big trouble. The spark that ignited the ensuing rebellion was unhappiness among selected members on both sides of the aisle with a last-minute provision that removed a tax advantage to retired government employees. Opponents seized an opportunity in a necessary procedural vote (to adopt a rule governing subsequent consideration) which could kill the bill without any overt statement on the merits of tax reform; this dealt the bill a stunning defeat before it was ever actually considered.

The bill would have been dead without the president's intervention. He chose to go to work to salvage his major domestic initiative, and lobbied many Republican members to change their votes. The device that apparently made the difference was an ironic letter, saying (in appropriately vague language) that the president disliked the bill and would veto it if it reached his desk in its current form, but urging the members to pass it on to the Senate where the Republican majority would surely improve it. The House Republicans were convinced in sufficient numbers, and the bill passed in a dramatic reincarnation on the House floor.

In the Senate, Chairman Packwood (who had said to a reporter shortly before that he "kind of like[s] the tax code the way it is") started with a bill that did far less base-broadening than the House's, and plugged the huge resulting revenue hole by denying businesses the deduction for their excise tax liabilities. The proceedings began much as had those of Ways and Means. The early votes went against the chairman, and his bill fell more and more behind on revenue – with the excise tax revenues extremely doubtful. As the series of defeats grew longer, Chairman Packwood, realizing that any more losses would destroy the bill's credibility, pulled it out of the committee.

There followed a dramatic transformation of Robert Packwood. After several days of soul searching over his own role in the growing debacle and conferring with his staff over some far-flung options, Packwood emerged as a true-blue tax reformer with a radical plan carrying a top individual tax rate of 27 percent (ignoring the 32 percent phase-out range). He told the press: "I came to believe that Bradley was right." The chairman's arguments carried an air of lobbying overload, of hearing too many times that one particular tax preference or another was the key to our prosperity. Packwood now responded to questions from the press and from other members by wondering aloud: "If tax incentives were so important, how did the nation's economy perform so well before the income tax even existed?"

The extremely low maximum rate in the chairman's proposal won several conservative members over almost immediately, and the bill had a strange coalition consisting of the ideological extremes of the committee. In time, the relative center was won over. Several threatening amendments were defeated through adherence to a revenue neutrality rule identical to that used in Ways and Means. Unlike in the House, there was little drama on the floor; after a few close votes on amendments, the bill passed 97 to 3.

Throughout the darkest days in the House and the Senate, some members of the press stated that the bill "had a life of its own," and that somehow the problems would be worked out and the bill would pass. The developments in the Senate most clearly gave meaning to this interpretation. There was a public reservoir of disapproval of the then current law, and that was the raw material with which the two chairmen could work; but they did their jobs in quite different ways. The House bill was brokered with enormous skill; the chairman worked closely with his members, discovered which particular preferences each member had to have to satisfy his most important constituent interests, and worked out a compromise that saved all of those preferences and used the repeal of the others to finance the bill. The problem with this approach was that the public, being far from expert on tax policy, saw this as another special interest tax bill; they were told that loopholes dear to important members were retained, and so remained lukewarm – even though the bill was a dramatic improvement over existing law.

The Senate bill, in contrast, operated in an entirely different dimension. Though far from perfect, it came close enough to the ideal of tax reform to capture the support of even the most reluctant. It repealed some preferences that were "essential" when measured by the scale of the Ways and Means proceedings, but compensated the offended senators with the extremely low rates. Tax reform has always been a motherhood and apple pie issue; almost every senator has said at some point, "I'm for tax reform, but. . . ." The Senate bill came close enough to the ideal so that the response could be, "Well, this is *real* tax reform – are you for it?" Thus it achieved Bradley's "power of the idea."

Early commentary suggested an easy melding of two good tax reform bills in conference. In fact, the process was extremely painful, for two reasons. The first was that the Democratic House demanded far more of a tax increase on corporations than the Republican Senate would accept. The second was that changes in the economic forecasts subsequent to the passage of both bills (including lower inflation), plus timing differences (the House bill was written to take effect on January 1, 1986, though that was obviously not feasible for a conference meeting in August 1986), plus fine tuning of estimating methods meant that both bills were now seen as revenue short. The reestimating continued, causing much anguish, even as the two chairmen were closing what they thought was a final deal.

The time for the Labor Day recess had come, and the chairmen responded to the new revenue totals with further painful revenue raisers. Then they called the full conference into session in private. Both sides balked, some hitherto supportive members expressed forceful opposition, and there appeared a serious risk that the process would break down. Some members had already left town, and others were sure to follow soon; both chairmen threatened to adjourn the conference for the holiday amidst a general fear that the inevitable intense lobbying pressure would make a subsequent agreement impossible. In this dramatic atmosphere, the chairmen, assisted by Bradley, found a formulation that provided the House with the middle-class relief it demanded without offending the majority of the Senate. The conference met in public session and signed a report late on Saturday, August 16, 1986.

Conclusion

The passage of tax reform required the most incredible confluence of circumstances – almost like an alignment of the planets. The bill could not have passed without Ronald Reagan winning over reluctant members of his own party; but Ronald Reagan almost certainly would not have taken the initiative without a firm shove from Bill Bradley. And the whole issue was motivated by its intense and broad impact on the public, and the ability to pose a vastly superior alternative to what was in place. Perhaps policy must really deteriorate before we can make fundamental advances.

It is not obvious that the Tax Reform Act of 1986 could be duplicated in other policy areas. Perhaps the most encouraging sign is that Congress voted for the bill despite the misinformation among the public. Whether the members believed that their constituents would soon learn of the bill's true impact, or whether the members were taking a political risk, is unclear. But either way, at least one dramatic step in economic policy has been taken; one economic idea, however old and shopworn, has spread into policy.

PART IV

Funding the spread of economic ideas

CHAPTER 14

Doing good and spreading the gospel (economic)

CRAUFURD D. GOODWIN

Economists (excluding those who are writing in this volume) like to think that the spread of their ideas proceeds ultimately according to some perfectly competitive model or Darwinian principle with "truth" like efficiency and fitness being the criterion for survival and success. They think people throughout society, just as the economists themselves, pick up and use economic theory that has been successfully tested and employ only analytical tools that have demonstrable utility. Similarly, they believe, society will reject falsified theory and unfruitful tools. The process of the filiation of economic ideas outside the discipline may be more complex than this.

Various groups in society outside the economics discipline use economics for specific tasks which are their responsibility: government officials to formulate and implement public policy; businesspeople to operate private enterprises efficiently in pursuit of various goals; and the media to interpret events for the public. But there is another, more amorphous, segment of society which makes use of economic ideas as well, and in several ways provides for their spread throughout the community. This segment resides in the private sector but is distinct from the various special interests such as firms, unions, and profitseeking individuals. It is the obverse of private interests; its sole declared objective is to safeguard the public interest, and the complexity of its existence is witnessed by the customary use of negatives rather than positives to describe its function: the units in this sector are "nonpartisan," "not-for-profit," and, customarily, "nontaxed." What makes this sector so important in American society is that it has come to control substantial wealth originating in firms, individuals, and governments. Under the designations philanthropy, endowment, trust, charity, or most generally "foundation," this segment of society is able both to subsidize and to propagate directly ideas and forms of inquiry that it approves and to discourage those it deplores. In addition, because of the decline in the authority of the church, government, and other sources of moral guidance within society, foundations and those who spend foundation money, such as "think tanks," assume an important role as dispensers of ethical precept. When society today looks for guidance on many large issues of public policy with important implications for efficiency or income distribution, it looks not to a priest or philosopher as it might have done in the past. It looks instead to the Brookings Institution (note how often the adjective "prestigious" is attached thereto) or to the National Research Council, both operating probably with support from the Ford, Rockefeller, or some other foundation. Similarly, when the intellectual elite in our society are annointed it is not with a knighthood or bishopric but with a grant from MacArthur, Guggenheim, or Nobel.

This last point is important because it suggests that the disciplines gain not just money from foundations but also reputability with the larger community and dignity within the institutions where they are employed. If the foundations in their wisdom give you grants, your right to be heard is much increased and your claim on support and encouragement from others in society, as well as from your colleagues, is vastly strengthened. One of the reasons for the prevailing gloom and insecurity in the humanities in recent years has been their general lack of success in gaining support from the private foundations.

Another way to view the relationship of the foundations to scholarly disciplines is as "patrons" in the old sense. Just as over time the purchase of a painting by the Medicis or Nelson Rockefeller has greatly enriched the artist both in treasure and repute, the "purchase" of economics or applied biology by foundations affects the income and the status of this field of inquiry. The other principal patrons of economics have been higher education, government, and corporations, with each dispensing wealth and approval for different reasons.

The relationship of economics to the philanthropic sector is, I believe, very important for both. Here I approach the question of how this linkage has evolved and attempt to reach some generalizations about it through reference mainly to the history over the past forty years of the largest American philanthropy, The Ford Foundation, where I was for some time employed and whose records I have been examining recently for another project.

My thesis, roughly stated, is that by the 1950s economics had acquired a highly privileged position with American foundations, which saw the new burgeoning social sciences as likely to provide the answers to many of society's looming problems. And because so many problems had economic roots, economics gained a special priority.

Consequently, the foundations came to be among the most powerful vectors for the spread of economic ideas – directly themselves, indirectly through the provision of funds to others, and very indirectly by placing their Good Housekeeping Seal on the work of economists. But over the years the foundations' ardor toward economics has substantially cooled. A marriage that seemed made in heaven has ended in some places at least in a trial separation or divorce. To my knowledge, with only one exception (headed by an economist), none of the major foundations today has a program aimed at assisting the discipline as such, and expressions of skepticism from foundation officers about the utility of the subject have become commonplace.

Why has the love turned sour? Is economics on its way to join the humanities in genteel poverty? (Is biotechnology perhaps set to pass the social sciences on the way up as the social sciences go down?) What can we learn from this experience that is relevant for our attempt to understand the spread of economic ideas more generally?

I identify below in a very preliminary way certain characteristics of the evolving economist-foundation relationship over the past forty years which help to explain the growing disillusionment of this important patron. Whether comparable tensions were growing in relations with the other patrons I cannot say.

The rise of foundations

Capital sums whose income is dedicated exclusively to some good works are not, of course, a recent phenomenon. Organizations to administer charity operated in ancient Egypt, Greece, and Rome. Dwight Macdonald, a historian of the Ford Foundation, reminds us that in the eighteenth century a citizen of Bath left fifty pounds to a church "on condition of their ringing on the whole peal of bells, with clappers muffled, various solemn and doleful changes . . . on the 14th of May in every year, being the anniversary of my wedding day; and also on every anniversary of the day of my decease, to ring a grand bob major[1] and merry mirthful peals unmuffled . . . in joyful commemoration of my happy release from domestic tyranny and wretchedness." Early thinkers who reflected on the creation of charitable institutions were often dubious about what they could become and their effects. Francis Bacon worried about "the painted sepulchres of alms, which soon will putrefy and corrupt inwardly." Adam Smith from his expe-

---

[1]"Grand bob major" is the name of a sequence of ringing bells, rung in the Church of England for especially joyful celebrations.

rience at well-endowed Oxford University could see how the transfer of a service like education from the marketplace to the philanthropic sector could have a deleterious effect on the performance of the suppliers.

Until the twentieth century, philanthropic endowments were established mainly on behalf of churches, schools, colleges, asylums, museums, libraries, and the like. Within the last century, however, philanthropists of various kinds have set out to harness science to the solution of the problems of mankind, first to find cures for ignorance and disease, and to discover better food crops, and then to take on more demanding tasks like bringing an end to overpopulation or human conflict. The attitude toward the social sciences within foundations before World War II was generally that the first task was to assist them to gain maturity as fields of inquiry. This was roughly the goal of the Laura Spelman Rockefeller Memorial, directed by the businessman-scholar Beardsley Ruml. The experience of the 1940s served to confirm by and large the conclusion that the social sciences, and especially economics, had reached the point where they would be directly beneficial to mankind. World War II demonstrated the usefulness of trained social scientists in market planning, price control, intelligence, human motivation studies, propaganda, and a variety of other areas. At the end of the war in 1945, economists were credited with helping to avoid the return of economic depression and with constructing a new international economic order, while political scientists became involved with the fledgling United Nations and with the challenge of creating new and independent societies out of colonies. Sociologists and psychologists were concerned increasingly with public policy toward crime, urban growth, family life, and a host of other areas.

The arrival on the national scene in 1949 of the Ford Foundation as the largest philanthropy thus far in history, by far, coincided with a mounting sense in various parts of the American elite that the social sciences had many more worlds to conquer and lacked only resources to effect the conquests.

One of the first studies of what areas the new Ford Foundation should support, commissioned from a management consultant by the foundation trustees in 1947 in anticipation of their impending new cornucopia of wealth, put the case as follows:

Rapid technological progress and development of mass production methods have, during the last forty years, at the same time produced unbelievable increases in our physical standard of living, and created a series of difficult problems of human relations – social, political, and economic. . . . It would seem fitting indeed if the Ford Foundation should give primary emphasis to encouraging and advancing the same scientific attack on problems of human relations which produced such spectacular advances in natural science.[2]

It has been suggested that the fact that Henry Ford II changed his major from engineering to sociology while an undergraduate at Yale is reflected also in this advice; but this is a mere canard.

Because the assets transmitted to the Ford Foundation by the Ford family were in nontraded, nonvoting Ford Motor Company stock, their total value cannot be given precisely. But most estimates placed it at several billions of dollars by the mid-1950s. Henry Ford selected as persons to lead the institution not professional social scientists, by and large, but rather men who had come to have high respect and great hope for what these new disciplines might achieve. The most prominent of the leaders was Paul Hoffman, the first president, former head of the Studebaker Corporation and of the Marshall Plan, and a member of the Committee for Economic Development, a businessmen's group with enlightened views about how to approach national problems. Another was H. Rowan Gaither, Jr., the second president, lawyer, and chairman of a special trustee study committee created to chart the Foundation's course over the early years.

The love affair between Ford and the social sciences began in these early days and has lasted (on and off) ever since. But it has been, at times, a rocky road. And it reveals, I believe, some of the obstacles to the sustained patronage of economics by foundations and thereby to the spread of economic ideas generally through society. I suggest in the following sections some of the difficulties along the path which have brought this foundation and this discipline into disagreement or even conflict.

Charity and self-interest

The first source of tension between foundations and economists arises out of the fundamentally contradictory mindsets of the two. An historian of foundations writes: "The adjectives philanthropic, eleemosynary, charitable, and benevolent are commonly used to describe certain activities which have as their aim the improving or uplifting of mankind."[3] In sharp contrast, the entire theoretical structure of economic science is based on self-directed rather than other-directed

---

[2]"A Scientific Attack on the Human Problems of an Industrial Society," attachment to Wyman Fiske, "Ford Foundation: Report and Recommendations on Policies and Programs," n.d., pp. 1–2. Ford Foundation Archives, Report 010621.
[3]Marion Fremont-Smith, *Foundations and Government: State and Federal Law Supervision* (New York: Russell Sage, 1965), p. 11.

activity. A young economist is taught at mother's (or mentor's) knee
that every important action is aimed at increasing one's own pleasure
and avoiding pain. Moreover, those who cloak their actions in appeals
to such goals as "uplifting mankind" are probably doing so for a self-
ish, ulterior, "rent-seeking" purpose. Moreover, society might fall
apart if it were not so. Indeed, the most celebrated fable in the history
of economics describes a "grumbling" beehive into which virtue and
the philanthropic instinct are introduced in place of the "vice" of self-
interest. When the firm moorings of self-interest are lost the hive effectively disintegrates. Bernard de Mandeville therefore concludes:

> So vice is beneficial found,
> When it's by justice lopt and bound;
> Nay, where the people would be great,
> As necessary to the state
> As Hunger is to make 'em eat.[4]

Practicing economists are seldom so indelicate as to doubt the desir-
ability of philanthropy (and of foundations) publicly, and especially
when it is directed toward themselves; but foundation officers who
deal with economists regularly soon detect a mixture of quizzical won-
derment or even contempt for the philanthropic process. A question
they sense in an economist's demeanor is: "What are you guys *really*
up to?" A reaction from some economists, when presented with the
notion of public welfare as the desideratum, is: "O.K., we'll play along
nominally if you let us do what we wanted to anyway." Philanthropy
has a very small place in economists' models or textbooks, and to
economists employment in the philanthropic sector has low prestige
(with the consequence that few foundation officers are economists).
This is not to suggest that economists and philanthropists are naturally
at each other's throats, but rather that at a minimum they are uneasy
with each other.

The nature of human welfare

Both economists and foundation staff and trustees find it necessary
from time to time to reflect on their professional values and on their
sense of what constitutes an ideal community. Economists trained in
mainstream doctrine present as their goals free choice and the efficient
use of resources. They treat various social and political objectives as

[4]Bernard de Mandeville, *The Fable of the Bees; or, Private Vices, Public Benefits* (London: Wishart and Co., a 1934 reprint of the work originally printed 1705–29).

someone else's business. They see a capitalistic economy achieving the economist's objectives, in the main, impersonally through the workings of interdependent markets. The economic system may fail to reach an optimum set of results as a consequence of improper distribution of income (in terms of some externally determined social values), monopoly, externalities, and macroeconomic instability. Indeed, attention to these four phenomena forms the rather limited public policy agenda for most economists and the focus for the subspecialty of welfare economics.

So how about foundations? The official "aim" of the Ford Foundation is "to advance human welfare." Accordingly, when the Foundation trustees were faced with the prospect of enormous new assets they went back to first principles. The study committee charged with the task of charting the path ahead entitled its first chapter "Human Welfare." A comparison of that chapter with the views of economists is instructive.

What is most striking about the Foundation's statement is its prescriptive character. Absent is the economist's notion of giving people a "fair" distribution of resources in an efficient market economy and then allowing them to establish their own hierarchy of wants. Instead, wants in the Foundation document are spelled out lexicographically. Presumably this list was established by the committee during the extensive empirical investigation which preceded the report in 1950, including 250,000 miles of travel and conversations with 1,000 experts. The highest priority is attached to "security." "Fundamental to any consideration of human welfare is human survival. All efforts to prolong life, to eradicate disease, to prevent malnutrition and famine, to remove the causes of violent accidents, and, above all, to prevent war, are efforts to forward the welfare of man."[5] Next is listed "improvement of physical standards of living." In the same fashion as some of the classical economists, the committee speaks of a natural hierarchy of wants: "Not until the physical requirements of life and good health are well met may men progress toward the fullest realization of their mental, emotional, and spiritual capacities."[6] The report lists as further prerequisites of advancing welfare "human dignity, personal freedom and rights, political freedom and rights, social responsibility and the duty of service. . . . These democratic ideals represent for the Committee a particularly significant expression of human wel-

---

[5] *Report of the Study for the Ford Foundation on Policy and Program* (Detroit: Ford Foundation, 1949).
[6] Ibid., p. 17.

164   Craufurd D. Goodwin

fare since they emphasize man's most crucial problems – the intricate relationships among human beings and social organizations, now so heavily marked by tension and disorder."[7]

It is clear at this point that the study committee is setting up a political and social agenda rather than an economic one. The problems of human welfare with which it is concerned are seen as prior to the issues of utility maximization that typically trouble economists. "While our ultimate concern is with the individual, it is clear that only in society can his full development take place. Modern man cannot forsake society in search of freedom; freedom, for him, exists only within and by means of the social order."[8] Causation is from the political and social to the economic, rather than vice versa. Democracy, not want-satisfaction, is the key to human progress and welfare. "When the democratic spirit is deep and strong in a society it animates every phase of living: economic, social, and political relations among groups and nations, as well as personal relations among men."[9] As a clarion call the Committee proposed "affirmative action toward the elimination of the basic causes of war, the advancement of democracy on a broad front, and the strengthening of its institutions and processes." The Foundation must not be "content to concern itself only with man's obvious physical needs; it seeks rather to help man to achieve his entire well-being – to satisfy his mental, emotional, and spiritual needs as well as his physical wants. It addresses itself to the whole man and to the well-being of all mankind."[10]

The significance of these general philosophical statements for our purposes is that they consign economics to a secondary or derivative role. The ultimate goal of foundation policy will not be simply increased want-satisfaction for its own sake (the economist's notion of improvement in human welfare). Economic improvement will be a means to other ends. For example, at one point it is made clear that growth in per capita income is important not for its own sake but because it eliminates one cause of war. "Half the people of the world are either starving or lack adequate food, and illness and disease are widespread. Such conditions produce unrest and social instability, and these, when aggravated by ignorance and misinformation, produce a climate conducive to conflict." Similarly, a sound economy is to be valued particularly as a prerequisite to political stability at home. "When morale is high, when men are free, when life is enriched, when

[7]Ibid., p. 19.
[8]Ibid., p. 19.
[9]Ibid., p. 20.
[10]Ibid., pp. 21 and 22.

self-government operates well, when production flourishes, when there is a pervasive sense of individual dignity and of national unity – only then is democracy internally strong and well armed."[11]

With this as a background and both the economy and economic science identified as instruments for the achievement of higher goals, the committee identified

three principal contemporary economic problems: first, the need to achieve increased economic 'stability', both at home and abroad, with a satisfactorily high output and the highest possible level of constructive employment; second, the need to discover the determinants of industrial peace in order to reduce the individual and social losses involved in labor–management strife; and third, the need, now acute with large-scale concentration of economic power, for determining a proper balance between freedom for the individual firm or industry and government planning and control of economic activity. In addition, the problems of conserving our natural resources, of achieving practical equality of economic opportunity for the individual, and of raising the level of economic understanding among the citizens of the nation, have been considered worthy of special note.[12]

The relative simplicity of an economist's goal and the relative complexity of a philanthropist's suggest a clear reason for the disillusionment of one with the other which would soon arise.

Modern methodenstreit

Just as there have been differences of opinion between economist and philanthropist about the purpose of economic inquiry and the goals held dear by each side, so there have been disagreements over method. Typically, foundation trustees and staff are close to the hurly-burly of affairs, both in their other careers and in their foundation lives where they travel widely and immerse themselves in the details of the social problems which they become so concerned to solve. As a consequence of this human condition, as well as their training which may well have been in law, public administration, or business management, they are programmed to think in terms of particulars. They are uncomfortable with abstractions, and especially those which depend on assumptions which they perceive from their own experience to be unrealistic. Milton Friedman's celebrated dictum that the realism of assumptions doesn't matter so long as predictions hold, has never played well outside the profession, and it has played especially badly in foundations. For a start, the rationality postulate seems to run in the face of much

[11]Ibid., pp. 26 and 28.
[12]Ibid., pp. 33 and 34.

everyday experience. Whereas on the one side foundation trustees and program staff accept optimistically the claim that social and economic theory can be crucially helpful to them in finding solutions to human problems, their own instinct is to plunge into an examination of the intricacies of these problems and trust sophisticated common sense in prescribing solutions.

Objections to the methodology of economics are presented as early as the study committee report in 1949. The failure of economists to concern themselves with facts and to really test their hypotheses by confrontation with evidence is noted and deplored. "In many instances theories which are highly plausible or which conveniently serve the interests of particular groups have had long acceptance without adequate efforts to verify them in real-life situations." The committee found even the use of simplifying assumptions in economics to be fraught with danger. "Dominant 'schools' of economic thought have from time to time constructed overall 'systems' through the use of convenient but unrealistic abstractions, such as 'other things being equal' or the fiction of the 'economic man,' and these systems have subsequently been adopted uncritically and consequently misapplied by economists and the lay public."[13] The study committee found hope for an improvement in the method of economics in "the recent growth of a practice of economics. Economists are now heavily relied upon by business, labor, and various branches of government and are represented at high policy levels by such bodies as the Council of Economic Advisers to the President. The increasing use of economists in practice should help bring together the development of theory and the solution of specific problems." The committee also found hope for the greater use of economics in the growth of economic statistics and "the studies and activities of voluntary groups and committees which have recently been organized in increasingly effective forms."[14] The Foundation over the next three decades did much to support the moves that it found salutary in economic science; it funded reforms of business schools and schools of public administration to feature applied economics, and it assisted empirically based institutes like the National Bureau of Economic Research and heavily empirical exercises like Wassily Leontief's input–output analysis. But, in general, the Foundation never gained full confidence that the economics profession as a whole had given up its "Ricardian vice."

[13]Ibid., pp. 71–2.
[14]Ibid., pp. 72–3.

Frustration with inaction

The modern economist's trained instinct is always to look and see if the invisible hand can be made to work. If the international trade deficit is frighteningly large or the number of persons on welfare distressingly great, the economist asks if these conditions are simply the result of market failures that can be corrected merely by reinvigorating the market. Is it really necessary, the economist wonders, to contemplate a tariff or a new welfare program? Cannot a free market, perhaps with changed rules, be instituted which will solve the problem once and for all rather than administer a palliative?

Foundation staff and trustees, especially those trained in law, business, or public administration, often find such a policy posture hopelessly utopian and, indeed, an impediment to constructive thought. Regardless of the merits of the case, the response "Let's see if the market will do it" is well calculated to raise foundation blood pressures to dangerous levels. There are probably at least three factors at work here. First, the training of foundation personnel frequently predisposes them to interventionist action. Second, the early Ford Foundation staff had extensive experience in the wartime and postwar government agencies where imaginative public policy seemed to have accomplished so much. And finally, the injunction to wait for the market to do it leaves open little opportunity for foundation programming upon which foundation careers depend. There is even the suspicion in foundations that economists play a conscious or unwitting blocking role for conservative forces in society who pursue their own self-interest under a cloak of public interest through appeals for laissez faire. The study committee asserted that much contemporary economic theory was an anachronism that could not be taken seriously in the modern world:

> Classical economic theory, for example, was developed long before the enormous expansion of government in economic life, before the technological developments which have led to increased concentration of economic control, and before organized labor acquired its important position in our economic structure. Yet such classical theory is still cited by certain groups in sweeping fashion as final authority for the particular economic policies they favor, even though the entire context of the questions now at issue differs radically from that existing when the theory was devised more than a century ago.[15]

It is striking how much these sentences resemble those of the leading German historical economists of the late nineteenth century in attacks

[15]Ibid., p. 72.

upon the Austrian Marginalists. But they represent much less the remnants of influence of this doctrinal position, filtered through American Institutionalism and pragmatism, than the natural predilections of persons in a position to "do something" and do it now. For those of restless vigor any doctrine which simply tells you that nothing can or should be done, except perhaps fiddle with the structure or the rules, is unacceptable. The study committee hoped that the answer to its unease about this aspect of economic science would lie in reform of the discipline. Later, Foundation trustees and staff, when they called for "action recommendations" and "policy agendas" at the end of program reports, were more inclined simply to reject or ignore this discipline that seemed to make a fetish out of saying "Nay."

Monodisciplinary myopia

Foundation officers and trustees are regularly importuned by representatives of particular academic disciplines that claim a monopoly on truth – some with great self-confidence, like economists and lawyers, and others more diffidently, like sociologists and historians. However, foundation staff are also constantly made aware of "problems" of human concern, like inflation or conflict, that on the face of it at least cry out for multidisciplinary attention. Consequently, a foundation finds it especially frustrating to be told by any discipline that "we don't deal with that question," "it is outside our sphere of interest," or "we don't work with that other discipline; we don't respect their research techniques or results." Comments from disciplines may not often be this direct or brutal. But they come close.

The study committee was pleased to note that a "sign of progress in economic thought is found in the growing recognition that man's economic behavior is only a part of his total behavior, and that it cannot be abstracted and studied in isolation. . . . Certain fields, such as psychology and sociology, and the new methods and approaches utilized in them, are now seen to apply to the conduct of economic research."[16] But as a prophesy of how the economics discipline would progress this statement was not deeply prescient.

Economics over the next three decades after the study committee report did extend its coverage to several policy fields of vital concern to the Foundation: population and economic development, to mention only two. But in other areas, such as national security studies and urban affairs, economists' contributions were disappointing. More-

[16]Ibid., p. 72.

over, in the creation of multidisciplinary centers, institutes, and programs, Foundation staff came to expect most problems from economics. In some cases economists simply wouldn't play, or play very long; in other cases they were a disruptive element characteristically exhibiting intolerance and arrogance toward their noneconomist brethren. During the 1970s even several subdisciplines in the field in which the Foundation had a longstanding interest, like economic development and institutionally based labor economics, came under attack for doctrinal heresy.

Frequently over the years, Foundation staff have felt highly ambivalent and frustrated about economics. Even the harshest critics feel a grudging respect for its accomplishments. Here, after all, is a social science that does seem to exhibit greater rigor than the others, and its achievement in some policy areas cannot be denied. In the early 1950s at least one optimistic Foundation consultant thought that economists themselves were beginning to see that they were overspecializing and withdrawing from contact with the general public and even from almost all the other disciplines. This consultant summarized his view of the history of the profession by ascribing to Adam Smith and Hume the belief that economics had a responsibility toward major political and social issues. Only beginning with the 1920s, the consultant decided, had economics defined itself as scientific study of a narrow aspect. He claimed to discern a trend toward broadening of the field and searching for interdisciplinary cooperation. But nowadays the feeling is that economics is seemingly inflexible and unwilling to approach its potential by addressing more of the interesting questions out there, and by cooperating with others where seemingly there can be mutual benefit.

Will it all make any difference?

In the early 1950s as preparation for implementation of the Trustee recommendations of a Program Area III, to be concerned with Economic Welfare, the Foundation engaged a consultant economist, Richard Bissell, to consider the matter in some depth. Bissell's reports, presented over several years before he left for government service, addressed the concerns of the Foundation as to how economic ideas could and should be diffused. Bissell's main message to the Foundation's officers and trustees is especially interesting because it epitomized the attitude that would be visible in foundation officials toward the discipline in years to come. As a respected member of the guild (Yale Ph.D., MIT faculty member), he presented as positive a picture

as was likely to be painted. But its color and style were not of the kind
that usually warm a foundation's heart. He emphasized that although
a scholarly discipline's objective was to seek truth and improve understanding, "It is clear that the Foundation is committed to doing what
it can to bring about changes in the real world. The problem is to find
the most appropriate and effective means of so doing."[17] It was *not*
clear that close ties with economics would pay off. He thought that
"fuller knowledge and deeper understanding of economic institutions
and processes" should not become for the Foundation ends in themselves, but simply "one means to influence the course of events in the
world." A cause of tension between the Foundation and the economics
discipline, he suggested, grew out of the Foundation's decision not to
accept "the conventional boundaries that divide up human knowledge
into separate fields" but instead to "start from observable phenomena
and discernable problems, in all their complexity, and organize activities around them." Bissell suggested that in fact the Foundation would
do the profession some real good by forcing it to think in these problematic terms.

Nevertheless, the Foundation had now to accept that economics was
locked into a set of disciplinary imperatives which inched it outward
on the frontiers of understanding, but probably not at a pace that
should be of much interest to the Foundation's "purposeful directed
operations" in the economic area, which he proposed should be: (1)
The nature and means of stimulating economic growth and development coupled with political stability; (2) the means of achieving and
maintaining a high level of output and avoiding inflation; (3) the con-
servation and development of basic resources – renewable and non-
renewable; (4) the international trading and payments position of the
United States; (5) the decentralization of initiative and decision making, both political and economic, in modern society; and (6) the
achievement of more satisfactory labor–management relations.

So where did this agenda leave economic science with respect to the
Foundation's program interests? First, to the extent that economists
themselves were willing to become involved, they could assist in
research which is purposeful and focused on a defined subject or problem. Second, some funds should be made available for "fundamental
investigation, . . . miscellaneous (undirected) proposals for research

---

[17]Richard M. Bissell, "Activities Designed to Advance Economic Well-Being," General
Correspondence, Area III, Ford Foundation Archives, April 3, 1952, p. 2. Bissell's ideas
are set forth in this paper and another, Richard M. Bissell, "Possible Activities of the
Ford Foundation Directed Towards strengthening the U.S. and World Economy,"
Ford Foundation Archives, Report 010598 n.d.

and intellectual inquiry," but it is not made entirely clear why these funds should be so allocated except as a sort of gratuity. In a letter to Foundation president Paul Hoffman, Bissell expressed his considered conclusion, after struggling with the question for some months, that even well-conceived economic research was not likely to bring the results that were the Foundation's raison d'etre.

It is tempting to believe that some useful research, pulling together of the facts, and skillful analysis of them, will move the world ahead. And there is a strong case to be made for supporting research in order to add to the sum of human knowledge. But this is *not* the way to influence action. If we are interested in action, then I am opposed to writing, financing, or having anything to do with any more reports unless and until I can see some chance that the reports will be acted upon.[18]

Finally, Bissell recommended that the Foundation explore the possibility of endorsing and diffusing economic knowledge that was accepted incontrovertibly by "intelligent and disinterested" economists of good will and high distinction. He confessed "the perhaps naive belief that among intelligent and truly disinterested people, agreement can be reached, without straddling, on many of the fundamental issues that are likely to be appropriate matters of concern to them." Even where public controversy surrounded a subject there was reason to believe that wise men, detached from their special interests, would arrive at a consensus: "The mere fact that there is genuine and valid disagreement on a public question does not necessarily indicate that a group of truly disinterested citizens could not reach agreement on it, even though they were thoroughly representative of different shades of opinion in the country. It is only when the members of such a group speak as the representatives of interested groups that the likelihood of general agreement on a number of major issues is reduced."[19] "Surely one of the functions that a private foundation can perform," he argued, "is to encourage, support, and lend the cloak of its prestige and authority to men who will, to the best of their ability, discern and proclaim the common interest, and support it in whatever ways they may." This diffusion role should be conducted with great care so as not to "take sides" in controversy over legislation, or simply add more to "the bookshelves and filing cabinets of the world . . . choked with unread reports and unadopted recommendations." Bissell seems to have envisioned diffusion of fundamental economic ideas at two lev-

---

[18]Memo to Paul Hoffman from Richard M. Bissell, Jr., February 15, 1952, Ford Foundation Archives, General Correspondence, Area III.
[19]Bissell, "Activities Designed to Advance Economic Well-Being," pp. 27 and 29.

els: among the governing elite, and among the mass of the people. In the latter case the implication is that a hard core of economic principles is a little like the Ten Commandments or rules for personal hygiene; no respectable person could possibly take issue with them. The persuasion which would be appropriate and legitimate for the Foundation to support would consist of the presentation of objectives, evidence, and disinterested conclusions; it would rely only upon the inherent reasonableness of the case, the honesty, intelligence, and disinterestedness of the individual by whom it was presented, and, perhaps, on the prestige attached to the views put forward. Tariff policy was suggested as one policy area where simple propagation of widely accepted notions was in order: "It is hard to see either the need to include intellectual inquiry among the activities to be supported or any possibility of refraining from taking sides in a controversy."[20] Clearly what was called for was public education, quite possibly on a large scale.

On the surface this attitude toward economics by a foundation advisor might be thought of as highly promising for the science. The discipline's conclusions on important issues of public policy were perceived as so important that they should be diffused vigorously among the populace not only to build up public opinion that would accept intelligent policies but also to give the men who were working for those policies at least enough political power so that doors would be opened to them and their arguments would be listened to and weighed. But the implications of Bissell's recommendations are complex. On the one hand he expressed little enthusiasm for foundation support of economic research of any kind because economists showed little inclination for the most promising problem-oriented and multidisciplinary approaches, while the potential payoff for policies from their discipline-directed research was not obvious. On the other hand, Bissell could see considerable benefit from the diffusion of economic principles presented as axioms or almost as self-evident truths. In his praise for economics in this latter sense Bissell is virtually at the same time denying its position as a vigorous advancing subject, identifying it instead, as John Stuart Mill had a hundred years before, as a subject virtually completed and closed to useful inquiry. Economics in the Bissell formulation is closer to religion than to science; and the Ford Foundation in its earliest deliberations determined to stay clear of religion!

[20]Ibid., p. 14.

Conclusions

So where does this leave us with respect to the relations between economics and one of its major actual and potential patrons, the charitable foundation, as they affect the spread of economic ideas? It may be complained at the outset that much of the evidence of relationships I have used is nearly four decades old and perhaps hopelessly obsolete. To this I can reply that my own personal experience of much more recent vintage supports the continuing force of the difficulties that are revealed.

It is significant to reaffirm, first of all, that foundations which identify social problems as their main concern are forced inevitably back on the social sciences for guidance and instruction. It may after awhile become a loveless marriage but a divorce is not really a possible path for foundations because there are few alternative partners available. What we see then is a condition where, even when disillusionment is greatest, some kind of contact and cooperation must be maintained.

From an examination of the early experience of the Ford Foundation down through its formative years I have suggested some of the sources of tension that have arisen between economics and philanthropy. These include different perspectives on philanthropic behavior, on the nature of human welfare, on methods of social scientific inquiry, on a proper policy posture, on multidisciplinary cooperation, and on policy impact.

The Ford Foundation did, in fact, during the 1950s, following a series of recommendations from a committee of the profession, establish a special program concerned with Economic Development and Administration which lasted until the 1970s. Even during this program's heyday, and certainly afterward, however, the tensions with the discipline discussed here were easily visible. It is not a purpose of this volume to reach policy conclusions. Our purpose is a respectable truth-seeking one. All the same I cannot refrain from suggesting that if these tensions of economics with one of its most powerful patrons and their origins were understood better the spread of economic ideas might be in all respects improved.

CHAPTER 15

Think tanks and the politics of ideas

JAMES A. SMITH

For eight years Ronald Reagan's presidency perplexed political commentators. From the outset his election was described as a revolution of ideas; at its conclusion it was still not altogether clear how deep or how sweeping the revolution was. It has been difficult for journalists and academic observers to describe and assess the play of ideas in American politics during the 1980s.

Reflecting early in the decade on the reasons for Ronald Reagan's sweeping 1980 electoral victory, one of the nation's veteran political observers, Theodore H. White, asked if his analysis during the months of campaigning and in the years before the election might have overlooked something. White wondered whether his reporting had somehow missed "the ferment of ideas within politics."[1] In the early 1980s, he was not alone in asking what role ideas had played in the conservative triumph. Richard Reeves looked back and saw the election as a momentous personal victory for Ronald Reagan. But he explained that while it had been a triumph of personality, it was "at least as much the triumph of conservative intellectuals." He described the growth of an "ideas industry" during the 1970s and gave it considerable credit for the Reagan success. Sidney Blumenthal also examined the conservative movement. He chronicled the rise of what he termed a "counter establishment" replete with conservative foundations, think tanks, and publishing operations. He argued that as the role of political parties has diminished, American politics has grown "more open to ideological appeals." In Ronald Reagan, he concluded, image and ideology were fused.[2]

---

[1]Theodore H. White, *America in Search of Itself* (New York: Harper and Row, 1982), p. 7.
[2]Richard Reeves, *The Reagan Detour* (New York: Simon and Schuster, 1985), p. 10, and Sidney Blumenthal, *The Rise of the Counter Establishment: From Conservative Ideology to Political Power* (New York: Times Books, 1986), p. 11.

Conservative activists and intellectuals were quick to celebrate their victory as a triumph of ideas. No doubt they were trying to temper the views of those who claimed that it had been only Reagan's personal charm and Jimmy Carter's lackluster appeal that accounted for the huge win. Conservatives preferred that the election be seen as a repudiation of liberalism and an endorsement of a set of conservative political ideas with programmatic consequences. The phrase they used time and again – "ideas have consequences" – seemed to be a simple truism. In fact, it echoed the title of a book by Richard Weaver, literary scholar and social critic, that had been popular in conservative circles for nearly forty years. But Weaver's book, a passionate argument for philosophical idealism, was not about electoral results and political programs. It did not explain how a body of ideas, convictions directly descended from the conservatism that had been so soundly repudiated in the 1964 election, had been able to win over a majority of American voters in 1980.

Many observers found at least a partial answer in the array of conservative research organizations and think tanks that had been established or had attained new prominence during the 1970s. In the three months between the election and inauguration, a number of staff members in these organizations were very visible, working on transition teams and jockeying for political appointments. A handful were appointed to high-level positions and several dozen more accepted second- and third-tier positions in the administration. Conservative think tanks also issued weighty volumes outlining broad policy positions or devising detailed blueprints for policy management; the Heritage Foundation's *Mandate for Leadership* was the most noteworthy of the publications, earning a brief ranking on the bestseller list in Washington.[3] In the first years of the "Reagan Revolution" there was considerable, often self-serving, talk among the various research institutions on the right about which ones deserved the most credit for the long-sought conservative intellectual triumph.

Disappointed liberals also looked at the conservative think tanks, hoping to draw useful lessons from their tactics and operations. In 1981 a group of Democratic activists and former office holders, sensing that the battle they had lost was indeed an intellectual one, organized their own progressive-minded think tank, the Center for National Policy (originally the Center for Democratic Policy). It is only one of the many dozens of new organizations to spring up in Washington in the 1980s with the mission of fostering talk and writing about new ideas.

[3] *Mandate for Leadership: Policy Management in a Conservative Administration* (Washington, D.C.: The Heritage Foundation, 1980).

The Center's president, Kirk O'Donnell, is convinced that national politics is now more "idea-driven" than "interest-driven," largely because regional and class differences have diminished as sources of political tension and conflict.[4] In Washington, the proliferation of research centers and advocacy organizations, well-attuned to both the press, which amplifies their messages, and to philanthropic foundations and the popular constituencies, which supply their funds, certainly helps to make it seem that ideas have become a more important political currency.

There are other widely recognized signs that a self-conscious politics of ideas has taken shape in the United States. The Reagan administration and its supporters continued to talk about fundamental values and to invoke metaphors of a "battle of ideas" and of a competition in the "marketplace of ideas." In other quarters, opponents of the administration struggled self-consciously to define a new "public philosophy" or to revive the liberal tradition. Gary Hart's 1984 campaign and his erratic effort in 1988 leaned heavily on the theme of "new ideas." He and other presidential candidates have either founded their own small centers and institutes or moved discreetly into the orbits of older research organizations. In the recent contests to confirm Supreme Court nominees or in debates about U.S. policy in Central America, the controversies have assumed, at least by traditional American standards, an unusually sharp ideological edge. Political advertising, direct mail fundraising technologies, and the point and counterpoint of Op-Ed page articles or television news programs reinforce the sense both that ideas matter and that our political debates in the 1980s became more divisive and fractious because of deep-rooted intellectual differences.

The politics of ideas, whether "ideas" are defined as discrete programmatic initiatives or as the larger framework of political beliefs and values, raises a number of questions about the way our political debates are conducted and about a set of characteristically American institutions – private, nonprofit, policy research centers.[5] If there is a

---

[4]Kirk O'Donnell, interview, June 2, 1987.
[5]Japan has gone further than other democracies in creating think tanks based on the American model. Until the 1960s there had been little organized private involvement in Japanese policymaking. By the early 1970s, however, there were over 70 Japanese think tanks, although in Japan computer software and consulting firms were often included in the tally of think tanks. Most of Japan's think tanks have a close corporate affiliation, and ties with universities are not as strong as in the United States. The Japan Center for International Exchange has kept track of think tanks and, more generally, Japanese philanthropy. See also the chapter on Japan by Hiroshi Peter Kamura in *International Relations Research: Emerging Trends outside the United States, 1981–82* (New York: The Rockefeller Foundation, 1982).

new politics of ideas in the United States, these organizations are certainly the primary participants in it. Their role over the years offers some perspective on the politics of ideas. Why has this nation spawned so many independent centers devoted to policy research and advocacy? What part do they play in public policymaking? What do they tell us about the politics of ideas and the shape and structure of our public discourse?

American think tanks

In the United States the phrase "think tank" is the imprecise and generic term we have coined to describe the many and diverse research centers and institutes dotting our political and academic landscapes. The term, a relatively recent colloquialism dating only from the 1950s, is used quite loosely. It is expansive enough to embrace endowed research institutes, contract research organizations, foundation-funded research enterprises, university-based centers, consulting firms, proprietary research laboratories, government research bureaus, and ad hoc public or private commissions. Their tasks can range from basic to applied research in all sorts of fields and from the most cloistered scholarly work to very public and political tasks of advocacy and policy activism. "Think tank" is an appropriately amorphous phrase to describe the various arrangements that this nation of institutional inventors and experimenters has devised over the course of the twentieth century to bring technical expertise, informed insight, and political judgment to bear on public matters.

More often than not, however, "think tank" is used to refer to a cluster of well-known organizations (and the less well-known aspiring to join their ranks) whose research staff members produce books, reports, and articles about public policy issues. The Brookings Institution, the American Enterprise Institute, the Urban Institute, and the Rand Corporation are, by anyone's definition, think tanks. If a broadly inclusive definition of think tank is used, there are upward of 1,000 private nonprofit research institutes concerned with public policy questions in the United States, most of them being university-based. My own informal survey of Washington's intellectual terrain reveals over 100 situated in the District of Columbia and environs.[6]

[6]It is exceedingly difficult to arrive at a precise estimate of the number of American think tanks. At the outset a listing would require a widely agreed-upon definition of "think tank" or of "public policy research center." Where are the lines to be drawn between public policy research and more general social science research? What boundary should be established between research and advocacy or research and public education? The estimate of more than a thousand is based on my scrutiny of the *Gale Research Centers*

These organizations are relatively small as institutions go in the late twentieth century. Even the largest ones in Washington – the Brookings Institution, the Urban Institute, the Heritage Foundation, the Center for Strategic and International Studies, the American Enterprise Institute – have only between 100 and 200 employees. Their annual budgets range between $9 and $14 million and only Brookings has a significant endowment. The Rand Corporation in Santa Monica, whose visibility in the 1950s and early 1960s brought the phrase "think tank" into our vocabulary, dwarfs the Washington-based organizations with its 1,000-member staff and $75 million budget, some $20 million of which is now devoted to domestic policy research and evaluation.

Far more numerous are research centers with budgets measured in six figures and staffs of ten or twenty people. Having little or no endowment income and seldom attracting long-term commitments from foundations, virtually all of these organizations, large and small, are on a financial treadmill. CSIS must raise over 90 percent of its income on an annual basis. AEI, after a relatively brief episode of administrative turmoil, saw its budget and staff shrink by 40 percent in a two-year period. And even the venerable Brookings has experienced occasional financial shortfalls in recent years.

American think tanks seem particularly small and fragile when compared to government research organizations and to the ranks of social scientists and policy researchers employed in government agencies or on legislative committee staffs. The Congressional Budget Office has a staff of about 200; the Congressional Research Service staff approaches 900; House and Senate committee staff number more than 3,000; and most cabinet-level departments have assistant secretaries heading up professional research and evaluation units, to cite only the most prominent places in government where public employees examine policy issues and provide information to decisionmakers.[7] Private policy

Directory (Detroit: Gale Research Company, 1984–5), ninth edition and supplement. My definition is much more expansive than that of the editors of the directory. During the course of my research, I have assembled a list of approximately 100 research centers in Washington.

[7]On the growth and role of Congressional staffs see: Michael Malbin, *Unelected Representatives* (New York: Basic, 1980), and Harrison W. Fox and Susan Webb Hammond, *Congressional Staffs: The Invisible Force in American Lawmaking* (New York: Free Press, 1977). According to Fox and Hammond, even though staffs have grown considerably, "Most offices do very little original research, relying on data from a wide range of sources" (p. 92). They examined the sources of information used by Congressional staffs: "The data confirm much of the previous evidence on information sources: heavy reliance on departmental personnel, a good deal of help from the congressional support agencies, and fairly close relationships with various interest groups" (p. 122).

On two of the federal government's analytic agencies see: Frederic C. Mosher, *A Tale* research institutions simply cannot compete with CBO, OMB, CRS, or other government agencies in supplying day-to-day data and information. It is ironic that over the past eighty years one of the greatest accomplishments of private research institutions, especially Russell Sage, the National Bureau of Economic Research, and Brookings, has been to encourage government to develop its own research and analytic capacities, thus rendering the private, outsider's role more problematic. Policy research institutions have been able to survive largely because they have been highly adaptable in the face of government's growing capacities for research and analysis.

But the question remains why are there so many of them in this country? What is it about American political culture and the structure of our political institutions that leaves us with so many private research organizations operating on the peripheries of public policy-making? The answer can tell us much about the structures through which policy ideas circulate, since the American political system seems to have all sorts of gaps and interstices in which research (or research cum advocacy) organizations can survive.

The Constitution created one of the most important gaps by establishing separate executive and legislative branches and setting in motion the perpetual struggle between the two. Over the years, policy research institutions have been able to supply data, analysis, technical help, and political argument because of interbranch rivalries. Some were actually established at moments when interbranch competition was keenest. The inspiration for the Brookings Institution came in the 1910s at a time when the federal executive seemed especially weak in relation to Congress. AEI was founded in the 1940s when Congress and conservative supporters outside were trying to redress an imbalance in its powers against a vastly expanded executive bureaucracy. Heritage was set up in the 1970s primarily to assist an ideologically conservative congressional faction in its battles against the Republican Party's then moderate legislative leadership and an Executive Branch that seemed unsympathetic to the conservatism of the hard right. Over the years, the increasingly fragmented committee and subcommittee structure of Congress as well as a balkanized bureaucracy have also offered openings in which outside research organizations can define a function for themselves.

---

of Two Agencies: A Comparative Analysis of the General Accounting Office and the Office of Management and Budget (Baton Rouge, Louisiana: Louisiana State University Press, 1984). On the role of policy analysts, in general, see: Arnold J. Meltsner, Policy Analysts in the Bureaucracy (Berkeley and Los Angeles: University of California Press, 1976).

The nature of our traditions of civil service and political appointments has also allowed private institutions to survive. The American civil service system first emerged in the 1880s after several decades of concern about a corrupt, spoils-ridden political process. The solution was not to create a permanent administrative class on the Continental or British model but to establish a relatively open and porous system in which "good" people could be appointed when administrations changed. There was considerable reluctance to build a cadre of policy experts within the Executive Branch. This long-standing distrust of bureaucrats, the deeply ingrained suspicion (or at least an ambivalence) toward experts in a democratic society, the absence of permanent departmental undersecretaries, and the large numbers of political appointees all help to explain why private repositories of expertise exist outside, but not far, from government. These organizations function in a political environment where the boundaries between public and private sector are less sharply defined than in other nations and where bureaucratic and legislative processes are more open to outside influences.

Over the years, policy research institutions have emerged on the peripheries and in the gaps of our formally organized political structures. They have arisen when administrations had no policy in one area or another, but some people thought there should be a policy. Institutions were established at moments when the government possessed little expertise on a subject, but some experts thought that knowledge could be organized and brought to bear on policy. Some were created when there was no formal mechanism for considering policy in a particular area. Others have been created when a group of people disagreed with a particular policy. They have been founded when a new problem called for research or when an existing policy needed monitoring and evaluation. They have been set up to help bureaucrats or Members of Congress when bureaucratic structures or partisan differences seemed too rigid to permit planning to take place or new initiatives to emerge. As a group, policy research institutes testify to the American proclivity, noted by Tocqueville and often remarked upon, to form new associations whenever novel circumstances demand.

These organizations embody our multifarious and shifting ideas about government in general and about policies in particular. And in a political system where parties have tended to function more as electoral coalitions than as focal points for ideological controversy or coherent policy planning and thinking (American political parties, unlike European and Japanese parties, have not had very significant research operations), policy research institutions have played an important role in building and sustaining policy consensus.

With the growth of the federal government's capacities for research and analysis and the proliferation of executive and legislative staff, policy research institutions have seen their roles change. In the 1910s, 1920s, and even into the 1930s, their staff members would be called on to draft legislation or serve in some temporary capacity on a government commission or in a federal agency. Since World War II, federal contracting arrangements have given birth to a number of new organizations, Rand and the Urban Institute among the more noteworthy, allowing policymakers to contract for technical and expert assistance. By and large, however, researchers in private institutions are now more often outsiders, summoned inside on occasion, but much more likely to act as critical observers and commentators on public issues (or when working on contract to serve as evaluators of policies and programs) than to be direct participants in policy formulation. It has become much more difficult to generalize about their role and influence.

As Herbert Stein, now in residence at AEI, recalled of his days in government service, "I never found that writings from outside organizations had any effect at all on policy. When it came time to act, we were well ahead of outside researchers. We had better and more timely data."[8] His views are endorsed by many others who have gone back and forth between government and private research institutes. Private research organizations, concludes Stein, deal almost exclusively with the broad climate of opinion among the well-informed and politically engaged.

The transfer of ideas from centers and institutes outside the governmental arena and the circulation of ideas within the policymaking process will frustrate any scholar who depends on the written word and precise intellectual formulations to chronicle the movement of ideas. A House commission found that in a typical eleven-hour day the average congressman devoted only eleven minutes to reading. Books and reports are seldom read; memos and action papers are quickly perused. Asking whether anyone in Washington has time to think, one observer concluded: "Some of the most thoughtful public officials admit that they have no time to develop new ideas but say they are working off intellectual capital built before coming into government."[9]

[8] Herbert Stein, interview, March 10, 1986.
[9] Bruce Adams, "The Limitations of Muddling Through: Does Anyone in Washington Really Think Anymore?", *Public Administration Review* (November–December 1979), pp. 545–2. The figure from the Obey Commission is cited by Adams.

Staff members on a congressional committee or in an assistant secretary's office may read the reports that emanate from private organizations, but it is the rare senior official who has time to ponder the latest book from Brookings or a report from the Urban Institute. And it is even rarer when a specific report or study, even in the summary form of memos and briefings or encapsulated in journalistic coverage, can be given credit for inspiring a particular decision. The forces at work in the policy process are far more complex. Even if their origins can be traced (and intellectual historians and political theorists have learned the difficulty of tracing ideas to their source), ideas interact with political events and contingent circumstances. Any claims about an idea's origins or consequences are problematic.

The research and publishing programs and the many conferences, seminars, and educational activities of the nation's think tanks suggest that ideas do, in various ways, emanate from these institutions. These institutions can and do serve as conduits bringing ideas from scholars and researchers into wider circulation, especially if "idea" is defined broadly. An "idea" might be anything from data collected about a government program (an evaluation revealing the deficiencies of a manpower training program) to some untried policy scheme (Individual Retirement Accounts or the Strategic Defense Initiative) to a broad theoretical perspective (strategic vulnerability or the opportunity theory of juvenile delinquency) that might begin to shape more specific policy approaches.

The channels policy research organizations have been able to open to policymakers and the public are numerous and varied. The ideas may, through briefings and private communications, circulate within the oral culture of Washington policymakers and their staffs. The articles and reports issuing from think tanks may, at times, be encountered when digested as Op-Ed page articles or summarized in the popular media. Books and reports may be read by experts or a knowledgeable public and over time a shared perspective and consensus may evolve. The politics of ideas is played out on many levels, its tools are varied, and its cycles often bear little relationship to the rhythms of the political process or to the formal analytic schema that try to explain the diffusion of an idea.

Frameworks of public discourse

In recent years, a politics of ideas has been contested in a way that concerns, at its core, the very meaning of "idea" and the basic purpose of public discourse in a democracy. The politics of ideas is about the ways in which we try to understand our society and economy and about the kinds of knowledge we will bring to our public debates. To understand the deeper dimensions of this politics of ideas it is worth recalling the circumstances that surrounded the origins of the nation's oldest policy research institutions.

In the mid-1860s the now familiar social science disciplines had not yet emerged distinctly from the older studies of history and political philosophy. In the United States there were no graduate and professional schools training people for research work or supplying the kinds of professional skills that would be demanded in a more complex urban and industrial society. Means of communication, whether they be the journals, associations, and conferences of professional groups or the mass circulation magazines and newspapers that inform and shape popular opinion, were limited and few. The research foundation and general purpose philanthropic trust were still unknown as mechanisms for funding research. And perhaps most importantly there was no coherent conception of the state and its duties. Localism, particularism, and a deeply ingrained individualism restricted the scope of public policymaking; and the moral and intellectual justifications of laissez-faire were as yet largely unchallenged.

The feeling that the nation was both saved and reborn after the Civil War kindled the hope that science might become an instrument of social and economic change. In 1865, only six months after Appomatox, nearly a hundred people – abolitionists whose battles were only recently won, doctors and public health reformers, charity workers, feminists, educators, and writers – gathered in Boston intent upon discussing "those numerous matters of statistical and philanthropic interest which are included under the general head 'Social Science.'" The members of the American Social Science Association, as the group came to call itself, were confident that science and its methods held the answers to the social and economic problems they saw around them and that social remedies would be within easy reach of their investigations. To those at the Boston meeting, social science and social reform were virtually synonymous.[10]

The reformers' science in the two decades following the Civil War did not go very far in exploring social processes, nor did it seek pat-

---

[10]On the origins of the A.S.S.A. see: Thomas Haskell, *The Emergence of Professional Social Science: The American Social Science Association and the Nineteenth Century Crisis of Authority* (Urbana: University of Illinois Press, 1977). The founding documents from which the quotations are taken were published in *Constitution, Address List of Members of the American Association for the Promotion of Science* (Boston: Wright and Potter, 1866).

terns and laws of social behavior. The social science that emerged in that era – in large measure a repudiation of the social Darwinism of Herbert Spencer and his American disciples – was a science that sought the facts about institutions and organizational life. It examined the conditions in asylums, prisons, and orphanages; it observed the practices of relief administrators, police officials, and charity workers. Social science was less concerned with investigative methods, which were rooted in simple Baconian ideas about organizing and collecting data, than with practical solutions, which were more often than not straightforward changes of institutional routine and bureaucratic habit.

Presentation and discussion of the facts were at the core of their notion of scientific practice. The A.S.S.A. members declared that their basic aim was "to bring together the various societies and individuals now interested in these objects [social reform], for the purpose of obtaining by discussion the real elements of Truth; by which doubts are removed, conflicting opinions harmonized, and a common ground afforded for treating wisely the great social problems of the day." They boldly asserted that they would "collect all facts, diffuse all knowledge, and stimulate all inquiry which have a bearing on social welfare." From our vantage point in the late twentieth century it is tempting to dismiss the naïveté of an organization like the A.S.S.A. But the amateur social scientists of the A.S.S.A. spurred the improvement of research methods, initiated the publication of journals, and spawned more specialized conferences and professional associations, including both the American Historical Association and the American Economics Association.[11]

Perhaps most significantly, the A.S.S.A. helped to reinforce in American social science, particularly in those fields most intimately concerned with social welfare issues, a strong commitment to the gathering of facts as well as a general hostility toward abstractions and theoretical discussion. For a time, it provided an institutional framework for those European-trained Americans who had heard the lectures of economists and sociologists of the German historical school and who had witnessed the role of the German professoriat's *Verein für Sozialpolitik* in the building of the Bismarckian welfare state.

The link between social reformers and the younger social scientists

---

[11]On the origins of the A.E.A. and A.H.A. see: A. W. Coats, "The First Two Decades of the American Economics Association," *American Economics Review*, 50 (September 1960), pp. 555–72, and Arthur S. Link, "The American Historical Association, 1884–1984: Retrospect and Prospect," *American Historical Review*, 90 (February 1985), pp. 1–17.

was strong at the turn of the century. It is this bond that helped shape and sustain the pragmatic, progressive tenor of social inquiry and political discourse. And it is this style which has been so typical of the American politics of ideas. Fact gathering leading to concrete proposals for reform, the repudiation of abstractions as either fixed principles justifying the status quo or as sources of ideological divisiveness, the belief that the facts properly aired and discussed would dissolve differences of opinion, ideology, and interest – all have been fundamental to the pragmatic tradition of research and public discourse. Those beliefs, shared by charity workers and professional social workers, philanthropists and progressive businessmen, and professionals in law, engineering, and social science, helped shape the first generation of public policy research institutions founded in the two decades following the turn of the century.

The Russell Sage Foundation, in many respects the prototype for all policy research organizations, the Institute for Government Research, the National Bureau of Economic Research, and the Twentieth Century Fund shared certain pragmatic assumptions, yet each owed its origins to different business and professional groups. Russell Sage (founded in 1907) throughout its first forty years remained the preserve of charity organizations and social workers; the Institute for Government Research (founded in 1916 and a forerunner of Brookings) was a creature of scientific managers and their counterparts in public administration concerned with government efficiency; the Twentieth Century Fund (founded in 1919) was E. A. Filene's contribution to the cooperative and scientific management movement; the National Bureau of Economic Research (founded in 1920) emerged largely through the efforts of Wesley Mitchell and others schooled in the traditions of institutional economics.

All were diligent fact-finding organizations and sought to use fact-finding processes as a mechanism for reconciling divergent beliefs and interests. Ideas were indeed plans for action, but they emerged only in the aftermath of fact-finding and discussion. The commitment to the facts echoes in charters, minutes of board discussions, prefaces to published works, and the organization of research programs. The pursuit of facts in the 1910s and 1920s is attested to in the social survey movement to which Russell Sage was so passionately attached, in Brookings' 60-odd monographs on the structure and administrative practices of federal agencies, and in the work on business cycles and national income accounts of N.B.E.R.

The founders of N.B.E.R. were explicit about their aims: "We believe that social programs of whatever sort should rest whenever possible on objective knowledge of fact and not on subjective impressions. By putting this faith into practice we are making a contribution to the working methods of intelligent democracy."[12] The investigation of facts would allow people of divergent views and interests (and from the beginning N.B.E.R.'s board members were selected for the diversity of their views) to reconcile their differences and work toward a common understanding of social and economic problems.

The labors of those social workers, institutional economists, and scholars of public administration seem today quaintly unscientific and naïve. Nevertheless, their devotion to fact gathering and to piecemeal reform and their aversion to ideological dispute have done much to shape our expectations of the social sciences and the expert's potential contribution to public well-being.

However, their approach did not pass unchallenged. Robert Lynd was among the more sympathetic critics of social scientists and their contributions to policy in the 1930s and 1940s. He contended that the atomism of the disciplines and the mindless accretion of factual knowledge so narrowed the focus on what could be known that knowing it became irrelevant.[13] It left the social sciences without a critical attitude toward existing practices and institutional structures. There were other, more severe critics whose voices also began to be heard at the end of World War II. Friedrich A. Hayek's *Individualism and Economic Order* and *The Road to Serfdom* attacked rationalism as an instrument to comprehend and manipulate society. Richard Weaver's *Ideas Have Consequences* is an even more penetrating attack on social science, positivism, and the pragmatic ways of understanding society and politics. Those who work in the conservative research and advocacy institutions have taken Weaver and his views about the role of ideas in politics seriously.[14]

From their inception, the conservative think tanks have challenged the pragmatic understanding of the role of ideas in the political process. They understand the operations of the intellectual marketplace differently, in part because they felt their wares had been excluded from that marketplace. Political journals, publishing houses, and research institutions began to be built in the 1940s and 1950s. The

[12]"A Bold Experiment," quoted in Lucy Sprague Mitchell, *Two Lives: The Story of Wesley Clair Mitchell and Myself* (New York: Simon and Schuster, 1953), pp. 355–6.
[13]Robert Lynd, *Knowledge for What?: The Place of Social Science in American Culture* (Princeton: Princeton University Press, 1939).
[14]F. A. Hayek, *The Road to Serfdom* (Chicago: University of Chicago Press, 1944), and *Individualism and Economic Order* (Chicago: University of Chicago Press, 1948); Richard Weaver, *Ideas Have Consequences* (Chicago: University of Chicago Press, 1948), pp. 12, 58, and 1.

dominant metaphor was one of intellectual combat and of an intellectual remnant fighting to preserve Western values.

William Baroody, Sr., who deserves most of the credit for turning AEI (founded in 1943) into a well-respected research organization in the 1960s and 1970s, often spoke of AEI as a combatant in the battle of ideas. He wanted to make AEI a credible voice for conservative views and to redress what he saw as an imbalance in the competition of ideas. Liberals had held the field too long, in his view. Baroody proved immensely successful in building a conservative research organization (though his son and successor proved less adept at maintaining it). AEI's intellectual credibility was heightened by Baroody's eagerness to seek out spokesmen for liberal views in order to sharpen the lines of political debate. But AEI did not pretend to be an organization representing all points of view; it engaged in serious research, but it knew what ideas and institutions it wanted to defend and strengthen. It saw other institutions as opponents in the war of ideas.

Some of the newer conservative and libertarian organizations seem to have pushed much farther in the advocacy of specific ideas and in viewing politics as intellectual salesmanship and combat. "We don't make any bones about packaging and marketing," says Burton Y. Pines, the Heritage Foundation's vice president for research. And Edwin J. Feulner, Jr., the president of Heritage, describes Washington think tanks in general as "second-hand dealers in ideas," contending that "it takes an institution to help popularize and propagandize an idea – to market an idea." He likens the process to keeping a brand name toothpaste before the consumer.[15] And the staff of Heritage, for the most part, bears more resemblance to the youthful staffs of public interest groups or campaign organizations than to the staffs of AEI and the more established research institutes.

Founded in 1973 by Feulner and Paul Weyrich, both of whom had served as staff members to conservative congressmen who were disgruntled and out of step with their own Republican leadership, Heritage came into full national view only after the 1980 election, with the publication of *Mandate for Leadership,* a project conceived nearly a year before the election. It was less a research project seeking to refine and articulate conservative policy positions than a self-described "'game plan' for implementing conservative policy goals under vigorous White House leadership."[16] Its release was orchestrated mas-

---

[15]Burton Y. Pines, interview, November 4, 1985, and Edwin J. Feulner, interview, December 17, 1985.
[16]Heritage Foundation Files, memorandum on "Mandate for Leadership: Policy Management in a Conservative Administration," June 1980.

terfully; and the Heritage Foundation itself became the subject of newspaper articles and editorial comment, reaping considerable institutional dividends as it came to be seen by many observers in the early 1980s as the most vigorous and aggressive of Washington's think tanks. Its staff eagerly described Heritage as a "new breed" of organization and at times seemed to relish the descriptive label "advocacy tank." Much of Heritage's considerable success is undoubtedly due to the election of a conservative president in 1980, but no small part of its ascendance has been the result of its very skillful and professional understanding of how information and ideas are used in Washington. Feulner and his colleagues understand both how the media operate and how congressional staff members and political executives must use ideas in their particular political contexts. They know that timing, brevity, and simplicity can be fundamental to the successful marketing of policy ideas and to winning political arguments.

The Heritage Foundation and those who imitate it have posed a considerable challenge to other Washington research organizations. At Brookings, the lament of one staff member is telling: "We are not good at getting attention. We feel the pressure to have Op-Ed pieces, to be on MacNeil-Lehrer, to be visible, even though none of these things have anything to do with what we do well – research. We now need to appear to be a player even though we have been a player all along."[17]

Since 1981, Brookings has had a public affairs department, though the resources devoted to it are miniscule compared to the efforts of Heritage, which, like a number of other conservative foundations, devotes roughly one-third of its budget to marketing. At Brookings and the older research organizations, shorter reports addressing more topical concerns are now published more regularly. More attention is being paid to the marketing of books and to using newspapers and broadcast organizations as avenues for bringing their policy ideas before the public. The Op-Ed page has become something of a battleground for research organizations; it is a handy indicator of the public visibility of an institution's research staff. The Hoover Institution points to well over 200 Op-Ed pieces published each year; Heritage, AEI, and, in recent years, Brookings now cite almost as many Op-Ed pieces and columns. Even smaller institutions will produce their monthly or quarterly digests of press clippings as evidence of their ability to influence public opinion.

Reflecting on the changes of the past decade, Bruce McLaury, the president of Brookings, concedes that his institution has felt a chal-

---

[17]Neil Cullen, interview, March 11, 1986.

lenge from the newer research institutes and admits that Brookings will never be as good a mass communicator as some of its rivals. He argues, however, that that is not its role. "We are targetting leaders," he says. He adds, "If one is specifically trying to mobilize ideas in a battle, that would be unthinkable for us. I bow at the altar of competition, but it is a perversion to mobilize it on one side of the spectrum. Ideas ought to be sold on their merits."[18] Nevertheless, the rhetoric of battle and salesmanship seems contagious, even though books remain Brookings' stock in trade and its principal medium of public influence.

Books have a more enduring influence in the political arena as part of the intellectual capital that the public servant brings to office or as a means of shaping the climate of elite opinion in which policy is made. Yet, it is sobering to contemplate the sales level of books on public policy topics. If policymakers have little time to read, the educated public, it seems, is no more likely to pick up a serious book on a contemporary policy concern. Sales of 10,000 copies of any book published by a policy research institution will certify it as a bestseller and, in most cases, it takes several years, at least, to reach that level; sales of one or two thousand copies are more likely. Where institutions have kept statistics, roughly half their books are sold as texts for college courses.

Books seldom work quickly to change the consciousness of a problem or alter perspectives on policy. The exceptions, such books as Michael Harrington's *Other America* or Rachel Carson's *Silent Spring,* are exceptional indeed. Ideas from social scientists and policy researchers are more likely to trickle gradually into the consciousness of the public and public officials or to be grasped when historical circumstances demand a novel response. Nevertheless, some policy research organizations do try to focus on more immediate lines of influence. They have turned to shorter reports, briefing papers (in some cases press briefings), and journalistic articles. Edwin Feulner explains that the work of Heritage must pass the "briefcase test"; that is, it must be thin enough to go into a policymaker's briefcase and short enough to be read in a limousine on the way to a hearing. It must get into the hands of the right people at precisely the right time.

All of this has given rise to a glutted and fast-moving marketplace of policy books and reports where many policy research institutions vie for the policymaker's ear and the media's eye. They expend considerable resources doing so. In recent years the largest two dozen policy research institutions have issued annually a total of about 250

[18]Bruce McLaury, interview, March 11, 1986.

books and over 1,000 reports, briefing papers, conference proceedings, and lectures. The totals point not only to the competition but to the fact that the pace of policymaking has changed. There is more on the public agenda – more bills and more committee and subcommittee hearings. Bigger staffs seem to generate more policy initiatives. There are more numerous and better-organized constituencies clamoring for particular policies. Some of the newer policy research organizations have relied more heavily on direct mail fund-raising techniques which require them to find ways of making their programs more compelling to a popular constituency. All of these things seem to put a premium on the topicality of research, the brevity of analysis, and the speed with which research reports can provide plausible answers, timely arguments, and evidence about immediate problems. Inevitably there are dangers in that marketplace of ideas: Perspective on public concerns can be foreshortened, public debate can become shallower, firm conviction and argument can drive out sustained analysis, and ambiguity and complexity can be lost.

Policy research institutions along the entire political spectrum have become much more conscious of the competitive environment they now inhabit. The competition for foundation grants, research contracts, Op-Ed space, and book sales, to name only the tangible objectives, is obvious. But those are only the most superficial manifestations of this nation's current politics of ideas. To be preoccupied with the marketing techniques of policy research organizations is to misunderstand an important dimension of the intellectual combat.

Pragmatists and idealists

The politics of ideas is much deeper and more important than competition among research organizations in promoting books and reports, in claiming credit for shaping opinion on particular policy issues, or in seeking funds from philanthropic foundations and corporations. At issue are two very different traditions of discourse, with implications for the way we organize social, political, and economic research and conduct our public debate. The rudimentary science of the fact, which emerged in the late nineteenth century, provided the point of departure for an empirical social science and the tradition of pragmatic political discussion that underlies the research and publication programs of many of the long-established policy research organizations. It is a tradition that tends to minimize disagreement over political values, and at times seems to ignore underlying values if not wish them away altogether.

The decades of the 1960s and 1970s eroded much of our faith in reasoned discourse and especially in what the social sciences could deliver to public debates. Too much was promised too quickly and too little was understood about intractable social problems. Science and reason seemed to falter and our tradition of pragmatic political discourse was thrown into question as well. It was challenged by partisans on both the left and right extremes of the political spectrum.

In the 1980s, however, the pragmatic tradition has been confronted more effectively and with more intellectual rigor from the right. The pragmatic tradition is now juxtaposed to an idealistic tradition that argues explicitly for the primacy of ideas and values. Many of the newer conservative institutions argue that "ideas have consequences." In doing so they consciously echo the title of Richard Weaver's 1948 book. It is more than a slogan to conservative thinkers and policy analysts. Weaver argued that Western society had gone astray, not with World War I, the Russian Revolution, or the New Deal, but in the fourteenth century, when nominalist philosophers came to conceive of ideas as mere words, mere logical categories, rather than transcendent truths. Weaver contended that the rejection of transcendent truths in the late Middle Ages led to a new approach to nature, to a search for knowledge of the particular rather than the universal, to an empirical science, and ultimately to an obsession with isolated fact instead of truth. "The whole tendency of modern thought, one might say its whole moral impulse," he contended, "is to keep the individual busy with endless induction." "The supposition that facts will speak for themselves," he concluded, "is of course another abdication of intellect." For Weaver, man had become "a moral idiot" obsessed not with truth but with a specious knowledge of the world.

To assert that ideas have consequences or that values have consequences is not to say merely that ideas have political consequences when they are shrewdly packaged to move an electorate or that they can alter the balance in a congressional debate. To a number of people, including Ronald Reagan, this assertion means that permanent truths, transcending human experience, must guide our political life. They reject the pragmatism that had seen the moral and political world as a realm of contingencies, change, and adaptation. Since the 1970s more and more institutions, on both the right and left, have placed an explicit set of ideas or values at the core of their research and publication programs. Ideas and assumptions are posited, but they are set outside the arena of reasoned discourse; they are truths that have been divinely ordained or derived as the permanent lessons of history and experience. The institutions are usually explicit about these truths, perhaps even more honest about the faith they defend than the research institutions whose pragmatic social science unconsciously and uncritically accepts a value system, or at least poses little challenge to prevailing views and values.

In the 1980s, these two conceptions of "idea" and of the role of ideas in politics have been poised in confrontation. This struggle between pragmatists and idealists has deep historic roots for it is about the way we organize our understanding of the world as well as our public conversation. To the extent that American think tanks have acted pragmatically, they have served to pull our debates toward the center, to narrow the range of policy discourse. They have, by and large, tended to temper and moderate public discussion and to search for compromise and consensus. In some respects, the idealistic conception of discourse and the institutions which ground their efforts in particular ideals and values have posed a vigorously healthy challenge to a century of pragmatic debate which has lost the capacity to discuss philosophical premises and fundamental values.

But what are the consequences of this conception of the role of ideas in public policymaking? Since the end of the nineteenth century the pragmatic tradition has extolled the role of the nonpartisan expert and tried to uphold the value of disinterested knowledge and dispassionate debate. Yet it often turns debate into a dialogue among experts who operate within narrower and narrower professional communities. Technical virtuosity and complexity create a gaping chasm between policy experts and the democratic citizenry. In contrast, the idealistic tradition is attentive to fundamental values and the moral implications of our policy choices. But it is susceptible to self-righteous fervor and certitude. It can foreclose open-minded discussion of contending values and moral contingencies. At times it has seemed that the idealist places a premium on forensic skills and argument, bearing a brief rather than engaging in a common inquiry. At the extremes, civil discourse gives way to the efforts to propagandize and convert; opponents are demonized and belittled.

The always fragile framework for discussing public concerns with civility and wisdom has been badly shaken during the past two decades. Public conversation has given way to fractious and sectarian disputatiousness. Consensus has been virtually impossible to arrive at or sustain, though the final years of the 1980s seem to hold out glimmerings of consensus in several areas of both domestic and foreign policy. An era of idealistic fervor seems ready to yield to one of pragmatic compromise. The American politics of ideas is grounded in this tension between two different conceptions of ideas and their place in our national life. The pragmatist is committed to the necessity of systematic social inquiry, to policymaking as a process of experiment, and to compromise and the search for agreement as the goal of political debate. The idealist begins with a set of values; policies and programs must reflect those values, and political discourse is a matter of exhortation and moral suasion. "Ideas" mean different things to pragmatists and idealists. And in the final analysis, the role of ideas in our political life cannot be understood without a grasp of the historical tension between these two contending intellectual traditions and their very different implications for our public discourse.

CHAPTER 16

The role of the NSF in the spread of economic ideas

DANIEL H. NEWLON

The National Science Foundation is a major arena in which economic ideas compete for funds. In fiscal year 1986 the Economics Program received 404 new proposals and funded 147. The total expenditure of the Economics Program was $11,292,000.

Proposals are processed as follows: Researchers prepare and submit proposals to the National Science Foundation. My two colleagues and I select six or more specialist reviews for each proposal. Twice a year pending proposals, with any written reviews received, are evaluated by a panel of fourteen distinguished economists. The panel makes recommendations. The staff uses the information in the written reviews and from the panel discussion and recommendations to make its own decisions, subject to approval of the Division Director and the Grants and Contracts Office. Funds are then given to the winning projects.

How does this way of proposal processing affect the generation and spread of economic ideas? One simple view of the connection between NSF and economic ideas has researchers thinking up new ideas and then submitting proposals to NSF. Those researchers whose projects are approved receive NSF funds and produce the ideas described in their proposals. Those who don't, choose other research topics or find other sources of support for their research.

Reality is more complicated than this. Let's begin with the preparation of proposals. Proposals usually describe research that is already underway because most work is incremental. Most successful economists develop broad lines of inquiry over a number of years and do not repeatedly shift from one new idea to another unrelated idea. Also, reviewers insist on detail. They want to know how the research will be

I would like to thank James Blackman, David Colander, Datiya Gunter, and James Slaugh for their assistance in preparing and revising this article. The views expressed in this paper are my own personal opinions and not National Science Foundation policy.

conducted. They want to evaluate the theory, the econometrics, and the data. Reviewers are usually unwilling to recommend funding for a vague proposal even if the investigator has been very productive in the past and the ideas are new and not yet clearly defined.

Since most research projects are already underway at time of submission and since it takes from four to six months from submission to grant for the typical proposal, it's possible that some research projects are completed before the grant is made. Researchers are at times misled by claims that NSF pays for already completed research. For example, I received an irate letter recently from an economist whose proposal was declined because the contemplated research had already been done. He claimed that reviewers were hypocritical for criticizing him, because "everyone knows" that NSF funds completed research. Another investigator submitted as a proposal only a brief introductory statement attached to his book. He ended his introduction with the statement, "I will now pause so you can read my book." This was not a very popular proposal format with reviewers.

In fact we have never knowingly funded work that was already finished. The successful proposal should have both the specifics that come from already starting the research or from related work and an interesting research plan of new ideas or worthwhile extensions of past work. The weight attached by reviewers to the detail and to the new ideas depends, in part, on the investigator. There is less insistence upon detailed research plans for someone with a brilliant record of significant research accomplishments than for an unproven scholar. But many reviewers feel, on principle, that everyone should write a detailed proposal, if he/she hopes to obtain NSF support. To paraphrase a statement I've heard many times from different members of the Economics Advisory Panel, "This person is very good, but he (or she) has to prepare an acceptable proposal just as I did."

But what of Gordon Tullock's suggestion (Chapter 18) that we make NSF a prize-awarding system as opposed to a new-research, or proposal-rewarding, system? Over the years NSF has moved toward awarding grants as prizes for past achievements. NSF now allows investigators to submit accomplishment-based renewals. The accomplishment-based renewal is no more than a four-page description of research plans with up to six appended papers completed under previous NSF grants. Reviewers are asked to concentrate on the investigator's accomplishments in evaluating the proposal.

Proposal processing is managed by the NSF staff. The NSF program director has been compared to a judge, an executive secretary of a committee, a journal editor, and even a czar. In reality the program director assumes at times each of these roles. The program officer manages the review process much as a judge manages a trial. Each proposal should receive a fair and accurate evaluation of its strengths and weaknesses. Investigators who feel they have not received fair treatment can appeal first to the program director and then to his or her superiors. The program director selects reviewers and provides feedback on proposals much as a journal editor handles articles submitted for publication.

NSF program officers could be viewed as czars when they do not follow reviewer advice. Occasionally the Economics Program staff will recommend that a proposal be funded in spite of reviewer criticisms and even a recommendation by the panel that the proposal be declined. The staff will also, infrequently, recommend that a project with very favorable reviews be declined. Researchers who have difficulty with the peer review process often want the NSF program officer to bypass peer review. But unlike the decisions of czars, program officers' recommendations need not be, and at times are not, followed by NSF. Staff recommendations that differ from reviewer advice must be especially persuasive or they won't be approved.

The program officer must strike a balance between independent judgment and reliance on the advice of others to fund consistently the best research. Program officers cannot be knowledgeable in every area of a broad field of research like economics, and they can be influenced by personal likes and dislikes, so a program director who frequently overrides reviewer advice risks making biased and wasteful decisions. But the program officer should not be solely the executive secretary of the advisory panel, recommending for funding only those projects approved by the panel, since committee decisionmaking is imperfect.

In the Economics Program the recommendations of the Economics Advisory Panel play the most important role of any aspect of the review process in determining what is or is not funded. Eighty-five to ninety percent of the time, staff decisions track panel recommendations. About five percent of the time the panel does not even reach a consensus. If there is a disagreement on the panel, the proposal is debated until it is sensed that the differences of opinion are clear and cannot be narrowed any further.

There have been many disparaging comments about the peer review process. I wish those who are critical of peer review could observe our panel meetings. The people who serve on the Economics Advisory Panels are extremely impressive. Their comments on the proposals are usually perceptive and well-reasoned. Panel members look for scientific rigor, imagination, and substantive significance in the proposals they evaluate. We rely heavily on our advisory panels because of the high quality and usefulness of the panel evaluation of proposals.

But the Economics Advisory Panel is a committee and does at times suffer from the deficiencies inherent in this method of evaluation. Occasionally panel recommendations reflect less the merits of the proposals discussed and more an especially forceful personality on the panel or compromises struck among panel members with differing views. Panel members also can place too much emphasis on technical details and not pay enough attention to the likely value of the proposed research. It is our job to discount these infrequent biases and distortions in the review process and make the best decision.

We also manage the peer review process in ways that make peer review especially responsive to new, and at times controversial, ideas. We tend to select young members for our advisory panels because older statesmen often are not as critical as their younger colleagues. The median age of past panels has hovered at about thirty-eight years with a minority of the panel in their mid-forties or older.

In selecting specialist reviewers for a controversial proposal, we choose those who will make the best case possible for the proposal, and then we rely on our advisory panel to provide balance. Sometimes researchers or investigators will send us the names of possible reviewers, and we try to use these or similar reviewers unless those suggested are close collaborators, relatives, or have some other conflict of interest. If the specialists' reviews are enthusiastic and the panel nevertheless recommends the proposal be declined, we can ask our boss, the Director of the Division of Social and Economic Science, to fund the project out of a special reserve that is at times used to support promising and controversial projects. If all of this fails and we think the project is worth supporting despite the controversy, then we will sometimes go ahead and recommend approval over the objection of the panel. We will not, however, repeatedly renew funding for a controversial line of research, if each time the project comes up for renewal the advisory panel is lukewarm or hostile to renewed funding.

Panel members usually serve two-year terms. New panel members are selected by the NSF staff based, in part, on the advice of departing panel members and, in part, on our own observations of potential panel members.

That's the process, but what are the results? Let me begin to answer this question with a challenge to those who remain critical of our peer review process: Give me the name or names of people the NSF's Economics Program should but probably did not support in the past thirty years. Where are the mistakes? Who are the economists that are now recognized for their contributions to economics, but who could not receive support for their research from NSF at the time they were doing the work for which they are noted?

Projects declined by NSF cannot be identified because of the confidentiality of the review process, but we can look at all the grants made from fiscal year 1958, the year NSF made its first grant to an economist, through fiscal year 1979 to see who did receive support. The eighties are not included because it is too early to tell whether research funded in the eighties will make a significant contribution and because the eighties were a period of severe budget cutbacks and from which NSF's Economics Program has only partially recovered.

It is not easy to identify mistakes, in part because so many economists received NSF support. From fiscal year 1958 to fiscal year 1979, over 650 different economists were principal investigators on at least one NSF-funded project, and an additional 250 economists were co-investigators. From 1965 to 1985 every one of the eleven John Bates Clark award winners, the economists selected once every two years by the American Economic Association as the best economist under 40 years of age, was an NSF grantee before winning this award. Eleven out of fourteen U.S. Nobel laureates in economics had NSF grants before winning the prize. The remaining Nobel prize winners never applied to NSF for grants, either because their research was supported from other sources or because they did not believe in federal government grants for research.

It is also difficult to find mistakes because of the broad range of different research ideas and types of economists supported by NSF. Tables 1a and 1b give some sense of the diversity of the exceptional NSF Economics Program grantees during the first 22 years of NSF support of economists. By exceptional grantee we mean the core of productive economists who repeatedly received NSF grants.

We used three criteria to identify exceptional grantees. First, the exceptional grantee received relatively large amounts (over $175,000) of support. Second, exceptional grantees received a large number (four or more) of different grants. Some of the "core" identified in this table received as many as fifteen different grants. Third, support for the core grantees spanned a relatively long period of time (five or more fiscal years from the first to last grants).

Moving from left to right across the top of Tables 1a and 1b, the first column describes the rank of the investigator as determined by the difference between the fiscal year for the first award and the fiscal year for

Table 1a. *Description of exceptional NSF economics program grantees 1958–79[a]*

Rank dif	Rank $	Prin investigator name	# grts	Awrd fy			Research emphasis
				1st	Lst	Dif	
79	1	Kurz Mordecai	13	69	79	10	conference, game theory, general equilibrium
2	2	Koopmans Tjalling C.	12	59	79	20	Cowles, dynamics
8	3	Klein Lawrence P.	11	61	78	17	large-scale models
57	4	Fromm Gary	13	66	77	11	large-scale models, conferences
13	5	Leontief Wassily W.	10	60	76	16	large-scale models (input–output)
1	6	Griliches Zvi	15	58	79	21	productivity
60	7	Juster F. Thomas	5	67	78	11	panel data
171	8	Brainard William C.	8	73	78	5	Cowles, large-scale models
34	9	McFadden Daniel L.	10	65	79	14	productivity, decisions under uncertainty
6	10	Ferber Robert	8	62	79	17	panel data
37	11	Zellner Arnold	7	63	77	14	Bayesian econometrics
172	12	Chow Gregory C.	6	72	77	5	engineering (control theory)
20	13	Baumol William J.	7	62	77	15	productivity
70	14	Samuelson Paul A.	7	68	79	11	dynamics
43	15	Radner Roy R.	10	65	78	13	decentralized choice
149	16	Feldstein Martin	8	73	79	6	public finance
10	17	Smith Vernon L.	11	62	79	17	experiments
4	18	Ando Albert K.	10	61	79	18	large-scale models
127	19	Hymans Saul H.	7	71	78	7	large-scale models
51	20	Taubman Paul J.	8	65	77	12	panel data
5	21	Nerlove Marc	8	61	79	18	time series
29	22	Debreu Gerard	11	64	78	14	general equilibrium
75	23	Goldberger Arthur S.	5	69	79	10	time series, panel data
25	24	Basmann Robert L.	8	64	78	14	demand
59	26	Holt Charles C.	5	64	75	11	productivity

23	27	Meltzer Allen H.	7	64	79	15	money, conference
7	28	Hurwicz Leonid	8	62	79	17	decentralized choice
33	29	Lucas Robert E. Jr.	9	64	78	14	rational expectations
67	30	Orcutt Guy H.	4	64	75	11	large-scale models
39	31	Eisner Robert	8	61	74	13	productivity (microsimulation)
177	32	Kadane Joseph B.	6	73	78	5	Bayesian econometrics
113	33	Theil Henri	7	69	77	8	demand
104	34	Kihlstrom Richard E.	8	70	78	8	decentralized choice
15	36	Mansfield Edwin	7	63	79	16	productivity
32	37	Jorgenson Dale W.	7	62	76	14	productivity
11	38	Arrow Kenneth J.	12	61	77	16	decentralized choice, dynamics
68	39	Reiter Stanley	8	68	79	11	decentralized choice
26	40	Brunner Karl	8	62	76	14	money, conference
36	41	Williamson Jeffrey G.	5	65	79	14	cliometrics
40	42	Fox Karl A.	5	62	75	13	index (measurement)
41	44	Phelps Edmund S.	6	66	79	13	rational expectations, public finance
14	45	Machlup Fritz	8	59	75	16	productivity
55	46	Fama Eugene F.	5	68	79	11	efficient markets
123	47	Fogel Robert	8	71	78	7	cliometrics
30	48	Diamond Peter A.	10	65	79	14	law
101	49	Hall Robert E.	8	71	79	8	productivity
161	51	Ross Stephen A.	7	73	79	6	decentralized choice
111	52	Solow Robert M.	6	68	76	8	dynamics, productivity
27	53	Buchanan James M.	7	64	78	14	public choice
46	55	Burmeister Edwin	6	67	79	12	dynamics
21	58	Harsanyi John C.	8	62	77	15	game theory
52	59	Telser Lester G.	7	64	76	12	dynamics, decentralized choice

[a]Exceptional investigators = number of grants >3, sum >$175,000, and difference >4 fiscal years.

Table 1b. *Description of exceptional NSF economics program grantees 1958–79[b]*

Rank dif	Rank $	Prin investigator name	# grts	Awrd fy			Research emphasis
				1st	Lst	Dif	
107	62	Morgenstern Oskar	4	60	68	8	time series
28	63	Chipman John S.	4	64	78	14	index, trade
35	64	Scarf Herbert E.	4	65	79	14	general equilibrium, game theory
66	65	Maddala G. S.	7	67	78	11	panel data
16	66	Morgan James N.	4	63	79	16	panel data
12	68	Jones Ronald W.	6	62	78	16	trade
181	69	Mincer Jacob	5	74	79	5	panel data
122	70	Fischer Stanley	7	71	78	7	rational expectations, money
126	71	Hickman Bert G.	4	67	74	7	large-scale models
121	73	Cyert Richard M.	6	72	79	7	Bayesian econometrics
146	75	Brock William A.	4	71	77	6	decentralized choice
134	76	Naylor Thomas H.	5	66	73	7	microsimulation
24	77	Tullock Gordon	7	63	78	15	public choice
87	79	Bhagwati Jagdish N.	5	70	79	9	trade
44	80	Williamson Oliver E.	9	64	77	13	productivity
64	81	Lindert Peter H.	8	68	79	11	cliometrics
62	83	Kendrick David A.	7	67	78	11	large-scale models, engineering (control)
49	87	Liu Ta-Chung	4	63	75	12	large-scale models
151	89	Gordon Robert J.	5	72	78	6	productivity
125	90	Green Jerry R.	5	72	79	7	game theory
90	91	Hester Donald D.	4	66	75	9	money
162	92	Shapley Lloyd S.	4	72	78	6	game theory
54	93	Engerman Stanley	6	67	78	11	cliometrics
19	95	Tolley George S.	5	63	79	16	location
97	97	Barro Robert J.	6	71	79	8	rational expectations

173	David Paul A.	4	73	78	5	cliometrics
83	Richter Marcel K.	6	68	78	10	general equilibrium
154	Leamer Edward E.	4	72	78	6	Bayesian econometrics
3	Zabel Edward	7	60	79	19	decentralized choice
31	Gallman Robert E.	6	65	79	14	cliometrics
48	Kuh Edwin	5	67	79	12	large-scale models
183	Plott Charles R.	4	73	78	5	experiments
53	Branson William H.	6	68	79	11	trade
88	Day Richard H.	5	64	73	9	engineering
77	Grossman Herschel I.	4	69	79	10	rational expectations
106	Mirman Leonard J.	4	71	79	8	game theory
164	Sonnenschein Hugo	5	71	77	6	general equilibrium
179	Majumdar Mukul K.	4	74	79	5	dynamics
132	Marschak J.	5	66	73	7	decentralized choice
115	Weil Roman L.	5	67	75	8	engineering
22	Lancaster Kelvin J.	5	63	78	15	demand
147	Brown Murray	5	65	71	6	productivity
137	Stern Robert M.	4	66	73	7	trade
112	Stein Jerome L.	5	68	76	8	money
128	Kamien Morton I.	5	67	74	7	productivity
144	Blinder Alan S.	4	73	79	6	productivity
18	Saving Thomas R.	4	63	79	16	money
100	Fisher Walter D.	4	63	71	8	productivity
105	Lovell Michael C.	4	62	70	8	inventory
38	Christ Carl F.	5	63	76	13	large-scale models, money

[b]Exceptional investigators = number of grants >3, sum >$175,000, and difference >4 fiscal years.

the last award. The second column is the rank based on the size of the sum of all grants received. The third column is the name of the principal investigator of the grants. The next columns are the total number of grants, the fiscal year of the first award, the fiscal year of the last award, and the difference between the two. The last column describes very briefly the type of research funded.

For example, Zvi Griliches obtained one of the first grants ever given by NSF to an economist, in fiscal year 1958, and a grant in fiscal year 1979. He received fifteen separate awards during this period. He ranks sixth in cumulative levels of support. The major emphasis of his NSF funded research is productivity.

Some very familiar names are not on the list. For example, Joseph Stiglitz received a series of grants starting in fiscal year 1975 and continuing to the present. He is not identified as part of the "core" because the period covered ends in fiscal year 1979 and we've defined an exceptional grantee as someone whose support spans five or more fiscal years. You can get some sense of the number of researchers excluded by this criterion if you examine the last entry in the table. Carl Christ is ranked 147 in cumulative support, but there are 102 names in the list. The missing names are of those who had substantial amounts of support but either did not have several grants or their grants did not cover a long enough period of time to meet the criteria of this table.

Some of the investigators received large amounts of support as principal investigators of grants that also provided support for many other researchers. Mordecai Kurz was supported as head of Stanford's annual summer program at the Institute for Mathematical Studies in the Social Sciences (IMSSS). Each of the IMSSS summer programs drew researchers to Stanford from all over the United States and the rest of the world for up to two months of seminars, workshops, and collaborative research on different topics in mathematical economics. Many of the distinguished mathematical economists at Stanford during this period were supported as co-principal investigators on this project.

The Economics Program funded the Cowles Foundation at Yale University during the sixties and seventies with large block grants. Tjalling Koopmans and then William Brainard were the principal investigators of these awards. You don't see in the table the names of many of the distinguished economists at Yale, such as James Tobin or Martin Shubik, because they obtained support from the Cowles block grants.

This table demonstrates that the process of peer review of unsolicited proposals resulted in support for extremely productive and distinguished scholars working on many of the most important economic ideas during this period. The diversity of topics shows that peer review does not necessarily result in support of only a narrow range of research topics or research methodologies. The presence of controversial lines of research on this list, such as Guy Orcutt's microsimulation, Robert Basmann's simultaneous equations, James Buchanan's public choice, or Robert Fogel's quantitative economic history, shows that peer review does not always lead to safe compromises. The numerous important accomplishments of these grantees show at the very least that NSF peer review recognizes genuine achievements and perhaps is responsible for a more rapid pace of research in economics than would have otherwise occurred.

The core of researchers supported in economics is not static. Over half of the people on this list no longer have active NSF awards. Some stopped submitting proposals because they had alternative sources of funds, shifted to other interests than research, or had their proposals declined. Others died. Most of these changes occurred after fiscal year 1979, due to the sharp reduction in NSF support for basic research in economics and, in part, to our effort to protect the younger economists from the brunt of the budget cuts.

To capture the dynamics of NSF support for different economic ideas, NSF grants can be grouped according to the themes of the core grantees in economics. For example, Lawrence Klein, Gary Fromm, and Wassily Leontief are core grantees for their research on large-scale models. Figures 1 and 2 describe the pattern of funding for large-scale macroeconomic models. In the early sixties major grants were made to Lawrence Klein, Albert Ando, Walter Isard, and James Tobin to develop large-scale quantitative models of different aspects of the U.S. economy. At times, over a quarter of the Economics Program's budget went to support the development of new models, the improvement of old models, and advances in the methodology of estimating, forecasting, and simulating with large-scale macroeconometric models. During the early seventies NSF supported several different large-scale macroeconometric models of the world economy. One was called Project LINK, a global model formed by linking a model of the U.S. economy with the most widely used national econometric models of our major trading partners. In the late seventies grants were made for better evaluations of the accuracy and scientific rigor of large-scale macroeconometric models.

Funding of large-scale macromodels peaked and then declined, first, as a relative share of the Economics Program budget, and then, toward the end of the seventies, in absolute amounts. If we had continued the

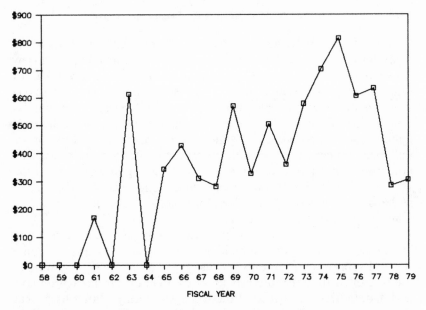

Figure 1   Large scale models and input–output (in thousands of dollars).

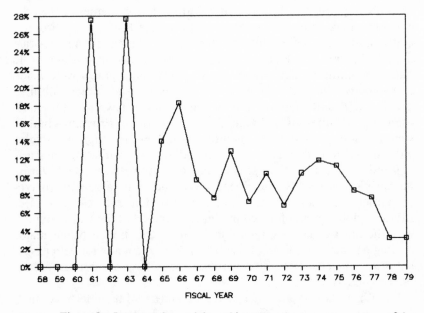

Figure 2   Large-scale models and input–output as a percentage of the Economics Program budget.

graph of expenditures into the eighties, it would have shown that funding for large-scale macroeconometric models disappeared except for an occasional grant. Funding stopped in part because large-scale macroeconometric models moved from basic to applied research. A substantial private industry of forecasters used, extended, and updated the national and international models to provide services to both the private and public sector. Government agencies developed their own forecasting models. Grants also stopped because the development of large-scale macroeconometric models was no longer competitive with other proposals for scientific research. Critics identified fundamental problems inherent with existing large-scale modeling techniques, and the efforts of many macroeconomists shifted to developing alternative ways of studying the U.S. economy that are not sensitive to these difficulties.

Table 2 and Figures 3 and 4 show the growth of funding for one of these alternative approaches, that is, the so-called rational expectations school. NSF started supporting most of the key contributors to this line of research, for example, Robert Lucas, Robert Barro, Herschel Grossman, Edward Prescott, and Edmund Phelps, while they were doing the work that would launch and define this new school of thought. Funding for rational expectations research rose rapidly in the late seventies as support for large-scale macromodels declined.

A major long-term objective of the Economics Program is to support the development of a new generation of large-scale macroeconometric models. These models will capture rigorously the underlying structure and interrelationships of entire economies in systems with many equations, and they will also incorporate the methodological advances in macroeconomics that have occurred in the last two decades.

These graphs and tables don't provide a comprehensive picture of NSF funding of macroeconomics. They leave out NSF support for monetarism in grants to Karl Brunner, Allen Meltzer, Anna Schwartz, Philip Cagan, and others; for the macrogrowth theory of Kenneth Arrow, Paul Samuelson, William Brock, David Cass, and many others; and for the macrofinance theory of Robert Shiller, Eugene Fama, Benjamin Friedman, Stanley Fisher, and others. But they do show that shifts in NSF funding reflected changes in economic ideas and that NSF supported large empirical projects even when that required using a substantial percentage of its budget.

There are other examples of NSF funding of new ideas in economics. Table 3 and Figure 5 show how support for laboratory experiments in economics started with a grant to Vernon Smith in 1962 long before experimental research became a widespread and significant line of eco-

Table 2. *Rational expectations awards from fiscal year 1958–79*

Fiscal year	Principal investigator	Co-principal investigators	Award $	Title
69	Grossman Herschel I.		$35,300	Market Disequilibrium in Macro-Economic Context
70	Lucas Robert E. Jr.	McGuire T. W. Rapping L. A.	$124,000	Theory of the Aggregate Supply of Labor and Output
71	Barro Robert J.		$30,000	Theory of Partial Adjustment and Expectations Mechanisms
72	Grossman Herschel I.		$29,600	Inflation, Employment, and the Theory of Markets
72	Lucas Robert E. Jr.		$63,200	Studies in Business Cycle Theory
73	Lucas Robert E. Jr.	Prescott E. C.	$89,000	Studies in Business Cycle Theory
74	Barro Robert J.		$3,100	Topics in Monetary Theory
75	Barro Robert J.		$47,400	Loan Market, Collateral, and Rates of Interest
75	Lucas Robert E. Jr.		$16,500	Collaborative Research on Business Cycle and Stabilization
75	Phelps Edmund S.		$81,400	Optimal Monetary Stabilization in Stochastic Equilibrium
76	Grossman Herschel I.		$66,700	Theory of Employment and Inflation
76	Prescott Edward C.		$24,600	Collaborative Research on Business Cycle and Stabilization
76	Lucas Robert E. Jr.		$51,300	Collaborative Research on Business Cycle and Stabilization
76	Barro Robert J.		$35,700	Economics of Loan Market, Collateral, and Rates of Interest
77	McCallum Bennett T.		$57,200	Rational Expectations, Price Rigidity, and Aggregate Income

Year	Name	Co-investigators	Title	Amount
77	Prescott Edward C.		Collaborative Research on Business Cycle and Stabilization	$28,600
77	Barro Robert J.		Money, Expectations, and Economic Activity	$94,700
77	Azariadis Costas		Optimum Economic Stabilization under Uncertainty	$47,700
77	Phelps Edmund S.		Stabilization Analysis under Rational Expectations	$88,900
77	Lucas Robert E. Jr.		Collaborative Research on Business Cycle and Stabilization	$51,600
78	Lucas Robert E. Jr.		Collaborative Research on Business Cycle and Stabilization	$57,594
78	Azariadis Costas		Optimum Economic Stabilization under Uncertainty	$47,647
78	Prescott Edward C.		Collaborative Research on Business Cycle and Stabilization	$36,600
78	Phelps Edmund S.	Taylor John B. Guillermo Calvo	Stabilization Analysis under Rational Expectations	$91,769
78	Wallace Neil		Theoretical Analysis of Alternative Exchange Rate Regulation	$69,300
79	Kidland Finn		Business Fluctuations and Stabilization Policy	$42,507
79	Polemarchakis Herak		Rationality, Observability and Indeterminacy	$9,272
79	Barro Robert J.		Money, Public Debt, Expectations, and Economic Activity	$41,679
79	Grossman Herschel I.		Employment Fluctuations and the Mitigation of Risk	$96,433

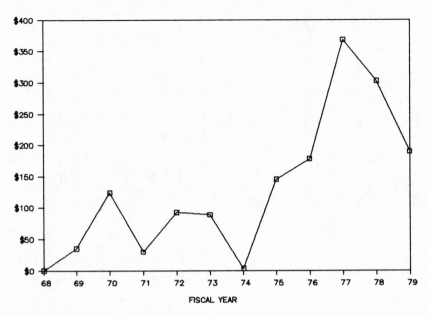

Figure 3   Rational expectations (in thousands of dollars).

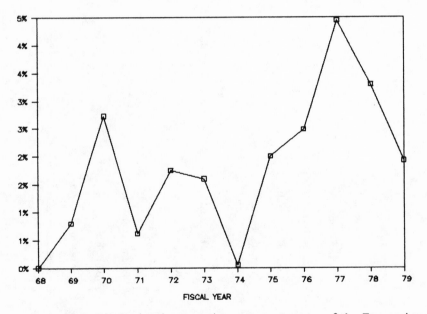

Figure 4   Rational expectations as a percentage of the Economics Program budget.

Table 3. Experimental economics awards from fiscal year 1 to 19

Fiscal year	Principal investigator	Co-principal investigators	Award $	Title
62	Smith Vernon L.		$39,500	Behavior in Competitive Markets
64	Smith Vernon L.	Starbuck W. H.	$63,800	Studies of Bargaining and Decision Behavior
69	Hoggatt A. C.		$65,300	Collaborative Research on Experimental Micro-Economic Games
70	Shubik Martin	Wolf G.	$62,300	Experimental Economic and Psychological Modeling
72	Shubik Martin	Wolf G.	$48,100	Experimental Economic and Psychological Modeling
72	Smith Vernon L.		$31,600	Explorations in Applied Economic Theory
72	Basmann Robert L.		$49,000	Interpretation Systems for Empirical Economic Theories
73	Blott Charles R.		$59,800	Political Economic Decision Processes
73	Basmann Rober	Battalio R. C. Kagel J. H.	$98,700	Interpretation Systems for Empirical Economic Theories
73	Smith Vernon L.		$32,300	Explorations in Applied Economic Theory
75	Smith Vernon L.		$40,300	Applied Economic Theory
75	Plott Charles R.	Fiorina Morris P.	$63,100	Experimental Examination of Group Decision Processes
76	Plott Charles R.	Fiorina Morris P.	$15,900	Experimental Examination of Group Decision Processes
76	Smith Vernon L.		$111,400	Explorations in Applied Economic Theory
78	Smith Vernon L.		$81,598	Explorations in Applied Economic Theory
78	Battalio Raymond	Kagel John H.	$52,958	Experimental Studies of Consumer Demand and Labor Supply
78	Plott Charles R.		$95,083	A Laboratory Experimental Investigation of Institutions
78	Smith Vernon L.		$153,259	Experimental Studies of Resource Allocation Mechanisms
79	Joyce Brian B.		$6,525	Experiments in Walrasian and Non-Walrasian Competition
79	Battalio Raymond	Kagel John H.	$38,087	Experimental Studies of Consumer Demand and Labor Supply

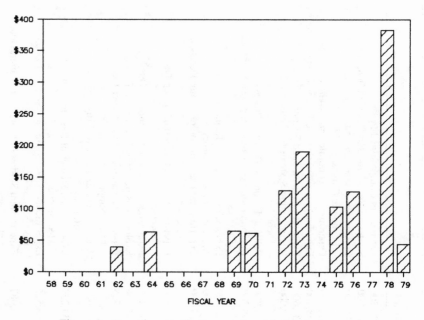

Figure 5   Experiments (in thousands of dollars).

nomics research. NSF financed the early pioneers in experimental research, Vernon Smith, Martin Shubik, and Charles Plott. The uneven pattern of funding means that the successful projects are bunched in the same year. Table 4 and Figure 6 describe NSF funding for three important research thrusts within public sector economics: public choice, law and economics, and public finance. In public choice, NSF supported the first meetings of the professional association that eventually became the Public Choice Society, the first issues of the journal devoted to public choice, and some of the research for which James Buchanan received the 1986 Nobel prize in economics. The leaders in the field of law and economics, George Stigler, Gary Becker, Richard Posner, and Peter Diamond, received support from NSF grants at an early stage in the development of this field. In public finance the many empirical studies by Martin Feldstein and his collaborators documenting the significance of the disincentives caused by the U.S. tax system were financed by NSF.

The Economics Program is not the only supporter of basic research in economics, even within NSF. The dynamics of funding for productivity research reflects the emergence in the seventies of support for productivity from the Research Applied to National Needs (RANN).

Table 4a. *Public choice awards from fiscal year 1958–79*

Fiscal year	Principal investigator	Co-principal investigators	Award $	Title
63	Tullock Gordon		$30,300	Models of Collective Decision
66	Buchanan James M.		$63,000	Decision Rules and Institutional Organizational Forms
68	Tullock Gordon		$6,200	Models of Collective Decision
69	Olson Mancur		$29,700	Property Institutions in "Precapitalist" Societies
69	Buchanan James M.		$13,600	Decision Rules and Institutional Organizational Forms
70	Rodgers James D.		$14,900	Collaborative Research in Utility Interdependence and Income Redistribution
70	Hochman Harold M.		$45,000	Collaborative Research in Utility Interdependence and Income Redistribution
72	Rodgers James D.		$24,100	Collaborative Research on Utility Interdependence and Income Redistribution
72	McGuire Martin C.		$11,400	Economic Theory of Government Formation and Organization
72	De Alessi Louis		$67,300	Resource Allocation Under Public Ownership and Public Regulation
72	Britto Dagobert L.		$12,400	Economic Models of Disarmament
72	Hochman Harold M.		$48,400	Collaborative Research on Utility Interdependence and Income Redistribution
72	Tullock Gordon	Buchanan J. M.	$45,000	Economic Analysis of Order and Disorder
72	Cheung Steven N. S.		$56,300	Theoretical and Empirical Investigations of Contracts
72	McKean Roland N.		$48,600	Implications of Different Resource Rights
72	Hochman Harold M.		$98,800	Studies in Metropolitan Political Economy
73	Rodgers James D.		$26,400	Collaborative Research on Utility Interdependence and Income Redistribution

213

Table 4a. *(cont.)*

Fiscal year	Principal investigator	Co-principal investigators	Award $	Title
73	Tullock Gordon	Buchanan J. M.	$59,900	Economic Analysis of Order and Disorder
73	Britto Dagobert L.		$3,700	Economic Models of Disarmament
73	McKean Roland N.		$43,700	Implications of Different Resource Rights
73	Hochman Harold M.		$35,000	Collaborative Research on Utility Interdependence and Income Redistribution
73	McGuire Martin C.		$40,400	Economic Theory of Government Formation and Organization
73	Musgrave Richard A.		$36,112	International Seminars in Public Economics
74	McKean Roland N.		$53,100	Implications of Different Resource Rights
74	Cheung Steven N. S.		$58,700	Theoretical and Empirical Investigations of Contracts
74	Intriligator Michael		$8,000	Collaborative Research on Economic Models of Arms Races
74	Britto Dagobert L.		$8,000	Collaborative Research on Economic Models of Arms Races
74	McGuire Martin C.		$57,100	Economic Theory of Government Formation
75	Britto Dagobert L.		$29,500	Collaborative Research on Economic Models of Arms Races
75	Intriligator Michael		$39,100	Collaborative Research on Economic Models of Arms Races
75	Buchanan James M.	Tullock Gordon	$58,100	Political Economy of Market Independence and Intervention
75	Hibbs Douglas A.		$10,000	Industrial Conflict in Advanced Industrial Societies
76	Buchanan James M.	Tullock Gordon	$61,500	Market Interdependence and Market Intervention
76	McKean Roland N.		$70,700	Direct vs. Indirect Regulation of Spillovers
77	Denzau Arthur T.		$55,400	Resource Allocation in the Public Sector
77	Romer Thomas		$108,700	Public Choice in Local Referenda

Year	Name	Co-investigator	Amount	Title
77	Shapiro Perry		$22,500	Private Preference for Nonmarket Goods and Services
77	Kramer Gerald H.		$11,200	Studies of Competitive Political Processes
77	Buchanan James M.		$62,900	Market Interdependence and Market Intervention
77	McKelvey Richard D.		$20,150	Agenda Design in Formal Models of Voting
77	Olson Mancur		$27,300	The Political Economy of Comparative Growth Rates
78	Britto Dagobert L.		$43,199	Collaborative Research on Dynamic Strategy Models for Arms Races
78	Wildasin David E.		$28,544	General Equilibrium Welfare Analysis of Intergovernmental Relations
78	Weitzman Martin		$42,914	Nonmarket Economics
78	Musgrave Richard A.		$32,200	The International Seminar Series in Public Economics
78	Hibbs Douglas A.		$6,050	Joint German-American Workshop on Politico-Economic Models
78	Tullock Gordon	Tideman T Nicolaus	$102,938	Theoretical and Practical Problems Involved in Improving Public Decision Making
78	Peltzman Sam		$58,000	The Growth of Government
78	Kramer Gerald H.		$11,480	Studies of Competitive Political Processes
78	Buchanan James M.		$119,714	The Implications of Positive Public Economics
79	Ferejohn John		$21,192	Collaborative Research in Social Choice
79	Ordeshook Peter C.	McKelvey Richard D.	$25,460	Collaborative Research on Voting
79	Wildasin David E.		$31,376	General Equilibrium Welfare Analysis of Intergovernmental Relations
79	Gramlich Edward	Courant Paul Robinfeld Daniel	$152,767	The Controllability of Public Spending
79	Weisbrod Burton A.		$53,952	Economics of the Private Nonprofit Sector
79	Wildasin David E.		$5,332	General Equilibrium Welfare Analysis of Intergovernmental Relations
79	Mackay Robert J.	Weaver Carolyn L.	$64,036	Resource Allocation in the Public Sector
79	Hibbs Douglas A.		$25,435	Comparative Studies in Political Economy
79	McKelvey Richard D.		$26,100	Collaborative Research on Voting
79	Packel Edward		$30,641	Collaborative Research in Social Choice

Table 4b. *Public finance awards from fiscal year 1958–79*

Fiscal year	Principal investigator	Co-principal investigators	Award $	Title
61	Musgrave Richard A.		$21,900	Empirical Analysis of Tax Incidence
69	Marglin Steve A.		$65,300	Criteria for Expenditure in the Public Sector
70	Bergstrom Theodore		$21,800	Consumer Preference, Externality and General Equilibrium
71	Hirsch Werner Z.		$106,500	A Conceptual Framework for State and Local Fiscal Analysis
72	Starrett David A.		$26,000	Intertemporal Allocation, Indivisibilities and Externalities
73	Feldstein Martin		$53,461	Effects of Taxation on Capital Accumulation
74	Heller Walter P.	Shell Karl	$75,300	Theory of Optimal Taxation and Markets
74	Starrett David A.		$9,600	Intertemporal Allocation, Indivisibilities, and Externalities
74	Feldstein Martin		$45,300	Effects of Taxation on Capital Accumulation
74	Hirsch Werner Z.		$9,700	A Conceptual Framework for State and Local Fiscal Analysis
74	Hamilton Bruce W.		$25,100	Studies on Zoning and Property Values
75	Feldstein Martin		$68,700	Effects of Taxation and Fiscal Programs on Accumulation
75	Feldstein Martin		$45,300	Effects of Taxation on Capital Accumulation
75	Heller Walter P.	Shell Karl	$6,300	Theory of Optimal Taxation and Markets
76	Kurz Mordecai	Wilson Robert	$201,200	Coalitional Power, Information, and Income Distribution

	Author	Title	Amount
76	Feldstein Martin	Effects of Taxation and Fiscal Programs on Accumulation	$62,000
77	Feldstein Martin	Effects of Taxation and Fiscal Programs on Accumulation	$80,600
78	Olson Mancur	The Political Economy of Comparative Growth Rates	$5,000
78	Brainard William C. Weber Robert J.	Comparison of Public Choice Systems	$28,164
78	Varian Hal R.	Optimal Taxation of Uncertain Income and General Equilibrium	$34,076
78	Shoven John B.	Business Finance and Taxation	$99,589
78	Thurow Lester C.	The Direct and Indirect Incidence of Government Expenditures	$148,079
78	Kurz Mordecai Wilson Robert B. Hart Sergiu	Coalitional Power, Incomplete Information and Income	$337,649
78	Raiffa Howard Zechauser Richard Weinstein Milton C.	Systematic Approaches to Improved Policy Decisionmaking	$156,014
79	Rader J. Trout	Externalities, Pareto Optimality and Decentralization	$108,654
79	Feldstein Martin	Macroeconomic Effects of Fiscal Programs	$151,901
79	Rosen Harvey	Individual Behavior and Personal Taxation	$54,570
79	Phelps Edmund S.	Collaborative Research on Theory of Optimal Taxation	$82,713

Table 4c. *Law and economics awards from fiscal year 1958–79*

Fiscal year	Principal investigator	Co-principal investigators	Award $	Title
67	Diamond Peter A.	Foley D. K.	$21,300	Theory of Public Finance
70	Diamond Peter A.	Foley D. K.	$42,000	Theories of Public Finance, Uncertainty and Information
71	Becker Gary S.	Stigler G. Posner R. Landes W. Ehrlich I. M.	$201,900	Research in Law and Economics
72	Diamond Peter A.	Foley D. K.	$35,800	Public Policy and Uncertainty
72	Becker Gary S.	Stigler G. Posner R. Landes W. Ehrlich I. M.	$80,000	Research in Law and Economics
73	Bergstrom Theodore		$20,500	Human Life and Legal Liability
73	Diamond Peter A.	Foley D. K.	$33,700	Public Policy and Uncertainty
74	Landes William M.	Posner Richard A.	$121,400	Economic Analysis of Law
74	Diamond Peter A.		$23,600	Public Policy and Uncertainty
75	Landes William M.	Posner Richard A.	$119,800	Economic Analysis of Law
75	Diamond Peter A.		$71,700	Public Policy and Uncertainty
76	Landes William M.	Posner Richard A.	$125,800	Application of Economic Techniques to Analysis of Law
76	Diamond Peter A.		$75,700	Incentives, Uncertainty, and Public Policy
77	Shavell Steven		$64,600	Economic Theories of Liability, Risk, and Insurance
77	Klevorick Alvin K.		$16,800	Topics in Law and Economics
77	Landes William M.		$56,100	Applications of Economic Techniques to Analysis of Law
78	Diamond Peter A.		$51,830	Uncertainty and Public Policy
78	Polinsky A. Mitch		$80,609	Legal Approaches to the Control of Externalities
78	Klevorick Alvin K.		$15,252	A Model of the Jury Decision Process
79	Ordover Janusz A.		$29,346	Collaborative Research on Theory of Optimal Taxation
79	Diamond Peter A.		$41,641	Uncertainty and Public Policy
79	Wittman Donald		$28,976	An Economic Analysis of Legal Rules and the Issues of Timing
79	Ordover Janusz A.		$47,490	The Impact of the Law on Economic Behavior

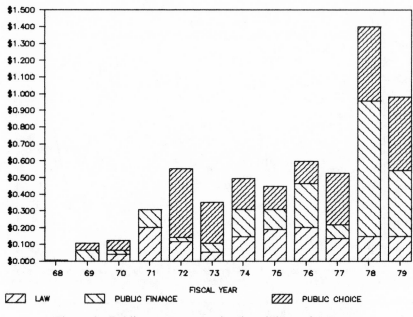

Figure 6   Public sector economics (in millions of dollars).

RANN was created within NSF to fund work that would help the government handle pressing national problems. The three major problems identified were energy, the environment, and the decline in U.S. productivity.

The first grants made by NSF to economists focused on technology and productivity. The theory of Robert Solow, the econometrics of Zvi Griliches, Daniel McFadden, and Dale Jorgenson, the careful industrial studies of Edwin Mansfield, and Fritz Machlup's pioneering research on knowledge institutions were supported during the sixties. Figures 7 and 8 describe how expenditures on productivity by the Economics Program peaked in 1973, both in absolute amount and as a percentage of the budget, and then declined as other NSF programs stepped in and made grants.

Unfortunately, most of the other NSF sources of funds for economists disappeared one by one during the eighties, victims of budget cuts or internal reorganizations. One of our goals is to rebuild funding of productivity and technology by the Economics Program, so that shifting NSF priorities won't hurt this important area of research.

Almost the whole Economics Program budget goes to support

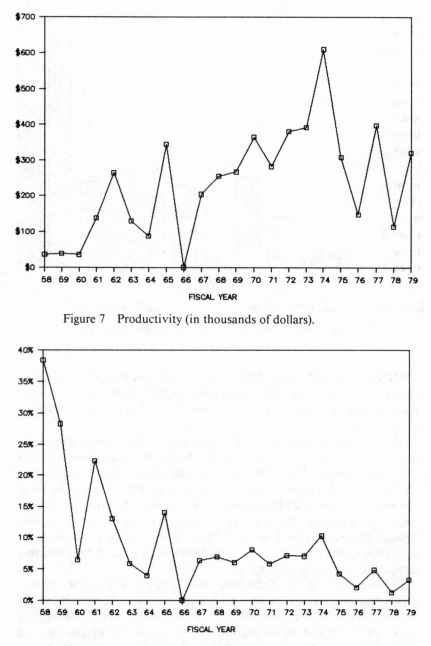

Figure 7   Productivity (in thousands of dollars).

Figure 8   Productivity as a percentage of the Economics Program budget.

research. As Table 5 and Figures 9 and 10 show, the Economics Program's annual funding of conferences, workshops, and institutes never exceeded $400,000, and for most of the seventies remained well below five percent of the budget. During the eighties the Economics Program cut back even further in its support of conference activities because we felt that conferences were more likely to be funded by private foundations or universities than was research because of the visibility conferences give the host institutions and their other sponsors. At the beginning of the eighties we declined all conference proposals no matter how favorable the reviews. We are now trying to restore support for conference activities in economics.

One frequent criticism of NSF peer review is that genuine interdisciplinary research cannot survive such an evaluation because scholars trained within a given discipline supposedly either will not understand or will not respect work that lies outside their discipline. This criticism is not valid for NSF support of the social sciences. Most of the programs in the Social and Economic Science Division are interdisciplinary, and the disciplinary programs for Sociology, Economics, and Political Science place a high priority on jointly supporting some research. The Political Science and Economics Programs started an initiative in political economy in 1987 to encourage more collaborative research between economists and political scientists.

Figures 11 and 12 show the dynamics of interdisciplinary research between economics and engineering. The Economics Program and the Program for System Theory Applications supported together the collaboration of distinguished economists and engineers such as David Kendrick of the University of Texas and Edison Tse of Stanford or Edwin Kuh and Michael Athans of MIT. The first meetings and the first issues of the journal of a new professional association of engineers and economists were supported by NSF. Control theory, nonlinear programming, system dynamics, and other methods widely used by engineers were applied to economic problems. During the seventies about three percent of the Economics Program's budget went to interdisciplinary grants to this area.

In conclusion, we at the National Science Foundation's Economics Program are proud of our version of the peer review process and its results. We think we've done a good job. Contrary to the beliefs of some economists, it is inappropriate to blame "closed-minded" reviewers for the relative lack of success experienced by researchers outside the mainstream of economics in publishing influential articles or obtaining research grants. In fact, peer review provides a reasonably open forum for new ideas. A wide variety of innovative alternative

Table 5. *Conferences, workshops, and institutes awards from fiscal year 1958–79*

Fiscal year	Principal investigator	Co-principal investigators	Award $	Title
60	Leontief Wassily W.		$20,400	Conference on Input–Output Analysis
61	McKenzie Lionel W.		$32,500	International Participation in Econometric Society Meeting
62	Leontief Wassily W.		$250,000	Conference on Input–Output Analysis
62	Stucky P. L.		$34,700	Inter-University Seminar Series in Quantitative Economics
64	Buchanan James M.		$5,100	Conference on the Theory of Collective Decision Processes
67	Moore G. H.		$57,500	Economic Research Conference Program
68	Stein Jerome L.		$5,600	Conference on Money and Economic Growth
68	Koopmans Tjalling C.	Nerlove M. Scarf H. E. Shubik M. Tobin J.	$370,000	Economic Theory and Econometrics
68	Brunner Karl		$2,000	Conferences on Econometrics
69	Stein Jerome L.		$2,900	Conference on Money and Economic Growth
69	Meyer John R.		$79,000	Economic Research Conference Program
70	Nadiri Mohammed I.		$39,400	Inter-University Workshop on Applied Econometrics
70	Koopmans Tjalling C.	Brainard W. C. Scarf H. E. Shubik M. Tobin J.	$242,200	Economic Theory and Econometrics
71	Koopmans Tjalling C.	Brainard W. C. Scarf H. E. Shubik M. Tobin J.	$243,200	Economic Theory and Econometrics
71	Promm Gary		$43,500	Conference on Econometrics and Mathematical Economics
71	Marschak Jacob		$4,500	Interdisciplinary Colloquium on Mathematics in the Behavioral Sciences
72	Wu S.		$6,300	Conference on Decision Under Uncertainty

222

Year	Name	Additional Names	Amount	Conference
72	Koopmans Tjalling C.	Brainard W. C. Scarf H. E. Shubik M. Tobin J.	$254,500	Economic Theory and Econometrics
72	Meyer John R.		$67,300	Economic Research Conference Program
72	Marschak Jacob		$2,800	Interdisciplinary Colloquium on Mathematics in the Behavioral Sciences
72	Andreano R. L.		$7,900	Conference on Problems in Economic History
73	Marschak Jacob		$5,900	Interdisciplinary Colloquium on Mathematics in the Behavioral Sciences
73	McCloskey Donald N.		$18,200	Seminars on British Econometric History
73	Lindert Peter H.		$16,100	Annual Econometric History Conferences
73	Koopmans Tjalling C.	Shubik M. Tobin J. Scarf H.	$73,100	Economic Theory and Econometrics
73	Fromm Gary		$47,500	Conference on Econometrics and Mathematical Economics
74	Meyer John R.		$72,600	Economic Research Conference Program
74	Fromm Gary		$10,700	Conference on Econometrics and Mathematical Economics
74	Perry George L.	Okun Arthur M.	$98,000	The Brookings Panel on Economic Activity
74	McCloskey Donald N.		$4,000	Seminars on British Econometric History
74	Brainard William C.	Shubik Martin Scarf Herbert Tobin James	$353,000	Economic Theory and Econometrics
75	Aaron Henry		$6,900	International Seminar in Public Economics Conference
75	Okun Arthur	Perry George L.	$98,000	The Brookings Panel on Economic Activity
75	Nadiri Mohammed I.		$41,000	Conference on the Computer in Economic and Social Research
75	Lindert Peter H.		$9,400	Econometric History Conference
75	Fromm Gary	Williamson Jeffrey G.	$65,500	Conference Series on Econometrics and Mathematical Economics

Table 5. *(cont.)*

Fiscal year	Principal investigator	Co-principal investigators	Award $	Title
75	Brainard William C.	Shubik Martin Scarf Herbert Tobin James	$348,100	Economic Theory and Econometrics
76	Okun Arthur	Perry George L	$98,000	The Brookings Panel on Economic Activity
76	McMains Harvey J.		$46,000	Economic Research Conference Program
76	Nadiri Mohammed L.		$7,900	Economics and Control Theory Workshop at Stanford
76	Perry George L.	Okun A. M.	$50,000	Brookings Panel on Economic Activity
76	Fromm Gary		$64,800	Conference Series on Econometrics and Mathematical Economics
76	Lindert Peter H.	Williamson Jeffrey G.	$14,000	Econometric History Conference to be held in Madison, Wisconsin
76	Brainard William C.	Shubik Martin Scarf Herbert Tobin James	$115,100	Economic Theory and Econometrics
77	Nadiri Mohammed I.		$6,000	Conference on Economics and Control Theory
77	Popkin Joel		$28,700	Conference Series on Research in Income and Wealth
77	Lindert Peter H.		$16,800	Econometric History Conference
77	Fromm Gary		$85,600	Conference Series on Econometrics and Mathematical Economics
78	Fischer Stanley		$13,988	Conference on Rational Expectations, Bald Peak VT
78	Lipsey Robert E.		$24,018	Universities-National Bureau of Economic Research Conferences
78	Meltzer Allen H.		$66,152	The Carnegie-Rochester Conference Series on Public Policy

78	Kendrick David A.		$4,800	Workshop on Economics and Control Theory
78	McLure Charles E.		$59,480	Institute in Applied Economics: Labor Studies and Business
78	McCloskey Donald N.		$19,400	A Conference on the Application of Economics to History
78	Okun Arthur	Perry George L.	$194,933	The Brookings Panel on Economic Activity
79	McLure Charles E.		$98,670	Workshop on Macroeconomic Fluctuations and Exchange Rates
79	Smith Vernon L.		$15,036	Support of a Conference-Workshop in Experimental Economics
79	McCloskey Donald N.		$20,730	Conferences on the Application of Economics to History
79	Hult Robert T.	Krueger Anne O.	$25,060	Three Conferences on International Economics
79	Meltzer Allen H.		$69,336	The Carnegie-Rochester Conference Series on Public Policy
79	Okun Arthur	Perry George L.	$0	The Brookings Panel on Economic Activity

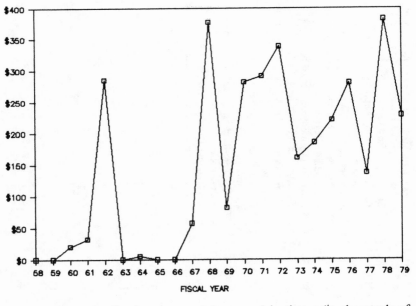

Figure 9   Conferences, workshops, and institutes (in thousands of dollars).

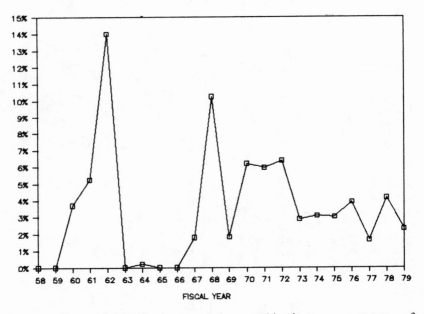

Figure 10   Conferences, workshops, and institutes as a percentage of the Economics Program budget.

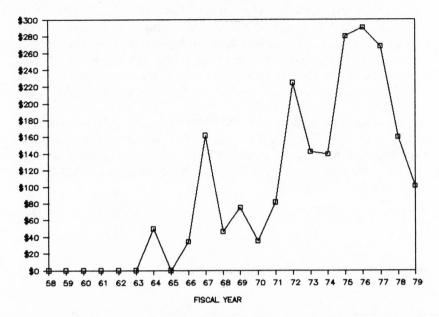

Figure 11   Engineering interdisciplinary work (in thousands of dollars).

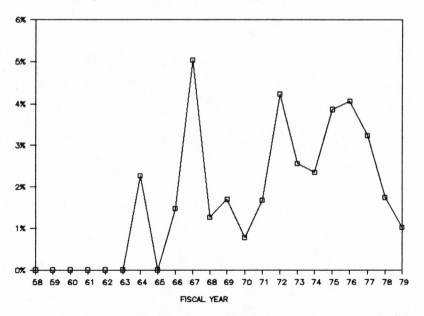

Figure 12   Engineering interdisciplinary work as a percentage of the Economics Program budget.

avenues of research have received NSF funding and have been thoroughly debated in articles in the leading economics journals. If these alternatives have not met standards of rigor and explanatory power and, as a consequence, are no longer pursued, then we need more and better ideas. We want to know about promising new researchers and original ideas not currently funded by NSF so we can avoid future mistakes.

My suggestion to critics of NSF funding is: Get your act together. Offer alternatives and not just criticism – it takes a paradigm to beat a paradigm. Rehashing criticisms will not have much impact on economics, no matter how lucid or perceptive the arguments, if better alternatives aren't offered.

CHAPTER 17

Money and the spread of ideas

DAVID C. COLANDER

For an economist it would be inconceivable to think of the spread of ideas without thinking of the funding of ideas. Money acts as a magnet, directing research and ideas. The papers by Goodwin, Smith, and Newlon considered specific aspects of the explicit funding of ideas: through government, through think tanks, and through private foundations. In this paper I summarize some of the concerns that have been raised about the funding of economic ideas and relate those concerns to the final paper in this volume, which offers some ideas about changing the method of funding.

In thinking about the role of funding in directing ideas, it is important to consider implicit, as well as explicit, funding. Of all the sources of funding for economic research, the largest is probably the implicit funding that comes from 3–2 or 2–2 teaching loads at liberal arts schools and 1–1 or 1–2 teaching loads at graduate schools. At junior colleges where no research is required the teaching load is often 5–5, so the net amount of funding that comes from implicit funding is large. In 1987 a rough estimate of the implicit funding might be $250 million, assuming 20,000 economics professors receive one-third time off to conduct research. This would be approximately twenty times the funding provided by NSF in that year. This money is generally without strings, in the sense that institutions do not explicitly state what type of research a person must do. There are, of course, the indirect silken cords imposed by institutions and historical precedent that were discussed in Part I. Since their institutions' departments are the most important factors in determining the fate, future, and success of economists, economic research is, in large part, internally directed within the profession. Younger researchers will do what older researchers

This paper is based, in large part, on discussion at the Middlebury Conference on the Spread of Economic Ideas. Special thanks go to Albert Rees for helpful comments.

think they should do. This means that departments are likely to acquire specific research characteristics. For example, everybody knows, in a commonsensical way, that we can't confuse UCLA with Berkeley or Harvard with Chicago.

The predominance of internal funding sources does not mean that the explicit funding sources discussed in the other papers in this section are unimportant. Because much of the implicit funding has no explicit strings, the influence of the marginal external funding in directing research can be much larger than is its quantitative importance. It can be; however, in practice it is not. For the most part, the other direct funding institutions, government and private, use the existing institutional hierarchy as the basis for choosing among ideas, so what we see in the direction given by private funding is a self-replication of the direction given within academic departments. Funding goes to top researchers, and top researchers choose who the top researchers are.

This comes out most clearly in the paper by Dan Newlon on NSF's role. NSF funds primarily mainstream, traditional research. Newlon makes a strong case that a conscious effort is made to include non-mainstream research, but there is, working against this attempt, an implicit sensibility on the part of peer reviewers, and hence, NSF, that nonmainstream work is not serious research. This sensibility lowers the probability of nonmainstream ideas being funded and, based on discussions with nonmainstream researchers, this bias is perceived by them as being much stronger that it may actually be. Thus, the probability of acceptance of a proposal is perceived as small, and generally, given the small chance of acceptance, it simply isn't worth it for non-mainstream researchers to apply. Good nonmainstream researchers know that if they play the game right they can get funding; many decide to do so – to play the game. And they get funding if they do so. That's why Newlon can make the challenge he makes. The NSF funding is for "selling out" to the mainstream, not for nonmainstream research.

Even among mainstream researchers the view of what is and what is not acceptable research influences the type of research submitted. The word goes out through the network about what research is and what research is not being considered for funding, and proposals are shaped accordingly. Thus we see a certain degree of faddishness in NSF funding with rational expectations catching on in one period, large-scale models catching on in another. One interpretation, the one suggested in Newlon's paper, is that the research on these issues has been completed, but an alternative interpretation is that the fad had run its course, and it's off to a new fad.

I'm not saying the process is bad, or that it could be different. There will inevitably be a problem of who will judge the judges, and if we do not rely on the recognized leaders, upon whom should we rely? What I am arguing is that we should not make out as if the system is more open than it is. Whether any change will improve the process is unclear. Gordon Tullock's delightfully enjoyable proposals are suggestive, but they don't leave me with a sense that I want to sign on.

Probably the most important contribution to the openness to funding nonmainstream ideas is the multiplicity of funding sources, nicely described in the papers by Crauford Goodwin and James Smith. Put simply, there are a large number of potential benefactors out there and an industrious researcher can often find funding, or can find sufficient research time available to self-fund ideas. But, although possible, it is not considered a wise strategy for young researchers to adopt if they want to remain within, or reach, an elite department. I've spoken with many young economists who do not feel their research is leading anywhere, but they feel they must continue in order to get tenure. One would think that after they do receive tenure, they would be free to direct their own research, but by that time they are so caught up in the profession that to change their research focus is impossible.

Probably the most important question to be asked about funding is whether the best ideas get funded. The answer is: Of course not. Some good proposals are going to get turned down. Everyone makes mistakes. Every journal editor, every foundation officer, is going to turn down some good proposals. In thinking about these mistakes it is important to remember that there is a problem of Type I and Type II errors. If a foundation wanted to make sure that it never turned down a good proposal, it would fund an awful lot of very bad proposals. No foundation has the money to do that.

The multiplicity of funding agencies provides some defense against the likelihood that some good ideas will not get funded. If a good proposal misses at one agency, it is likely to make it at another, and funding agencies make a conscious effort to fill the niches.

For example, the Sloan Foundation, which provides about $4 million in funding to economics, focuses on applied fields because theorists and econometricians have the highest prestige in the profession and fare best in the peer review process. Also, rather than funding individual investigators, or even groups of investigators, Sloan tends to fund workshops within leading graduate departments.

Perhaps the best way one can see the complementary role that foundations play is with an example, which Albert Rees of the Sloan Foundation provided at the Conference. In 1981, as Danial Newlon writes, there was a very sharp cut in the NSF budget. One of the things that happened at that time was that the panel study of income dynamics at the University of Michigan, which had been funded by NSF, and which was the data base for a tremendous amount of applied research in economics, was threatened with being interrupted. There were fourteen years of longitudinal data on the same five thousand families and the split-off from those families, and the study was going to be halted. To get that kind of longitudinal data base again you would have to start from square one and it would have taken fourteen more years.

Tom Juster, the head of the project, came to the Sloan Foundation in great consternation. Sloan said yes, they'd try to help out, but the most they could give was $250,000. Juster needed a million dollars. He eventually got $250,000 of that from NSF. That left him half a million short. Juster and Rees went together to the Rockefeller Foundation; Juster went alone to Ford – and the panel study of income dynamics got support from both of these foundations. Why? Neither of these foundations had much interest in the preservation of the data base for the good of the economics profession. But at Rockefeller the head of the equal opportunity program saw the data base as a potential source of data on black/white differences in income and family composition and agreed to contribute $250,000. The Ford Foundation was interested in the study because it was interested in alleviating poverty and the panel study gave wonderful data on poverty and who moved in and out of poverty and who stayed in poverty. So Ford contributed $250,000 under the rubric of alleviating poverty. So there were three foundations supporting the same project for rather different kinds of reasons. Once the NSF budget returned to its previous level, NSF picked up the panel study on income dynamics, and it's now entirely supported on NSF funds.

What lessons can be drawn from this experience? The lesson Albert Rees drew at the conference is that the agencies work together to see that a good project receives continuous funding. The lesson some non-mainstream economists drew was that there is almost an interlocking directorate of funding agencies and elite academic departments which eliminates the multiplicity of funding sources and makes the source loom as one source.

That argument is, of course, overstated. Some additional niches are filled by a third group of private foundations that support economics in a much more direct way. For many of them this means that they support research if it is supportive of the free enterprise system. This group includes the J. M. Olin Foundation, the Smith Richardson Foundation, and the new Bradley Foundation. In economics the largest of these is the J. M. Olin Foundation, which funds chairs in economics and related fields. There is a much smaller set of funding possibilities on the other side and probably the most difficult ideas to get funding for are radical ideas. Put in blunt terms: Institutions seldom fund research devoted to the tearing down of those institutions. But, even here, there remain the rich former student radicals who provide funding for various radical ideas.

Where does this leave us in our consideration of the funding of ideas? In my view, it leaves us in a relatively neutral position. The funding system of ideas certainly isn't perfect; changes could make it better, But it is not at all clear what the nature of these changes would be, or how they could be accomplished.

CHAPTER 18

Changing incentives to make economics more relevant

GORDON TULLOCK

The social sciences have made less progress than the natural sciences; and the application of social science ideas tends to be much less well developed than the application of natural science ideas. There are several explanations for this. One, which might be offered by unfriendly critics, is that social scientists just aren't as good as the physicists and chemists are. Certainly, we don't have as much in the way of resources to play around with.

Another explanation is that the problems are inherently harder. I don't see how anybody who is familiar with modern physics could actually believe this, but the explanation is sometimes offered. In this paper I want to focus on a third reason: the incentive system for funding the producing and applying of ideas in the fields of the social studies is weaker than that in the natural science area. Put simply, without property rights in ideas, the market cannot adequately produce and develop ideas. What we need is a patent system for ideas, or its equivalent.[1]

In my opinion, the invention of the patent was an important, even vital, step in the development of modern technology. Consider the patent system in some old-fashioned field, like mechanics. First, there is an incentive for inventing new ideas because they can be patented. Perhaps more important than this incentive actually to invent new ideas in a direct sense is the secondary incentive to entrepreneurial activity. Once the idea has been invented, it must then be sold, and frequently more resources are invested in that and the profits from it are markedly greater than from the invention itself. Indeed, in many cases, entrepreneurial effort takes the form of hiring somebody to make inventions which will then later be sold by the entrepreneur.

[1]Gordon Tulluck, *The Organization of Inquiry.* New York: American University Press, 1987; and Durham, NC: Duke University Press, 1966, especially pp. 21–6.

The extension of the patent system to biological systems in recent years has already shown signs of sharply improving the rate at which new species are invented by geneticists. (Note that I am not talking about genetic engineering, although that is relevant, but the more conservative breeding techniques.) Since the expansion of the patent system into biology, these techniques have been applied more vigorously.

Unfortunately, direct copying of the patent system by the social sciences is probably impossible, but it is possible to move in that direction, and that is the point of my paper.

To see the value of that move, begin by assuming that, quite literally, social science ideas can be patented and that I "invent" a new social science idea. The new idea which I propose to invent is to permit Korean and Japanese cars into the United States without restriction. I realize, of course, that this is not a new idea to most of you, but there are a surprising number of people for whom the argument for such unrestricted imports would be completely and totally new.

Let us assume then that an academic in some outlying part of the world – Scotland, for instance – invents this idea and is granted a patent. He is not, himself, very much of an entrepreneur. He sells the patent to a stockbroker in, let us say, London, who proceeds to promote it. The stockbroker must convince governments that it is a good idea and then collect from them a fee for using it. There is a very difficult and expensive sales problem here. I take it none of us would dispute that the value of the application of this particular idea by the government would be up in the level of billions of dollars, and hence a good deal of money could justifiably be spent in attempting to sell it.

There is nothing here quite equivalent to the marginal value of the idea since to a large extent it has to be sold as a unit.[2] We can simply assume that whatever price the entrepreneur is asking, it leaves a considerable consumer surplus. Granted the value of such an idea if applied, there is plenty of room to make the entrepreneur immensely rich while benefitting the rest of us.

The other problem here if we look at our present institutions, of course, is that there is no reason why the government should in fact pay at all. If it were planning on paying, presumably a number of other people would dash in with a claim that they were legitimate recipients. This is particularly true if the invention is old and only the entrepreneurial activity recent.

---

[2]The same is true of certain types of patented inventions. Satellites, for example, frequently contain pieces of equipment which will be installed in that one satellite and no other.

But let us temporarily ignore these problems and just assume that there are ideas like this out in the world, and it is possible for companies to hire people to engage in such research. Furthermore, assume the entrepreneur-inventor will receive, let us say, half of the social value of the idea if it is applied. Presumably, the entrepreneurial activity of selecting areas in which research is to be concentrated and then selling the ideas would be at least as valuable and as highly paid as inventing the idea itself.

We would like, if we could have this patent system, to make it possible for an individual inventor simply to invent something and then find an entrepreneur who would buy it from him, or directly sell it to the government himself. Houdry would be a natural science example. He combined the invention and the entrepreneurial activity and became extremely wealthy. Thomas A. Edison and Jay Gould would exemplify an entrepreneur seeking out an inventor, financing him, and then taking his fee out of the organization of, in this case, General Electric.

But how can we do this in the social sciences, and, in particular, in economics? The first thing to be said here is that an idea of how we could do it of necessity is going to be invented in our current environment. Thus whatever reward system I propose, I will not myself receive the reward. Therefore, I am less than ideally motivated to work out the optimal institutions. I can, however, give it a try.

Once more there are two problems: inventing new ideas and getting the government or private citizens to adopt them. I suspect that the latter is the more difficult of these problems because there are so many good ideas for government policy that have been invented a long time in the past and are not now being applied. Indeed, an entrepreneur who simply succeeded in getting the government to carry out a policy recommendation randomly selected from the pages of *The Wealth of Nations* would in all probability deserve extremely high rewards.[3]

Nevertheless, idea creation faces somewhat simpler problems than does idea adoption, and so we can well start with creation. Suppose, then, the following simple institutional setup: anyone who has a new idea which he thinks might benefit the government may apply for an intellectual patent on it, and then the patent office treats this application much as it treats present-day patents. Since I have written a good deal on the current patent law, which I think is basically a good idea,

---

[3] In many cases, of course, we could do better than Adam Smith now. We have two hundred years of additional study. Still, it is surprising on how few practical matters we can improve his advice.

but very badly administered, I take it no one will assume that I am overly idealistic here.[4] There doesn't seem to be any reason why the patent office would have any more difficulty with this kind of a "patent" than it does with the mechanical devices, electronic devices, lasers, and so forth that it now patents.

But although getting the patent would raise no significant problems, its reward would. The government – indeed, all government – would in fact be able to make use of it without paying anything if it wished to economize. If the idea was such that it could be used by private citizens (an improved sales technique, for example), then I presume the government would be reasonably willing simply to enforce the patent monopoly. But when the government itself is the customer, it is not obvious that it would choose to pay.

Even if the government does choose to attempt to stimulate new ideas by agreeing to pay for them, it is not at all clear how it could do so. Indeed, it seems likely, as I have said several times so far, that the entrepreneurial task of selling the idea would involve at least as great resources as the creation of the idea and hence there would be a reward both for the idea and for its selling. Let us simplify our problem, however, for the time being by ignoring the resource investment in selling and simply talk about the idea itself.

Note that one characteristic application of patents could not be applied here. In general, ideas for improvement in policy are either applied or not applied and there is no unit-by-unit production. A repeal of an existing quota on Japanese and Korean goods would not be something for which the traditional royalty agreement would work, because it would be a once-and-for-all operation.

I mentioned Houdry above, and, of course, his invention, which was an improved oil refinery, had somewhat the same characteristic. There weren't very many oil refineries built which were big enough to use the Houdry process. Indeed, many companies already had an oil refining process. Still, he at least was bargaining with a number of private oil companies rather than with just one. Furthermore, the oil companies were in direct competition with each other in the product market. The sale of such an idea to government is much more difficult.

It seems likely that the best type of contract here would be one in which the potential benefits of application of the idea were specified and some division of them between the inventor and the government

---

[4]Unfortunately, the patent office currently does not work very well. It would be nice if we could improve the patent office, both for the new and for the old patents.

provided. Once again, return to the abolition of quotas on imports of cars. A contract could contain a specification of the way in which the net social benefit from having the imports enter was to be computed.[5]

But here it will be noted that I have chosen an area where I think such calculations would be relatively easily done. Indeed, calculations of the social cost of these quotas now exist, and aren't particularly controversial. Furthermore, it would make no great difference if the calculations were not perfect. I don't think anyone maintains that the royalty system used in ordinary patents is a perfect measure of the value of the patent.

The real problem comes when it isn't so easy to measure, and a great many things would meet that specification. Suppose the inventor, for example, works out a method of breaking the principal codes in use by an enemy. Even a rough approximation of its value may be very, very difficult to produce. Still, it is likely that an expected return of, let's say, $500 million would no doubt improve our cryptanalytic technique.

But these problems of calculation are basically less important than the other difficulties here. Once again, the patent system does not offer perfect rewards. Large rewards, even if there is a strong element of randomness in the way that they are calculated, would certainly stimulate much effort. Furthermore, the type of person who devotes large resources to invention is apt to be decidedly short on risk aversion anyway. Hence, this additional gamble on top of the great gamble he makes in his ability to penetrate into the unknown might not have very much negative effect.

Entrepreneurial activity in order to sell the thing to Congress would be more difficult. As I said before, a number of people might claim that they were the entrepreneurs. If it is a new idea, we could use exactly the same technique that is now used for patents in mechanics, which is simply to provide that whoever owns the patent is the one who gets paid for the entrepreneurial work. If Lilly were to engage in sales efforts for a drug, the patent for which was owned by Seba, it would just be a waste on their part. Seba would send Lilly a letter of thanks. Hence, once the idea has been invented and patented, the arrangement between whoever held the patent and potential entrepreneurs would almost of necessity be exclusive. No one else would be willing to invest entrepreneurial effort in attempting to sell the idea.

Note that it is likely that the kind of thing we are now talking about

---

[5]Strictly speaking, this contract should also involve the Japanese automobile producers.

will require a great deal more entrepreneurial effort than do most regular scientific inventions. Material scientific devices which are new can be sold to a few people, and then other people can tell by observing the results whether they want the devices or not. It was not necessary for Henry Ford to convince the U.S. government that mass production of a cheap and simple car was a good idea. It was only necessary for him to get a certain number of customers and then let other people copy them in purchasing his car.

Note that sometimes it is easier to get governments than to get private businessmen to buy these things. Porsche, a well-established automobile designer, invented the Volkswagen and failed in all of his efforts to get any of the big German automobile manufacturing companies to produce it. He did, however, succeed in selling the idea to Hitler. As a result of World War II, no civilian Volkswagens were actually produced until the late 1940s. The Volkswagen factory was completed, however, and produced an amphibious jeep during the war. At the end of the war the factory was in the British zone. The British government offered the factory, either in place or with all of its equipment moved to England, and all of the patents and designs to the major English automobile manufacturers. All of them rejected it. Consequently, the plant remained in the ownership of the German government and, of course, turned out to be one of the great success stories of our time.

Note that this particular method of making certain that the entrepreneurial rewards go to the right person, by giving only one person a motive to engage in them, won't work for those ideas that have already been invented. Since the overwhelming majority of the reforms that any of my readers would recommend to modern governments are indeed previously invented ideas, it is not obvious how one could invest in the necessary entrepreneurial activity. One way would be simply to let people who are, let us say, potential entrepreneurs select (perhaps as a result of a lottery) ideas which have been invented in the past and which they think would be useful now. They would then be given an equivalent patent on them which would be available to any entrepreneur interested. Presumably in this case we would want to arrange it so that the payment to the entrepreneur would be at least somewhat less than if there was both a true inventor and an entrepreneur available.

Let us turn to a minor idea, which, in fact, I did invent myself (others may have thought of it independently) and which I did make a very slight effort to get adopted. As you know, under present circumstances, almost all of the data collected and eventually published by the government first accumulates in the memory of a computer. I suggest that this memory be always accessible either to anyone who has a modem or, alternatively, to some specialized institution which, as a result of competitive bidding, has acquired the right to access it and distribute it.

There are a number of advantages to this. First, there are considerable resources involved in the effort to keep these numbers secret until they're formally announced. There is also a considerable volume of resources invested in attempting to penetrate the secrecy for many, although not by any means all, of these series. There is also the random noise thrown into the market process by the appearance of this information from time to time, in a discontinuous way. Continuing access would mean that information would become available gradually instead of once a week or once a month.

I've tried a little bit to sell this idea, not much but a little bit, and have gotten nowhere mainly because it obviously is not a major idea. At most it would save the government $15 to $20 million a year, and the economy perhaps $50 million. It is, however, an idea area where, I believe, sales effort would pay off. The only people possible positively injured by the change would be those bureaucrats who enjoy the press conferences, or those who are selling the information before the press conference. The politicians would gain because instead of being compelled to have a press conference regularly whether the news be good or bad, they could be selective. I suspect that if there was some organization that would, in the event somebody sold this idea to the government, pay that somebody $5 million, the idea would be sold.

There are some basic problems with the patentlike ideas I have so far presented, one of which is that I have great difficulty believing any government would adopt them. A second, which in a way is simply a generalization of the same thing, is that the entrepreneurial activity in these areas would be both very, very expensive and very, very risky. One would have to create specialized companies willing to put, let us say, a quarter of a billion dollars into a one-in-four chance on an idea whose social payoff is large enough so that their fee would be a billion dollars. That is not impossible, but it certainly would involve a drastic reorganization.

Furthermore, selling such an idea is particularly difficult because innumerable politicians would feel that if they did adopt a new idea, it was really the result of they themselves having understood it, or of one of their constituents having really urged it on them rather than whoever the entrepreneur was. The entrepreneur would not be physically providing anything to them, except perhaps some propaganda material. Furthermore, giving him the right to collect the large fee, regardless of whether or not he actually did anything, would seem unfair. I don't know why this objection is rarely made for regular inventions. Here again, a person who buys a patent, or hires somebody to invent something which is later patented, may make a great deal of money with almost no entrepreneurial activity. We don't seem to be bothered by that, but I suspect we would be if the inventions were governmental ideas.

Let us turn from this, my original and most radical idea, to somewhat more moderate proposals, of more direct relevance to the funding of ideas. Let me begin by talking about simply inventing new ideas, something that professional economists are, on the whole, rather more likely to do than conduct the large-scale entrepreneurial activity necessary to sell the ideas to Congress.

This moderate proposal, which accomplishes some of what a patent system would, is for the government to institute prizes for economic ideas. This proposal is not outlandish. The Department of Agriculture is now giving six annual prizes for the best new vegetables. Prizes have the advantage of being ex post rewards for research. That is, instead of trying to guide the research in advance by research grant proposals, we simply pay people in terms of the potential merit of the research after the research is done. It is easier to judge the value of a research project after it is finished than before it is started; and before the research project begins, whoever is carrying it out is undoubtedly the best judge. This is, of course, the way the patent system rewards people for research in the natural fields.

If the prizes are to be feasible, I'm afraid I'm going to have to shy away from the immense rewards which a number of government reforms would merit, and suggest much smaller rewards. It is easier to think of Congress offering rewards of the order of $1 million or, better yet, $10 thousand, than of the order of billions. Indeed, if we switch down to those relatively small rewards, one can readily imagine a prize system which is analogous to the patent system that I discussed. As a specific proposal, we might change NSF from a prefunding organization to a prize-giving organization, raising its budget from about $12 million to $50 million.

Before looking at new ideas, however, let me briefly survey what we already have in this area. First, of course, there is a good deal of just plain accidental transmission of new social science ideas to the government by way of the usual scholarly publication process. Second, there are a number of organizations which exist for the purpose of propagandizing the government and which are perfectly willing to make use of new ideas invented in the social sciences. CATO and Heritage on the right, Brookings and the Resources for the Future on the (mid) left, are examples, although in all four cases they also do other things. Note, however, that they do not receive any direct reward when they are successful. Presumably, that has some effect on their fund-raising activities.

In addition, CATO, Heritage, Brookings, and so forth sometimes hold conferences or arrange to have publications on topics which they think are of general interest. Usually, the papers or books produced from these are the result of scholars simply repeating what they have already published, but in somewhat more popular language. Sometimes, however, particularly with Brookings and Resources for the Future, original research is produced as the result of this activity and it usually is designed to have political effect.

A further area here is that of Congressional investigations and the special investigating commissions. Once again, normally what these do is simply permit scholars to regurgitate previous work, but there is no doubt that on occasion, particularly among presidential commissions, serious research in important political areas is commissioned. The ending of the military draft and the ending of the CAB were, in part, the result of commissioned research.

Special interest groups also may commission perfectly genuine research, although they are a bit reluctant to do so. In general, they want to know what the outcome will be before they put their cash down, and, hence, they tend to get recyclings of previous research or strong statements by well-known scholars who actually haven't done any research but are willing to make strong statements for a fee. Still, all of these are examples of entrepreneurial activity.

What I suggest is that we strengthen this, and in order to protect myself from attacks on the right, I should point out that at the moment the government in fact does astonishingly little in the way of research into its own functioning. This research would in general be an almost perfect example of a public-good-generating activity, and hence it is obviously an area where government expenditure is called for. Furthermore, any organization is well-advised to engage in research to improve its own efficiency. In a way, we may think of the government as an entity in itself for whom this is a private good.

If we look at the present situation, we observe that, with the exceptions mentioned above, government economists are normally engaged in either a rather routine way, pursuing hobbies that they have one way or another fallen into, or doing fairly cut-and-dry statistical work. It is apparently the opinion of most Congressmen and other political leaders that the economist is the person who can get you the right number. If you want to find out quickly what the balance of payments between the United States and Lichtenstein is, ask an economist. You may get the number, but giving that kind of information is not what economists are primarily trained to do.

The second activity, firefighting, is the basic reason that most really influential government economists haven't read anything for the last twenty years. They find themselves in a government job and are asked to deal with some problem right now. They do so in terms of what they can remember. If they are successful, they are asked to do something else right now, and the process continues with the result that the higher ranks of government economic advisors aren't able to read. Furthermore, their work tends to be very hasty so that it is almost by definition of low quality.

That is not a statement that they personally are of low quality. Indeed, I know a number of them who are really first class. The organizational structure in which they operate, however, is such that their advice is of somewhat limited value.

Even though it is a public good, I do not now want to recommend that really vast amounts of money be spent, but $50 million a year is a mere bagatelle from the standpoint of the government, and it is a lot of money from the standpoint of the academic profession. I am therefore going to assume that such an appropriation is available.

First, as an economist I of course believe in competition so I do not suggest that this amount all be given to the NSF. Not only do I not recommend it be given to the NSF, I don't recommend that just a single organization be set up to disburse it. In fact, I suggest five organizations, each of which is given $10 million. On the whole, I would like these five separate organizations each to be organized rather differently from the other four, but in order to save time I'm going to describe only two such organizations. I'm sure that a group of brilliant individuals, such as the other contributors to this volume, and the readers who recognize its importance, can think of the other three quite easily.

Note that the objective here is to obtain applied research for the benefit of the government, and, hence, government should be involved in it. On the other hand, I myself have a strong aversion to the civil service organization.[6] Thus, I would suggest for one group a body of seven directors. The majority and minority leaders of the House and Senate would each select one. Another would be selected by the president of

---

[6]My aversion may simply represent the fact that I spent a good deal of time in the foreign service.

the United States and two would be selected by the president of the American Economic Society. It would be sensible to have the last two selected for two-year terms with overlaps so that in fact they would be selected by different AEA presidents. The directors' jobs would be largely honorary in the sense that they wouldn't be heavily compensated but also that they wouldn't have a great deal of work to do except to press in certain directions and select projects.

It would be their duty from time to time to decide on problems which they thought were important, and, each time they had decided on an important problem, issue two research grants to two different research organizations. If Harvard University were one of the research organizations, this would not require that Harvard spend all of the money, although presumably there would be some bias in that direction. Harvard could contract the work out. The award would not only specify a general topic, and who was to do it, but also set a deadline. If the deadline were missed, the award would be reduced by one percent for each day's delay.

Once the two separate reports had been received, they would be submitted to general criticism by publication, and in particular each report would be sent to the other research organization for comment. Sometime later, preferably six to eight months later, the board would meet again and offer a bonus of twenty percent of the original research award to *one* of the two research organizations.

There would of course be no reason why this group should not commission another pair of studies on the same topic if they felt either that this particular pair had been inadequate or, alternatively, that the studies had opened up an important research channel which should be further explored. This is my proposal for one of the five research organizations. The existence on the board of representatives of five different politicians sort of automatically provides for at least some entrepreneurial effect from these ideas.

Personally, I would be delighted if it turned out that some of the appointees by the politicians were themselves members of Congress. It would surely lower the quality of the judgment of excellence used in rewarding the twenty percent, but it would also surely increase the likelihood that any concrete proposal became known to the political part of the government and, hence, implemented.

My second proposal follows on that idea. I suggest that all former U.S. presidents and vice-presidents be invited to join a board of which they will make up half of the members. They're each permitted to appoint one academic economist as another member. The size of this board would of course vary from time to time. It would clearly be dominated by politicians, but there is no reason why these retired politicians should have any very strong axe to grind. We would have to worry about their competence more than their bias.

This board would then simply reward regularly published research by cash prizes. I think it would be desirable to have quite a large number of small prizes. Since they would have $10 million to spend and the administrative cost would be low (the appointments would once again be primarily honorary), it would be possible to award almost two hundred prizes of $50 thousand each year. There probably should be some rule that these prizes not be given for research funded by the first group. The terms of reference would emphasize that the research is intended to have at least theoretical and distant practical application rather than being part of pure theory.

I would assume that in this case, the politicians would in fact tend to dominate the selection process, but that they would also pay attention to the advice of their academic colleagues. A little bit of logrolling would take place with trades under which a project much-liked by one ex-president would be approved in return for approval of one liked by, let us say, a professor from Harvard.

Once again, this should provide a sort of automatic entrepreneurial effect. Furthermore, the ex-presidents would probably occasionally decide that they were interested enough in one of the ideas to do something about it. They can pull a good many strings.

So much for two of my five commissions. Although I do indeed believe this is a legitimate government function, I would obviously not have any objection at all to a private foundation moving in the same track. The objective is quite literally to change the structure of economic research in the direction of greater practical application.

At the moment, economic research is very heavily dominated by nonapplied activity. I suspect any reward system for existing research administered solely by academics would tend simply to reward the person who first applied differential topology to Ramsey pricing. There is also undeniably a strong element of fashion consciousness in any scholarship. Where there are very few practical applications, this is apt to become overwhelming.

Furthermore, most economists find themselves in a rather unfortunate situation. If they work on direct practical problems they're almost certain to have fights with members of the English department at faculty cocktail parties. Consider trying to convince the typical noneconomist faculty member that the Minimum Wage Act is not terribly helpful for poor laborers. Or think of trying to argue successfully that in a bitterly poor agricultural country, "land reform" which converts the landlords' domains into cooperative farms will probably reduce food supplies.

Suppose an economist, in an applied effort to help a very poor country, recommends to its government a program for attracting foreign capital. The suggestion is that bringing in plants to use semiskilled labor to produce low-quality textiles is possible, if you are willing to pay their workers a dollar a day, which is twice what they are now making on the farm. The economist feels that getting them off the farm and into industry is the only real way of raising living standards in the country. The suggested wage is so low that the average member of the faculty at the university where the economist works would regard it as inhumane exploitation.

Suppose further that the *nation* chooses to attack this program. Clearly, life in the university would be much less pleasant than if the economist had concentrated on Ramsey pricing. Indeed, it is notable that, at the moment, land reform is pushed a good deal more than is industrialization with low wages in public discussion of the poorer parts of the world.

My objective is to provide countervailing rewards to overcome the strong social pressures that now exist within the university for abstract and fashionable research. I would assume that if my recommendations are followed, a great deal of money would be wasted on projects that seem sensible to politicians, although most economists know that they are pointless. I suggest, however, that this waste would be less than the waste in our present research.

So much for recommendations. I would be delighted if any of you could do better. But if you cannot do better, please do not let the desire for a truly optimal solution lead you to oppose what I think would be an improvement. We don't want to let the best be an insuperable barrier to the better.

Bibliography

Abbott, George C. (1976). "Why Visiting Economists Fail: An Alternative Interpretation." *Public Administration* (Australia) **54** Spring, pp. 31–43.

Ackley, Gardner (1982). "Providing Economic Advice to Government." In *Economics in the Public Service: Papers in Honor of Walter W. Heller,* eds. Joseph A. Pechman and N. J. Simler. New York: Norton, pp. 200–34.

Adams, Bruce (1979). "The Limitations of Muddling Through: Does Anyone in Washington Really Think Anymore?" *Public Administration Review* **39** Nov.–Dec., pp. 545-52.

Agassi, Joseph (1981). *Science and Society: Studies in the Sociology of Science.* Dordrecht, Holland; Boston and Hingham, MA: Reidel.

Allen, William R. (1977). "Economics, Economists and Economic Policy: Modern American Experience." *History of Political Economy* **9** Spring, pp. 48–88.

Anderson, Gary M., William F. Shughart, II, and Robert Tollison (1985). "Adam Smith in the Customhouse." *Journal of Political Economy* **93** Aug., pp. 740–59.

Baldwin, George (1986). "Economics and Economists at the World Bank." In *Economists in International Agencies: An Exploratory Study,* ed. A. W. Coats. New York: Praeger.

Barber, Clarence (1955). "Canadian Tariff Policy." *Canadian Journal of Economics and Political Science* **21** Nov., pp. 515–30.

Barber, William J. (1987). "The Career of Alvin H. Hansen, in the 1920s and 1930s: A Study in Intellectual Transformation." *History of Political Economy,* **19** Summer, pp. 191–205.

 (1981). "The United States: 'Economists in a Pluralistic Polity,'" in *Economists in Government: An International Comparative Study,* ed. A. W. Coats. Durham, NC: Duke University Press.

 (1975). "The Kennedy Years: Purposeful Pedagogy." In *Exhortation and Controls: The Search for a Wage-Price Policy, 1945–1971,* ed. Craufurd D. Goodwin. Washington, D.C.: The Brookings Institution.

Bissell, Richard M. (1952). "Activities Designed to Advance Economic Well-Being." General Correspondence, Area III, Ford Foundation Archives (April 3).

(1952). Memo to Paul Hoffman. Ford Foundation Archives, General Correspondence, Area III. February 15.

(n.d.) "Possible Activities of the Ford Foundation Directed towards Strengthening the U.S. and World Economy." Ford Foundation Archives, Report 010598.

Blumenthal, Sidney (1986). *The Rise of the Counter Establishment: From Conservative Ideology to Political Power.* New York: Times Books.

Brander, James A. (1986). "Rationales for Strategic Trade and Industrial Policy." In *Strategic Trade Policy and the New International Economics,* ed. Paul Krugman. Cambridge, MA: MIT Press, p. 23.

Brittan, Samuel (1973). *Capitalism and the Permissive Society.* London: Macmillan.

   (1973). *Is There an Economic Consensus? An Attitude Survey.* London: Macmillan.

Buzzell, Robert D., and Bradley T. Gale (1987). *The PIMS Principle: Linking Strategy to Performance.* New York: Free Press.

Campbell, R. H., and A. S. Skinner, eds. (1976). *An Inquiry into the Nature and Causes of the Wealth of Nations,* by Adam Smith. Oxford: Clarendon Press.

Carson, Rachel (1962). *Silent Spring.* Boston: Houghton Mifflin.

Caves, Richard (1971). "International Corporations: The Industrial Economics of Foreign Investment." *Economica* **38,** pp. 1–27.

Clarke, S. V. O. (1973). "The Reconstruction of the International Monetary System: The Attempts of 1922 and 1933." *Princeton Studies in International Finance,* No. 33. Princeton: International Finance Section, Princeton University.

Coats, A. W. (ed.). (1986). *Economists in International Agencies: An Exploratory Study.* New York: Praeger.

   (1985). "The American Economic Association and the Economics Profession." *Journal of Economic Literature* **23** December, pp. 1697–1727.

   (1981). "Britain: The Rise of the Specialists." In *Economists in Government: An International Comparative Study,* ed. A. W. Coats. Durham, NC: Duke University Press, pp. 27–66.

   (1981). *Economists in Government: An International Comparative Study.* Durham, NC: Duke University Press, pp. 27–66. Also a complete issue in *History of Political Economy* **13** Fall, 1981.

   (1981). "Report of Discussions" at the Royaumont Conference on the Role of the Economist in Government, April 1974. Unpublished.

   (1967). "Sociological Aspects of British Economic Thought, Ca. 1885–1930." *Journal of Political Economy* **75** October, pp. 710–11.

   (1960). "The First Two Decades of the American Economic Association." *American Economics Review* **50** Sept, pp. 1697–1727.

Colander, David, and Arjo Klamer (1987). "The Making of an Economist." *Journal of Economic Perspectives* **1** Fall, pp. 95–111.

Constitution, Address List of Members of the American Association for the Promotion of Science (1866). Boston: Wright and Potter.

Corden, Max (1971). *The Theory of Protection.* Oxford: Clarendon Press.

Craver, Earlene. (1986). "Patronage and Directions of Research in Economics: The Rockefeller Foundation in Europe; 1924–1938." *Minerva,* **24** Summer–Autumn, pp. 205–22.

Derthick, Martha, and Paul J. Quirk (1985). *The Politics of Deregulation.* Washington, D.C.: The Brookings Institution.

Discovery Processes in Modern Biology: People and Processes in Biological Discovery (1977). Ed. W. R. Klemm. Huntington, NY: Krieger.

Edgeworth, Francis Ysidro (1881). *Mathematical Psychics, an Essay on the Application of Mathematics to the Moral Sciences.* London: Kegan Paul.

Einstein, Albert (1920). *Relativity: The Special and General Theory.* New York: Holt.

Ezekiel, Mordecai (1938). "The Cobweb Theorem." *Quarterly Journal of Economics* **52** Feb., pp. 255–80.

Fisher, Irving (1919). "Economists in Public Service." *The American Economic Review* **9** March, Supplement, pp. 5–21.

Flash, Edward S., Jr (1956). *Economic Advice and Presidential Leadership: The Council of Economic Advisers.* New York: Columbia University Press.

Fox, Harrison W., and Susan Webb Hammond (1977). *Congressional Staffs: The Invisible Force in American Lawmaking.* New York: Free Press.

Fremont-Smith, Marion (1965). *Foundations and Government: State and Federal Law and Supervision.* New York: Russell Sage.

Frey, Bruno S. et al. (1984). "Consensus and Dissensus Among Economists: An Empirical Inquiry." *American Economic Review* **74** pp. 986–94.

Gale Research Centers Director (1984–85). Detroit: Gale Research Co.

Goodwin, Craufurd D. (1972). "Economic Theory and Society: A Plea for Process Analysis." *American Economic Review* **62** May, pp. 409–15.

Goodwin, Craufurd D., and I. B. Holley, Jr., eds. (1968). *The Transfer of Ideas: Historical Essays.* Durham, NC: Duke University Press.

Graham, Dan A., and E. Roy Weintraub (1975). "On Convergence in Pareto Allocations." *Review of Economic Studies* **42** pp. 469–72.

Grossman, David M. (1982). "American Foundations and the Support of Economic Research." *Minerva,* **20** Spring–Summer, pp. 59–82.

Halberstam, David (1986). *The Reckoning.* New York: Morrow. (Paperback 1987. New York: Avon.)

(1981). *Breaks of the Game.* New York: Knopf.

(1972). *The Best and the Brightest.* New York: Random House.

Hargrove, Erwin C., and Samuel A. Morley (1984). *The President and the Council of Economic Advisers.* London: Westview Press.

Harrington, Michael (1962). *The Other America: Poverty in the United States.* New York: Macmillan.

Haskell, Thomas (1977). *The Emergence of Professional Social Science: The American Social Science Association and the Nineteenth Century Crisis of Authority.* Urbana, IL: University of Illinois Press.

Hayek, Friedrich A. (von) (1948). *Individualism and Economic Order*. Chicago: University of Chicago Press.

(1944). *The Road to Serfdom*. Chicago: University of Chicago Press.

Heilbroner, Robert (1980). *The Worldly Philosophers: The Lives, Times, and Ideas of the Great Economic Thinkers*. New York: Simon and Schuster.

Heller, Walter W. (1966). *New Dimensions of Political Economy*. Cambridge, MA: Harvard University Press.

Helpman, Elhanan, and Paul Krugman (1985). *Market Structure and Foreign Trade: Increasing Returns, Imperfect Competition and the International Economy*. Cambridge, MA: MIT Press.

Henderson, David (1986). *The BBC Reith Lectures: Innocence and Design: The Influence of Economic Ideas on Policy*. Oxford: Blackwell.

Herman, Edward S. (1982). "The Institutionalization of Bias in Economics." *Media, Culture and Society* **4** July, pp. 175–91.

Hutchison, T. W. (1977). *Knowledge and Ignorance in Economics*. Oxford: Blackwell.

(1968). *Economics and Economic Policy in Britain. Some Aspects of Their Interrelations*. London: George Allen and Unwin.

Hymer, Stephen (1976). *The International Operations of National Firms: A Study of Direct Foreign Investment*. Cambridge, MA: MIT Press.

Kamura, Hiroshi Peter (1982). "Japan." In *International Relations Research: Emerging Trends outside the United States, 1981–82*. New York: Rockefeller Foundation.

Keynes, John Maynard (1936). *The General Theory of Employment, Interest, and Money*. New York: Harcourt Brace.

Kindleberger, Charles (1963). *International Economics,* 3rd ed. Homewood, IL: Irwin.

Klamer, Arjo (1984). *Conversations with Economists: New Classical Economists and Opponents Speak Out on the Current Controversy in Macroeconomics*. Totowa, NJ: Rowman and Allanheld.

Krugman, Paul (1986). "New Trade Theory and the Less Developed Countries." Paper delivered at the Carlos F. Diaz-Alejandre Memorial Conference, Helsinki. Aug. 23–25.

(1986). *Strategic Trade Policy and the New International Economics*. Cambridge, MA: MIT Press.

Kuhn, Thomas S. (1962). *The Structure of Scientific Revolutions*. Chicago: University of Chicago Press.

Linder, Staffan Burenstam (1961). *An Essay on Trade and Transformation*. New York: Wiley.

Lynd, Robert (1939). *Knowledge for What?: The Place of Social Science in American Culture*. Princeton: Princeton University Press.

Macdonald, Dwight (1956). *The Ford Foundation: The Men and the Millions*. New York: Reynal.

Machlup, Fritz (1980–4). *Knowledge, Its Creation, Distribution, and Economic Significance,* 3 vols. Princeton: Princeton University Press.

(1962). *The Production and Distribution of Knowledge in the United States.* Princeton: Princeton University Press.

Malbin, Michael (1980). *Unelected Representatives.* New York: Basic.

Maloney, John (1985). *Marshall, Orthodoxy, and the Professionalization of British Economics.* Cambridge: Cambridge University Press.

Mandate for Leadership: Policy Management in a Conservative Administration (1980). Washington, D.C.: The Heritage Foundation.

Mandeville, Bernard (1934); rpt. London originally published over the period 1705–29. *The Fable of the Bees; or, Private Vices, Public Benefits.* London: Wishart.

Marris, Stephen (1986). "The Role of Economists in the OECD." In *Economists in International Agencies: An Exploratory Study,* ed. A. W. Coats. New York: Praeger.

Mas-Colell, Andreu (1985). *The Theory of General Economic Equilibrium: A Differentiable Approach.* New York: Cambridge University Press.

McCraw, Thomas K. (1984). *Prophets of Regulation: Charles Francis Adams, Louis D. Brandeis, James M. Landis and Alfred E. Kahn.* Cambridge, MA: Harvard University Press.

McKinnon, Richard I. (1963). "Optimum Currency Areas." *American Economic Review* **53** Sept., pp. 717–25.

Meade, James (1971). *The Controlled Economy,* vol. III of *Principles of Political Economy.* London: Allen and Unwin, Ltd.

   (1955). *Trade and Welfare.* London and New York: Oxford University Press.

Meltsner, Arnold J. (1976). *Policy Analysts in the Bureaucracy.* Berkeley and Los Angeles: University of California Press.

Mirowski, Philip (1982). "What's Wrong with the Laffer Curve?" *Journal of Economic Issues* **16** September, pp. 815–28.

Mitchell, Wesley Clair (1953). "A Bold Experiment." Quoted in *Two Lives: The Story of Wesley Clair Mitchell and Myself,* by Lucy Sprague Mitchell (1953). New York: Simon and Schuster.

Mosher, Frederic C. (1984). *A Tale of Two Agencies: A Comparative Analysis of the General Accounting Office and the Office of Management and Budget.* Baton Rouge, LA: Louisiana State University Press.

Mundell, Robert A. (1961). "A Theory of Optimum Currency Areas." *American Economic Review* **51** Sept., pp. 657–64.

Mundell, Robert A., and Alexander K. Swoboda, eds. (1969). *Monetary Problems of the International Economy.* Papers and Discussions of a Conference on International Monetary Problems, 1966. Chicago: University of Chicago Press.

Nagel, Ernest, and James Roy Newman (1958). *Godel's Proof.* New York: New York University Press.

Nelson, Robert H. (1987). "The Economics Profession and the Making of Public Policy." *Journal of Economic Literature* **25** March, pp. 49–91.

Neville, J. W., ed. (1981). *Economics, Economists and Policy Formulation.*

CAER Paper No. 13, September. Australia: Centre for Applied Economic Research.

Occupations of Federal White-Collar Workers. Published periodically (officially, every two years) by the Office of Personnel Management (formerly Civil Service Commission). Washington, D.C.: U.S. Government Printing Office.

Okun, Arthur (1981). *Prices and Quantities: A Macroeconomic Analysis.* Washington, D.C.: The Brookings Institution.

Orlans, Harold (1986). "Academic Social Scientists and the Presidency: From Wilson to Nixon," *Minerva* **24** Summer–Autumn, p. 174.

Pagels, Heinz (1985). *Perfect Symmetry: The Search for the Beginning of Time.* New York: Simon and Schuster.

    (1982). *The Cosmic Code: Physics as the Language of Nature.* New York: Simon and Schuster.

Pearson, James B., and Abraham Ribicoff (1984). *Report of the Study Group on Senate Practices and Procedures to the Committee on Rules and Administration.* S. Prt. 98-242. Washington, D.C.: U.S. Government Printing Office.

Peters, Thomas J., and Robert H. Waterman (1982). *In Search of Excellence: Lessons from America's Best-run Companies.* New York: Harper and Row.

Prigogine, Ilya, and Isabelle Stengers (1984). *Order out of Chaos: Man's New Dialogue with Nature.* Toronto: Bantam.

Reder, Melvin (1982). "Chicago Economics: Permanence and Change." *Journal of Economic Literature* **20** pp. 1–38.

Reeves, Richard (1985). *The Reagan Detour.* New York: Simon and Schuster.

Reich, Robert (1983). *The Next American Frontier.* New York: Times Books.

Reich, Robert B., and Ira C. Magaziner (1983). *Minding America's Business.* New York: Harcourt Brace Jovanovich.

Report of the Study for the Ford Foundation on Policy and Program. (1949). Detroit: Ford Foundation.

Riesman, David (1950). *The Lonely Crowd: A Study of the Changing American Character.* New Haven: Yale University Press.

Rivlin, Alice (1987). "Economics and the Policy Process." *American Economic Review* **77** March, pp. 1–10.

Robbins, (Lord) Lionel (1971). *The Autobiography of an Economist.* London: Macmillan.

Roberts, Paul C. (1984). *The Supply-Side Revolution: An Insider's Account of Policymaking in Washington.* Cambridge: Harvard University Press.

Rosen, George (1985). *Western Economists and Eastern Societies: Agents of Change in South Asia, 1950–1970.* Baltimore: Johns Hopkins University Press.

Salant, Walter S. (1975). "Introduction to William A. Salant's 'Taxes, the Multiplier and the Inflationary Gap.'" *History of Political Economy* **7** Spring, pp. 3–18.

Samuels, Warren J. (1980). "Economics as a Science and Its Relation to Policy: The Example of Free Trade." *Journal of Economic Issues* **14** March, pp. 163–85.

(1977). "Ideology in Economics." In *Modern Economic Thought,* ed. Sidney Weintraub. Philadelphia: University of Pennsylvania Press, pp. 467–85.

Samuelson, Paul (1948). "International Trade and the Equalization of Factor Prices." *Economic Journal* **58** June, pp. 163–84.

Schneider, Erich (1975). *Joseph Schumpeter: Life and Work of a Great Social Scientist,* trans. W. E. Kuhn. Lincoln, NE: Bureau of Business Research.

Schumpeter, Joseph A. (1954). *History of Economic Analysis.* New York: Oxford University Press.

Schultz, Theodore W. (1982). "Distortions of Economic Research." In *The Social Sciences, Their Nature and Uses,* ed. William H. Kruskal et al. Chicago: University of Chicago Press, pp. 122–33.

"A Scientific Attack on the Human Problems of an Industrial Society," attachment to Wyman Fiske, "Ford Foundation: Report and Recommendation on Policies and Programs," n.d., pp. 1–2. Ford Foundation Archives, Report 010621.

Sederberg, Peter (1984). *The Politics of Meaning: Power and Explanation in the Construction of Social Reality.* Tucson, AZ: University of Arizona Press.

Seers, Dudley (1962). "Why Visiting Economists Fail." *Journal of Political Economy* **70** Aug., pp. 325–8.

Shinn, Terry, and Richard Whitley, eds., (1985). *Sociology of the Sciences,* vol. IX of *Expository Science: Forms & Functions of Popularisation.* Dordrecht, Holland; Boston; and Hingham, MA: Reidel.

Silk, Leonard et al. (1972). "Economists Consider Economic Reporters and Vice Versa." *American Economic Review* **62** May, pp. 373–90.

Smith, Adam (1796). *An Inquiry into the Nature and Causes of the Wealth of Nations.* London: A Strahan and T. Cadell jun. and W. Davies (successors to Mr. Cardell).

Spencer, Barbara J. (1986). "What Should Trade Policy Target?" In *Strategic Trade Policy and the New International Economics,* ed. Paul Krugman. Cambridge, MA: MIT Press, p. 69.

Spengler, J. J. (1970). "Notes on the International Transmission of Economic Ideas." *History of Political Economy* **2:1** pp. 133–51.

Stein, Herbert (1986). "The Washington Economics Industry." *American Economic Review* **76** May, pp. 1–9.

(1984). *Presidential Economics. The Making of Economic Policy from Roosevelt to Reagan and Beyond.* New York: Simon and Schuster.

(1981). "The Chief Executive as Chief Economist." In *Essays in Contemporary Economic Problems: Demand, Productivity and Population,* ed. W. Fellner. Washington, D.C.: American Enterprise Institute.

Stevenson, Adlai III (1976). *Report of the Senate Select Committee to Study the Senate Committee System.* Washington, D.C.: U.S. Government Printing Office.

Stigler, George J. (1982). *The Economist as Preacher and Other Essays.* Chicago: University of Chicago Press.

(1967). "The Foundations and Economics." In *U.S. Philanthropic Foundations: Their History, Structure, Management, and Record,* ed. Warren Weaver. New York: Harper and Row.

Stockman, David (1987). *The Triumph of Politics: The Inside Story of the Reagan Revolution.* New York: Avon.

Taussig, F. W. (1931). *Some Aspects of the Tariff Question.* Cambridge: Harvard University Press.

(1931). *The Tariff History of The United States,* 8th ed. New York and London: Putnam.

Thurow, Lester C. (1984). *Dangerous Currents: The State of Economics.* New York: Random House.

Tinbergen, Jan (1954). *International Economic Integration.* Amsterdam: Elsevier.

Tullock, Gordon (1987 and 1966). *The Organization of Inquiry.* New York: American University Press; and Durham, NC: University Press.

Viner, Jacob (1924). *Canada's Balance of International Indebtedness, 1900–1913: An Inductive Study of the Theory of International Trade.* Cambridge: Harvard University Press.

Ward, Benjamin (1979). *The Ideal Worlds of Economics: Liberal, Radical and Conservative World Views.* New York: Basic.

Weaver, Richard (1948). *Ideas Have Consequences.* Chicago: University of Chicago Press.

Weinberg, Steven (1984). *The First Three Minutes: A Modern View of the Origin of the Universe.* Toronto and New York: Bantam.

Weintraub, E. Roy (1985). *General Equilibrium Analysis: Studies in Appraisal.* Cambridge and New York: Cambridge University Press.

Weller, Patrick, and Michelle Grattan (1981). *Can Ministers Cope? Australian Federal Ministers at Work.* Richmond, Victoria (Australia): Hutchinson.

White, Theodore (1982). *America in Search of Itself.* New York: Harper and Row.

Whitley, Richard (1984). *The Social and Intellectual Organization of the Sciences.* London: Oxford University Press.

Winch, Donald (1983). "Science and the Legislator: Adam Smith and After." *Economic Journal* **93** Sept., pp. 510–20.

Zeleny, Milan (1981). *Autopoesis: The Theory of Living Organizations.* Oxford: Oxford University Press.

Zeleny, Milan, ed. (1980). *Autopoesis, Dissipative Structures, and Spontaneous Social Orders,* AAAS Selected Symposium 55. Boulder, CO: Westview Press.

Ziman, John (1968). *Public Knowledge: An Essay Concerning the Social Dimension of Science.* London: Cambridge University Press.

Index

multiplier, 28, 80, 88; foreign trade, 50, 58
Mundell, Robert, 44, 46, 47, 52, 54, 92

National Bureau, 45
National Bureau of Economic Research, 166, 186–7, 188
National Research Council, 158
National Science Foundation. *See* NSF
neoclassical synthesis, 27
New Classical Revolution, 33
new international economics, 56
Newlon, Daniel H., xv–xvi, 18, 230
Newtonian framework, 23, 51
New York Times, 98–100
Niskanen, William, 89
Nissan Motors, 88
Nixon, Richard, 115
Nobel Foundation, 158
Nobel prize, 24, 87; NSF, 212
NSF, 18, 195 (n.), 195–228; econometrics, 219; funding growth, 207; grant process, 195–9, 204–5; incentives, 244; laboratory experiments, 207, 212; Nobel prize, 212; productivity, 212, 219; public choice, 212; research, 219, 221; technology, 219
Nurkse, Ragnar, 50, 52

O'Donnell, Kirk, 177
Office of Management and Budget. *See* OMB
Okun, Arthur, 28, 95–6, 104, 126
Okun's Law, 96
OMB, 18, 180
O'Neill, Tip, 134
Op-Ed, 18, 91, 126, 177, 183, 189, 191
Oppenheimer, Peter, 54
Orcutt, Guy, 205
orthodoxy, 10

Packwood, Robert, 137, 152
Pagels, Heinz, 72
Pareto-optimal state, 77
Peacock, Alan T., 118 (n.)
Pechman, Joseph A., 104, 143, 144
Pedersen, Jorgen, 50
Peirce, Charles S., 6
Pertchuk, Mike, 91
Peters, Thomas J., 89
Phelps, Edmond, 207
physics, 24, 33, 39, 40, 72, 235
Pines, Burton W., 188
Planck, Max, 24–5
Plott, Charles, 212

policy, 127–30, 143–53
policymakers, 12, 14–15, 17
political science, 32
politicians, 9; leadership, 133; policies of, 129; and tax reform, 141–53
politics, 24, 124–40
Poole, William, 49
Posner, Richard, 212
pragmatists, 6
Prescott, Edward, 207
project LINK, 205
protection, 78
public choice, 131; and NSF, 212
public choice theory, 127
published books, 102–15
publishing, academic, 48–73; books published in 1985, 97; lessons from, 100–5; and reviews, 98

Rand Corporation, 178, 179, 182
rational expectations, 33, 207
Rayburn, Sam, 132 (n.)
Reagan, Ronald, 115, 123, 136, 141, 148, 150, 152, 154, 175, 177, 192
Reder, Melvin, 47, 229 (n.), 232
Reeves, Richard, 175
Reich, Robert, 85, 90–1
reporters. *See* journalists
research, 32, 33, 37; institutes, 9; mainstream, 9, 230–1
research institutions, 187; Brookings, 180; Institute for Government Research, 186; National Bureau of Economic Research, 180, 186–7; Russell Sage, 180, 186; Twentieth Century Fund, 186
Resources for the Future, 243
Reynolds, Clark, 55–6
Ricardo, David, 86, 101
Riesman, David, 43
Rivlin, Alice, 13
Robbins, Lionel (Lord), 116
Robinson, Joan, 59
Rockefeller Foundation, 158, 232
Rockefeller, Nelson, 158
Roosevelt, Franklin D., 120
Rosenstein-Rodan, Paul, 52
Rostenkowski, Dan, 138, 151
Rostow, W. W., 55
Rowen, Herbert, 100
Ruml, Beardsley, 160
Russell Sage Foundation, 180, 186

Salant, Walter, 49
Salant, William A., 125
Salin, Pascal, 47